Fundamentals of
and

MW01613451

Also by Robert Langs

A Clinical Workbook for Psychotherapists (1992)
Science, Systems, and Psychoanalysis (1992)
Empowered Psychotherapy (1993)
Doing Supervision and Being Supervised (1994)
The Dream Workbook (1994)
Clinical Practice and the Architecture of the Mind (1995)
The Daydream Workbook (1995)
The Evolution of the Emotion-Processing Mind: With an Introduction to Mental Darwinism (1996)
The Cosmic Circle: The Unification of Mind, Matter and Energy (with A. Badalamenti and L. Thomson) (1996)
Death, Anxiety and Clinical Practice (1997)
Ground Rules in Psychotherapy and Counselling (1998)
Current Theories of Psychoanalysis (editor) (1998)
Psychotherapy and Science (1999)
Dreams and Emotional Adaptation (1999)

Fundamentals of Adaptive Psychotherapy and Counselling

ROBERT LANGS, MD

First published 2004 by
PALGRAVE MACMILLAN
Houndmills, Basingstoke, Hampshire RG21 6XS and
175 Fifth Avenue, New York, N.Y. 10010
Companies and representatives throughout the world

PALGRAVE MACILLAN is the global academic imprint of the Palgrave
Macmillan division of St. Martin's Press, LLC and of Palgrave Macmillan Ltd.
Macmillan® is a registered trademark in the United States, United Kingdom
and other countries. Palgrave is a registered trademark in the European
Union and other countries.

ISBN 1–4039–0342–5

This book is printed on paper suitable for recycling and made from fully
managed and sustained forest sources.

A catalogue record for this book is available from the British Library.

A catalog record for this book is available from the Library of Congress.

10   9   8   7   6   5   4   3   2   1
13 12 11 10 09 08 07 06 05 04

Printed in China

Contents

Contents

PART I

Basic Concepts

1

Two Modes of Psychotherapy and Counselling*

This book is addressed to all manner of students and practitioners of psychotherapy and counselling. It offers a compendium of deep psychological and interpersonal insights and precepts that can serve as a solid foundation for all of the diverse efforts at emotional healing that are in vogue today. While its bias is psychodynamic, the knowledge and principles of technique that will be espoused have a bearing on, and can serve to illuminate, the practice of all present-day treatment modalities regardless of their theoretical underpinnings.

The broad applicability of this book stems from its grounding in explorations of emotional realms where humans share a set of universal attributes that are inherent to *the emotion-processing mind* that marks us as members of the hominid species (Slavin and Kriegman, 1992; Badcock, 1994; Langs, 1996). Regardless of whether they are addressed by a given psychotherapist, these psychobiological features of the human mind are operative at all times and they exert many powerful effects on emotional life and the therapeutic process.

---

* For ease of presentation, I shall hereafter use the terms 'psychotherapy' and 'therapy' to allude to all forms of mental healing, much as I shall use the terms 'psychotherapist' and 'therapist' to refer to all types of mental health professionals. Similarly, the term 'patient' shall imply all types of recipients of psychological treatment.

Historically, the various schools of psychotherapy have had little to say about shared, psycho-biological fundamentals. The prevailing trend is to stress the distinctive features of a given theory and mode of practice, and the uniqueness of each patient–therapist couple, to the neglect of universal features (Slavin and Kriegman, 1992; Langs, 1998a). This attitude supports the employment of a wide range of ill-defined techniques of therapy which are buttressed with the use of highly abstract, uncertain, clinically distant concepts like 'symptom relief', 'psychic defence', 'transference', 'cognitive retraining', 'intersubjectivity' and 'the unconscious'. This way of thinking also finds support through the avoidance of model-making, a most important scientific tool. The few models of the mind that have been generated tend to be naïve, static, lacking in clearly defined entities and devoid of a precise definition of the unconscious domain and unconscious adaptation (Gedo and Goldberg, 1973). Freud's (1923) well-known model of ego, id and superego is a case in point (see Langs, 1992b).

The field of psychotherapy is sorely in need of a far more precise definition of terms, theories and techniques (Little, 1951; Szasz, 1963; Smith, 1991). It also requires the development of suitably complex, adaptation-oriented models of the mind that take into account both conscious and unconscious efforts to cope with the many, ever-present adaptive challenges that humans face from day to day. It is for this reason that this book is being written from *a strongly adaptive perspective*. This vantage-point has heretofore been called *the communicative approach* because the theory and techniques that it offered were derived largely from careful investigations of the processes of conscious and unconscious communication between patients and therapists. The shift to the terms *adaptive or strong adaptive approach* was made because, with time, it became clear that the most distinctive feature of the approach is its emphasis on *conscious and unconscious emotional adaptation* as carried out by the psycho-biological structure that has evolved for this purpose – *the emotion-processing mind*. In this context, it's well to stress that the propositions of the approach have been clinically derived and unconsciously validated, and that they are based on a new way of listening to and formulating the clinical material of the therapeutic interaction and the conscious and unconscious implications of that meterial. Throughout the book I shall refer to clinical findings that have been developed though the methods of the strong adaptive approach. These references allude to 30 years of unconsciously validated cumulative clinical experience rather than any specific clinical research study.

Adaptation

We begin our pursuit of psychological fundamentals with a cardinal set of questions: As human beings, what is our most essential task? What activities are most basic to our very existence and survival? What are we first and foremost designed to do? And how does this central devotion apply to the emotional realm?

Biologists offer a clear and incontrovertible answer to these questions. Granted that there are basic needs for boundaries, nourishment, metabolism and excretion, nevertheless the most fundamental *task* for all living beings including humans is that of *adapting to their environments* – a term used in its broadest sense to include living conditions, interactions with other living beings, natural events, and the state of our body organs and our inner feelings, fantasies and other affects and thought processes (Dawkins, 1976; Plotkin, 1994; Dennett, 1995; Langs, 1996; Rose, 1997). Except for serious or life-threatening physical illnesses, however, the latter internal events are of lesser importance to the vicissitudes of emotional life than those that arise and impact from reality and the external environment. Thus, fantasies and memories, conscious or unconscious, are far less evocative of major adaptive responses and emotional consequences than disturbing outside incidents – so-called *emotionally-charged traumas* or *anxiety-provoking triggering events*.

Defining the unconscious domain

It seems axiomatic that a fundamental and universally applicable theory of emotional life and psychotherapy must, of necessity, include a sound conceptualization of both the conscious and unconscious realms of experience and coping. Current psychoanalytic conceptions of unconscious factors in emotional life are extremely vague and poorly conceptualized. Virtually anything that a patient is unaware of that a therapist believes to have been expressed in the patient's behaviours, words or feelings has been defined as operating unconsciously. This includes patterns of thinking and acting, relational trends, self-attitudes, the need for so-called narcissistic supplies, fantasies, memories, and many of the implications of patients' manifest communications (see for example, Kohut, 1971; Kernberg, 1975; Mitchell, 1988; Bacal and Newman, 1990; Orange *et al.*, 1997; Langs, 1998a). The appellation 'unconscious' has thereby been reduced to a waste-basket term that is lacking in specificity, credence or clinical utility. Much of this arises because the bulk of psychotherapeutic work carried out today deals with conscious experiences and, in respect to communication, with the manifest contents and the evident implications of patients' material. From a strong adaptive perspective, it appears that many therapists have a rather vague conceptualization of the unconscious realm and are truly lacking a sense of the distinctiveness and specificity of unconscious experience, communication and processes (Langs, in press a).

This situation can be traced to Freud's (1900) abandonment of his *topographic (map) model of the mind* in which the term *unconscious* (UCS) referred to a system of the mind, and thus to the state of a particular set of mental contents and to a distinctive type of mental processes that he called the *primary processes*. This system was sharply distinguished from the other system of the mind, the *preconscious–conscious system* (PCS–CS) which had its own set of contents and mode of operation, which Freud called the *secondary processes*. These distinctions were based on the study of patients' communications in psychoanalysis, in which attention to symbolic unconscious expressions played a definitive role. Almost all of this was lost with Freud's (1923) adoption of his *structural approach*, in which the term *unconscious* no longer alluded to a system of the mind and its modes of communication and processing. Instead, the term referred to a quality of human experience and, thereby, soon became a secondary consideration in formulating material from patients and in intervening.

Of importance in this regard is the realization that Freud's models of the mind were grounded in a basically inner mental or intrapsychic focus, with minimum attention to coping with external realities – a position that is sustained to this very day by virtually all forms of psychotherapy. In contrast, the strong adaptive approach that informs this book is based on a view of emotional life and psychotherapy that is organized around the human need to adapt first and foremost to emotionally-charged external events and their meanings; inner mental issues are seen as a secondary concern. Because this adaptation-centred approach was developed as an extension and revision of mainstream psychoanalytic approaches, it shares features with Freud's and other present-day thinking, yet differs in significant ways as well – fundamentally, theoretically and clinically.

One difference of relevance to the present discussion is that, in being stimulus-oriented, the adaptive approach views unconscious communication as a means of conveying *encoded unconscious perceptions* rather than *encoded unconscious fantasies and memories* – although these may be encoded secondarily. And because unconscious communications and processes are evoked and organized by events that can be specified, the strong adaptive approach has been able to define the unconscious realm in relatively specific terms. In addition, its focus on communication has led to an appreciation of the dramatic differences between *manifest (unencoded) or conscious* and *latent (encoded) or deep unconscious* modes of expression. This in turn has led to the development of a model of the emotion-processing mind that basically is a return to Freud's topographic model, albeit greatly modified – that is to a model of the mind with conscious and deep unconscious systems. And despite differences in attributes, the adaptive model shares with Freud's model a relative precision in defining for each system a set of clearly identified operations, moral values, mode of expression, degree of defensiveness, perceptive capabilities and adaptive intelligence.

The weak adaptive position

The proposition that adaptation is at the very centre of emotional life, as well as the psychotherapeutic process and the operations of the emotion-processing mind, is the basis for a classification of forms of psychotherapy into two basic groups – *the weak and strong adaptive approaches*. There's an in-built, natural tendency for us as humans and psychotherapists to adopt a mind–centred, weak adaptive position. By evolved design, the human mind tends to look away from external realities and to think of its troubles as its own. Emotional problems are then thought to arise when the mind thinks terrible or conflicted thoughts or has unfounded beliefs, or when it's learned poor ways of relating or has been conditioned to respond badly to certain kinds of situations. It's also believed that the mind's forbidden wishes and fantasies, and the conflicts that they cause both consciously and unconsciously, are the root causes of emotional ills. External realities are seen as a backdrop for the mind's struggles or as creating coincidental events that set off inner struggles and then fall by the wayside. Even in the case of extreme traumas, the focus is almost entirely on how the mind is affected by and handles these situations.

These are, then, *mind-centred approaches* which are exemplified by classical psychoanalysis and its off-shoots, self-psychology, relational and intersubjective theories and the like, which view inner mental conflicts, self-nurturing needs, and relational difficulties as the primary issues in emotional life (see for example, Freud, 1923; A. Freud, 1936; Greenson, 1967; Kohut, 1971; Kernberg, 1975; Atwood and

Stolorow, 1984; Stolorow *et al.*, 1987; Mitchell, 1988; Bacal and Newman, 1990; Orange *et al.*, 1997; Langs, 1998a, in press b). Also included here are behavioural and cognitive approaches to the human mind and its psychotherapy. Their basic principle when it comes to psychotherapy is: Heal the mind – train it to think more clearly, rid it of its bad habits and poor patterns of thinking, behaving and relating, and/or render its unconscious tendencies and conflicts conscious – and the patient's emotional problems will be solved. Healing is believed to stem from interpretations along these lines and from the patient's constructive identifications and interactional experiences with an assumed soundly functioning psychotherapist.

In respect to communication and listening, therapists who adopt these approaches work with manifest contents and the purported implications that can be extracted from these contents – an *extraction process* that is very different from the strong adaptive *trigger-decoding process* described below. When unconscious contents or processes are considered by weak adaptive therapists, if at all, it's done in three ways:

First, by defining unconscious expressions as previously unavailable or unmentioned mental images, thoughts, fantasies or memories that suddenly appear or break through into a patient's awareness. This phenomenon is understood to be the result of changes in intrapsychic defenses that allow previously repressed or unrealized mental contents to enter awareness.

Second, by classifying as unconscious expressions any implication of a manifest message of which the patient is unaware. Here, the focus is on meanings unrecognized by the patient that can be extracted from the surface contents of his or her free associations – that is, from the manifest contents of their messages.

Third, by viewing unconscious expressions as any behavioural tendency, pattern of behaviour or mode of relating that a therapist can deduce from a patient's behaviour in therapy or his or her self-descriptive free associations that the patient does not consciously acknowledge.

The study of these efforts from the vantage-point of the strong adaptive approach accepts the validity of some of these weak adaptive conceptualizations, but finds that they tend to pertain to emotional issues that have only minimal impact on the vicissitudes of emotional life and the psychotherapy experience. More tellingly, they appear to serve as ways of avoiding and defending against far more powerful, anxiety-provoking, emotionally-charged experiences and issues of a kind that serve as the deeper sources of both emotional health and emotional suffering. These more compelling problems have been found to stem not so much from the inner mind as from the external world and life itself with its never-ending traumas, large and small, including the overwhelming prospect of personal demise.

The strong adaptive position

To the best of my knowledge, the strong adaptive approach is the only school of psychotherapy that has adopted a primarily adaptive view-point of emotional life and its vicissitudes (Langs, 1982, 1993, 1998a; Smith, 1991). As a result, as noted by Raney (1984), it is a new para-digm of psychoanalysis, one that illuminates all manner of therapeutic efforts. As noted above, its basic proposition is that the single most important function of the *emotion-processing mind* is that of adapting to external environmental challenges, which mainly take the form of blatant and more subtle traumas; adapting to inner mental processes and affects is seen as a secondary function. It also proposes that the emotion-processing mind adapts on two levels of emotional experience – *conscious and unconscious* – and that it's comprised of two relatively independent, distinctive processing systems – the *conscious system* and the *deep unconscious system*. Reality and the two-system emotion-processing mind are seen as equal partners in determining the course of our emotional lives.

As for the process of cure, the emphasis is on the healing qualities of the insights garnered through the interpretation of patients' uncon-scious perceptions as evoked by current or recent triggering events and their effects on the vicissitudes of patients' symptoms and resistances, as well as their unconscious links to responses to past traumas. Also salutary are a therapist's offer and maintenance of a secured setting and ideal set of ground rules for the treatment experience – a reflection of the healing powers of a soundly structured therapeutic space. And, finally, there are the curative effects of the positive unconscious identifications patients make with their psychotherapists when they function well and, in general, confine their therapeutic endeavours to unconsciously validated interventions – mainly trigger-decoded interpretations and efforts to keep the framework of a treatment well-secured.

These modes of insight and healing enable patients to modify their existing maladaptive behaviours and resolve their emotional symptoms, and to develop the ability to cope favourably with future emotionally-charged triggering events. By and large, this is a *reality-centred approach* that views the mind's efforts to adapt to actual traumatic events and their multiple meanings as the primary issue in emotional life. It sees the mind as continuously activated by environmental events and rejects the idea that the mind is an isolated entity that goes off on its own to fight its own battles.

Communicatively, this approach is grounded in the understanding that messages from the deep unconscious system of the emotion-processing mind are *encoded* within the manifest contents of narrative vehicles such as dreams, conscious fantasies and daydreams, and stories that attract the interest of a patient. These messages reflect the deep unconscious experiences and adaptive processing efforts of this system, and they are determined by undoing their disguise in light of their evocative triggers. The means by which this so-called process of *trigger decoding* is carried out involves deciphering the encoded meanings of narrative themes in light of the unconsciously perceived triggering events that have prompted deep unconscious processing activities. In essence, then, trigger decoding entails using the trigger – the stimulus – for an encoded narrative message as the decoding key for undoing its camouflage or disguise. For example:

A male patient seeing a male psychologist in psychotherapy reports a dream of being examined by a male physician in front of a group of medical students. The doctor looks up at the students and announces that he's discovered evidence that the patient has syphilis. The patient tries to close the doctor's mouth so he'll stop talking.

Among the many possible meanings of this narrative, those that are relevant to and organized by the event that triggered these disguised themes are most pertinent to the patient's deep unconscious experiences and adaptive processing activities. In this case, the trigger was the therapist's request that the patient permit him to use his case material in a presentation that he was planning for his psychoanalytic society. The patient had agreed to the request and consciously stated that he felt pleased and flattered – little more. But in light of this trigger – which is a departure from the ideal, secured frame that guarantees the patient total privacy and confidentiality for his treatment experience – the dream trigger decodes as an indication that deep-unconsciously, the patient is experiencing the presentation as his therapist exposing his secrets to others. The syphilis encodes the fact that the patient is homosexual and is suffering from AIDS. The dream also decodes as indicating that while the patient consciously acceded to his therapist's request, deep-unconsciously he has the very opposite wish – that the therapist not present his case and expose him and his secrets to others.

As can be seen, I have used the trigger to select the most likely meanings of the encoded dream and have transposed the themes in the dream into the therapy situation, thereby undoing their disguise. This process of decoding narrative themes in light of their unconsciously experienced triggers is distinctive to the adaptive approach and it accounts for its many unique findings and relevance to all emotion-related healing efforts – deep unconscious experiences affect all attempts at cure.

A clinical illustration

To illustrate the differences between the weak and strong adaptive approaches, let's consider the following psychotherapy session:

Mrs Hall, a depressed woman, begins the hour with her male therapist, Dr Benton, by talking about her fear of men. She ruminates a while and then decides that she must be afraid of men because all they want is to have sex with her. She recalls an incident in college when her psychology professor tried to seduce her during a visit to his office. When he got physical with her, she panicked and thought he was going to murder her. She reacted by pulling away from him and dropping the class. It was a disgusting, immoral thing for him to do.

Weak adaptive psychotherapists would propose a wide range of formulations based on the manifest contents of this material. In addition to simply addressing the evident surface messages, they would attempt to extract from these contents a variety of *unconscious implications* that pertain to the patient's behaviours, inner mental conflicts and state of mind. For example, the story could be seen to imply an undue, unconscious fear of men or as indicating that the client has unconsciously identified men in general with this seductive professor and therefore mistakenly mistrusts all men. Another reading of the story might lead to the proposal that the professor is a stand-in for the patient's father and that the incident with the professor represents a repressed, unconscious memory of seduction or harm at the hands of her parent. Projection of the patient's own repressed wishes to seduce men and/or of her murderous rage at them might also be considered, as might dysfunctional patterns of relating to or thinking about men. Also possible is the idea that the professor is a stand-in for the therapist and that, 'in the transference', the patient is entertaining the fantasy that he wants to seduce or murder her – a purported *unconscious misperception* that might then be traced to a seductive experience that the patient had endured with her father in her childhood. On the other hand, the story might be thought of as a projection of the patient's own seductive and murderous wishes towards the therapist.

All of these formulations take the manifest contents of this material at face value and considers its themes in their own right. Adaptation is vaguely implied, but the main focus is on the inner mental world of the patient and how her thoughts, fantasies and behaviour patterns are disturbing her relationships with men. The search is made for possible meanings inherent to the tale; the main technique involves *extracting implications* from the surface story *per se* – that is, from the isolated narrative. No other information is needed. And there is, of course, a degree of logic and some likely elements of truth to these mind-centred, vaguely adaptive, arbitrarily extracted implications of this manifest tale. Why then is there a need for something more?

The answer lies with an event – *an adaptation-evoking, traumatic triggering event*, a trigger that is ignored in these formulations – something that happened in the therapy situation that calls for a very different line of reasoning and formulating. In escorting the patient into his consultation room, Dr Benton's arm inadvertently had brushed against Mrs Hall's arm.

While many therapists would think of this as an innocuous event, such an assessment reflects the naivety of, and proneness to the use of denial by, the conscious mind. Clinical observations made in the context of the strong adaptive approach indicate otherwise. A boundary violation of this kind, which is often disregarded consciously, is experienced deeply unconsciously as a highly traumatic intervention by the patient – and therapist as well. And the evidence that the patient had indeed unconsciously experienced and reacted to the physical contact with her therapist, which she ignored consciously, is found in *the encoded theme in the narrative images that bridges from the story to the trigger* – that of a professor who 'got physical' with her. This is how the deep unconscious system communicates with the conscious mind: by telling a story about someone else and some other event that is analogous and thematically similar to a disturbing event that has taken place elsewhere – for patients in psychotherapy, this other locale is almost always the treatment situation and the other person is the therapist.

It appears, then, that whatever her conscious intentions in telling this tale, Mrs Hall unconsciously chose to tell this story to convey her unconscious perceptions of the meanings of the physical contact that Dr Benton made with her arm. Thus, while the narrative reflects her *conscious* attempt to understand her general problems with men, it also reflects her *unconscious* efforts to understand and adapt to the traumatic triggering event created by the therapist's lapse − the story is a two-tiered, two-meaning communication.

Once the trigger has been identified, it's no longer possible to be satisfied with mind-oriented, weak adaptive formulations of the story about the seductive professor. Instead, the unconscious meanings of the story must be formulated first and foremost in light of the trigger that evoked the recollection. But in order to do this, and to thereby discover the *encoded level of deep unconscious experience*, the therapist needs to have consciously noticed the physical contact with his patient and to have kept it in mind as he listened to her material. If the trigger goes unnoticed − as often is the case with disturbing interventional triggers − then weakly adaptive, intellectualized, intrapsychically-oriented but highly defensive formulations hold sway. But if the trigger is noticed − as it should be − then strong adaptive formulations are an utter necessity. The critical point is to appreciate that these manifest narratives contain two stories and two sets of messages − one consciously fashioned and stated directly, the other unconsciously honed, camouflaged or encoded, and indirectly stated.

To complete the picture, a strong adaptive psychotherapist would trigger-decode this narrative about the seductive mentor who made inappropriate physical contact with his student as conveying the patient's unconscious perception of her therapist's physical contact with her as being a seductive gesture on his part, and as something that was disgusting, immoral and murderously destructive. The incident was so damaging to the patient that she was thinking − again, quite unconsciously − of leaving treatment. All of this is logical and undistorted because the trigger, for which the therapist must bear full responsibility, is a violation of the ground rule that precludes physical contact between patients and their therapists. It is therefore correctly appraised deep-unconsciously by the patient, who has unconsciously chosen from among the many universal meanings of the event, those that are most relevant to her mental state and emotional history. *Selection rather than distortion* is the operative mechanism here.

Unconscious experience tends to be raw, undefended and very much to the point. For these reasons, the trigger-decoding of these manifest themes does not entail formulations that propose that the patient was making use of her imagination, engaged in expressing her fantasies or projections, or conveying disguised unconscious distortions or misperceptions of the therapist. Instead, the formulation is developed in terms of valid unconscious perceptions, accurate readings of the actual meanings of the traumatic triggering event – meanings that the patient unconsciously and selectively experienced. Also included in this formulation are the patient's efforts to adapt to the incident by under-standing its implications and responding accordingly. All of these cognitive processes took place outside of her awareness, as there is no sign of her conscious recognition of the physical contact with her therapist (nor was there any in the remainder of the session).

It's important to appreciate the extent to which the weak and strong adaptive interpretations of the *unconscious meanings* of this material are at odds with each other. These differences stem from the fact that weak adaptive approaches *extract implications from the story as such*, while the strong adaptive approach *decodes the themes of the story in light of their activating trigger*. In the first approach, the story is believed to be sufficiently revealing on its own that no additional information is needed. In the second approach, which is basically adaptive, the trigger for the story must be identified – without it, no active unconscious meaning can be assigned to the narrative. In add-ition, the various weak adaptive formulations of the patient's story are propositions about her inner mental psychopathology, while the strong adaptive formulation are propositions about her deep uncon-scious strengths. Put another way, one view reflects the belief that the material primarily reflects problems in the patient, while the other view sees the primary problem in the therapist and in his inadvertent boundary violation.

As for the genetic connections between this material and a likely seductive incident between the patient and her father, the weak adap-tive position has it that the unconscious effects of the memory of that event prompts the patient to *mistakenly believe* that the counsellor is behaving seductively when he's not – the past is viewed as a source of present-day distortions. In contrast, the strong adaptive approach has it the other way around: the link to the past takes the form of an unconscious appreciation that the counsellor is *actually repeating* in some form the seductive behaviour of the patient's father – the past is actually being re-enacted in the present.

All in all, the weak adaptive line of thought is based on the premise that fantasy is stronger than reality, while the strong adaptive approach postulates (and has observed) that reality is stronger than fantasy. Furthermore, traumatic events do not fall to the wayside leaving the mind to fight its own battles – these events are as much a part of ongoing inner mental conflicts as the fantasies and memories that they arouse. Residuals of traumatic events continue to be processed unconsciously – and more rarely consciously – for long periods of time, often for one's entire life.

The following table summarizes the key differences between the weak and strong adaptive approaches:

	Weak adaptive approaches	Strong adaptive approaches
1	Emotional adaptation is a peripheral consideration	Emotional adaptation is the central thesis
2	Sees narratives and intellectualizations on an equal par	Distinguishes between intellectualizations and narratives
3	Extracts unconscious implications of manifest contents	Trigger-decodes narrative themes
4	Stresses fantasy and memory	Stresses unconscious perception
5	Focuses on the mind in isolation	Focuses on the mind as activated by traumatic events
6	Gives full credence to manifest contents and their implications	Acknowledges surface meanings, but works mainly by decoding encoded narratives
7	Models the ego, id and superego	Models the conscious and deep unconscious systems of the emotion-processing mind
8	Stresses individual differences	Stresses universals
9	Favours a subjective-relativistic view of reality	Favours an absolute view of reality
10	Unconscious realm ill-defined	Unconscious realm specifically defined
11	Accesses the superficial unconscious system of the conscious mind	Accesses the deep unconscious system of the emotion-processing mind
12	Focuses on relatively weak, intrapsychic issues: relating, interacting, imagining, fantasizing and remembering	Focuses on powerful environmental traumas such as illness, injury and death

2

Two Modes of
Communication

While it's true that there are many avenues of emotional expression –
for example affects, physical symptoms, behaviours, body posture and
so on – none is more concisely expressed and deeply revealing than
the words spoken by the participants in psychotherapy sessions. For
this reason, we turn now to a study of the verbal exchanges between
patients and their therapists. To begin this pursuit, let's look at another
brief clinical vignette:

Ms Exeter is a young woman in her early twenties who has been
hospitalized on an inpatient unit because of a serious depression.
Her therapist, Dr Frank, had inadvertently forgotten and missed the
session prior to the hour whose opening minutes I shall now briefly
excerpt.

The therapist begins the session by apologizing for having missed
the previous session and for not being able to offer a make-up session. The patient then says it's all right, she's okay with it, she knows
how busy he is these days. The unit's been very disorganized lately.
It's the kind of situation that could confuse anyone. What's really
bothering her is Eddie, her boyfriend. He promised to visit her last
night, but he didn't show up. It's just like a man to do something like
that. He doesn't give a damn about her. His saying one thing and
doing another is driving her crazy. It's what he wants to do to her.
He must hate her. Something must be wrong with him. She feels

betrayed and hurt. He needs to work out his problems with women, his hostility. Her friend Kate knows how to deal with men like that. She once had this boyfriend, Ben, who had tried to choke her to death while he was bombed out on alcohol. He disappeared after the incident and showed up weeks later. She took a knife and cut his arm just to have her revenge. A little trick with a knife will teach Eddie to keep his promises, which is exactly what he's got to learn to do.

Perspectives on listening and formulating

Therapists have several tasks in respect to facilitating patients' open and meaningful communication in psychotherapy sessions. The first is to create the conditions and framework – that is, to offer a set of ground rules and boundaries – that facilitate the unencumbered expression of directly stated, conscious perceptions, thoughts and feelings, as well as those that are indirectly, unconsciously stated through narrative vehicles. The ideal or secured frame, in which total privacy and confidentiality are assured, is optimal for this purpose. In addition, the use of a ground rule that speaks for unencumbered communication is of value. Thus, patients should be advised to say everything that comes to mind without censoring their thoughts and feelings – an application of the so-called *fundamental rule of free-association* (Freud, 1913). In addition, strong adaptive therapists now favour adding the suggestion that the patient begin each session with a dream or story and associate further stories to these initial images – an application of *the basic rule of guided associations*, which is designed to maximize the communication of encoded deep unconscious perceptions and adaptive processing activities (Langs, 1993).

A key adaptive finding is that patients' communications are at all times under the unconscious influence of both the conditions that a therapist sets for a given therapy experience, and his or her moment-to-moment verbal and behavioural interventions. Thus, whatever a patient does and does not say is based on and adaptively reactive to what the therapist does and does not do, most of it unconsciously mediated. Clinical studies have shown, for example, than in less than ideal conditions for a psychotherapy experience – for example in therapies in which reports are sent to third-party payers – patients are less inclined to express themselves openly, especially in respect to their deep unconscious experiences of the compromised treatment situation. Even so, many of these patients will, from time to time, encode these experiences in their narratives in

ways that lend themselves to trigger decoding, so meaningful communication is possible in modified therapy frames. The point is to realize
that patients' communications are interpersonally crafted and inter-
actionally framed.

As for listening and formulating, the therapist's goal is to identify
and take into account all of the meanings that are expressed both
directly-consciously and in encoded-unconscious form in a patient's
material. This is especially important because, as we have begun to
see, each of the two systems of the emotion-processing mind not
only communicates in its own special manner, but also adapts on the
basis of its own distinctive perceptions, values and coping strategies.
Furthermore, quite often the conscious system is processing one set
of triggering events and their meanings, while the deep unconscious
system is processing another, more powerful set. It's essential, then, for
therapists to adopt two different levels of listening and formulating
because their patients – and all humans – live mentally within two
very different worlds of emotion-related experience.

Modes of expression

The first step in the listening process involves the determination of
the mode of expression that a patient is using from moment to
moment in a session. The question to be answered pertains to
whether the patient is *intellectualizing or telling a narrative tale*, be it a
dream or storied vehicle. These are two very different modes of communication. Intellectualizations – speculations, ruminations, analyses,
interpretations, opinions, explanations, general descriptions and so on –
by and large are single message units that are derived mainly from
conscious experiences. They do not have substantial encoded meaning and seldom facilitate entry into the realm of deep unconscious
experience. They may, however, be communicated by patients in the
service of deep unconscious interpretations directed to an errant
therapist – a reflection of the remarkable ability of this system to
analyse and comprehend, within limits, some of the psychodynamic
sources of therapists' erroneous interventions.

In the above excerpt, this mode of expression is seen in Ms Exeter's
comment that her therapist's absence was all right, that she's okay with
it, that she knows how busy he is these days, and that the unit's been
very disorganized lately. The analyses of her boyfriend's behaviour is a
reflection of this same mode of expression, although here we may
postulate encoded attempts to interpret some of the dynamic sources

of the therapist's lapse. Thus, there may well be a measure of inter-pretive effort in her comments that it's just like a man to forget to appear for a promised visit, that he doesn't give a damn about her and is trying to drive her crazy, that he must hate her, that something must be wrong with him, and that he needs to work out his problems with women. Nevertheless, it's well to notice that these appear to be weakly adaptive of the kind made by the conscious mind, and they may well have been in the patient's conscious thoughts as she mulled over her therapist's absence. At most, they are best thought of as super-ficially unconscious and easily brought into the patient's awareness. They are without the mystery and surprise that is seen in encoded expressions of deep unconscious experiences of triggering events.

The second type of message is narrative in nature. Because almost every dream is configured as a story, they are the best-known example of this mode of expression. Nevertheless, other narrative forms have comparable structures and functions. This includes patients' daydreams, stories that they make up, and incidents that they recall in some detail, drawn from their personal lives, movies, novels, newspapers and the like. In the excerpt presented above, this mode of communication is seen in Ms Exeter's brief stories about her boyfriend Eddie's absence and her girlfriend's cutting her boyfriend, Ben, with a knife when he returned to her after a long absence. These narratives convey two sets of meanings: one set is directly and manifestly stated and consciously intended, while the other set is disguised or encoded in the same message, and therefore indirectly stated and unconsciously intended. Both sets of meanings convey adaptive responses to triggering events, the manifest message pertaining to consciously experienced incidents, while the encoded message pertains to incidents, or meanings of incidents, that have been unconsciously experienced.

In the excerpt above, the patient's manifest story is about her boyfriend Eddie's unexpected absence. The triggering event for her conscious concerns is his absence, and the conscious adaptive response, which is also manifestly developed and communicated, involves getting angry at him, analysing the situation and arriving at a tentative adaptive response – namely, to harm him in order to teach him how to behave. At the same time, the story about Eddie encodes the patient's responses to a very different triggering event, namely the therapist's absence – a ground-rule violation that constitutes a failure to honour his pledge to be present at all scheduled sessions. Encoded in the story, which bridges to the trigger through the theme of absence in the face of a promise to appear – is the patient's adaptive response to the therapist's lapse. Here, too, she is feeling angry, albeit with her therapist whom she wants to harm in order to teach him a lesson – reactions that the patient, for good reason, needed to experience unconsciously and encode rather that experience consciously and enact.

Because this trigger was alluded to consciously, we can compare the patient's conscious and unconscious responses to the therapist's lapse. The conscious response is limited, forgiving and dismissive – the therapist was simply confused. But the encoded, unconscious response is expansive and very different. To ascertain its nature, we lift the themes from the story about Eddie and relocate them, connecting them to the triggering event – a process that is the essence of trigger decoding. The story's themes are those of not giving a damn about the patient; trying to drive her crazy; hating, betraying and hurting her; and something being wrong with the perpetrator of the harm who has unresolved problems with hostility towards women. The trigger-decoded, transposed translation of these themes is that in light of the therapist's absence (the triggering intervention), the patient unconsciously perceives the therapist as not giving a damn about her. The remaining themes appear to be an unconscious attempt to interpret the underlying cause of the therapist's error, namely that he is trying to drive her crazy; betraying, hurting and hating her; and has problems with unresolved hostility towards women. There is also, as noted, a responsive wish to harm the therapist for what he did and to teach him how to keep his promises in the future.

These are the patient's personally selected, but valid deep unconscious perceptions of the implications and sources of the triggering event, along with her adaptive reaction to the event. The latter includes an *encoded corrective or model of rectification* – namely, that the therapist should be present, as promised, for all scheduled sessions.

We can see, then, that a dream or story is an end-product – that it's told at the end of an unconscious adaptive processing effort that begins with an unconscious perception of aspects of a triggering event. That is, after a traumatic incident or some of its meanings are perceived and processed deep-unconsciously, the system seeks out or creates a dream or story through which it reports on these unconscious activities to conscious awareness. Typically, patients' narratives are about events outside of therapy and the incident is chosen because it's analogous to, and therefore shares themes with, the unconsciously experienced trigger created by the therapist. In the vignette, for example, the theme of Eddie's unexpected absence is analogous to the therapist's missing the patient's scheduled session. This is the *bridging theme* that supports the thesis that the manifest story encodes responses to unconsciously experienced aspects of the latent trigger.

Notice, too, the extent to which the encoded, unconscious view of the triggering intervention is different from the unencoded, manifest view. The conscious response is based on the evident *use of denial* – it was nothing. In contrast, the deep unconscious reaction is forthright and incisive – it conveys disturbing unconscious perceptions of the actual implications of the triggering event that apparently had not registered consciously. We can also see that the trigger that the patient is trying to cope with consciously (her boyfriend's absence) is different from the trigger that she's trying to cope with at the deep unconscious level (the therapist's absence). This is typically the case.

Finally, we may trigger-decode the story about the patient's girl-friend, Kate, by first noting another bridging theme – again, that of an absence – and then identifying themes of an attempt at murder, abandonment, revenge through a violent act, and teaching wayward men a lesson so they don't disappear again. It seems clear that this story truly encodes the patient's deep unconscious perceptions of her therapist's absence as an attempt at murder and abandonment, while Kate's attacking her boyfriend on his return speaks for the rage that the patient is feeling unconsciously towards her therapist and the harm she intends for him. There's a striking difference between the patient's consciously bland response to the therapist's absence and her intense deep unconscious experience and reaction to the lapse. This is an especially important point because deep unconscious experiences have enormous effects on patients' symptoms, resistances in therapy, behaviours within and outside of treatment, and overall emotional life. It's one reason why trigger decoding and adaptive interpreting is so important for all forms of psychotherapy – without these efforts, there's considerable danger of harm to the patient, even as its sources go unrecognized.

Single-message units

In listening to patients' material, the first task of an adaptive-oriented psychotherapist is to distinguish narrative from non-narrative communications. If both types of expression are in evidence, the intellectualizations, along with the manifest contents of dreams and other narratives, are put into one bin and treated as conscious system communications and adaptive responses. While often of little conse-quence, they may indicate the status of a patient's symptoms and emotional life in general, or reflect his or her attitudes towards treatment. But they do not encode unconscious perceptions and adaptive processing activities and therefore do not lend themselves to trigger decoding. Attempts to extract implications from such material is of limited value.

Narrative themes need to be separated into a second bin, their manifest contents duly noted, and then treated as encoded reflections of deep unconscious perceptions and processes. With the themes in hand, the search is directed towards finding the trigger – usually an intervention by the therapist – to which the themes are attached and the patient is responding to on the deep unconscious level of experience. It's this type of effort and the use of trigger decoding that opens a window into the realm of deep unconscious experience and the adaptive activities of the deep unconscious system of the emotion-processing mind. In general, the absence of narrative material is a sign of *communicative resistance* and, as such, should initiate a search for the triggers that have evoked this unconsciously wrought avoidance of encoded themes. In most cases, the answer lies with intellectualized interventions by the therapist that have been made on the basis of extracting implications from manifest contents – a surface-oriented way of intervening that unconsciously invites the patient to communicate unencoded, intellectualized messages and to avoid expressions of deep unconscious experience.

The recognition of a sharp distinction between, and in the functions and meanings of, narrative versus non-narrative communications is basic to the strong adaptive approach. Therapists who do not recognize this distinction are generally unable to appreciate the unique role played by encoded narrative communications. They tend to treat all messages as if they were identical in structure and limit themselves to extracting implications from the surface of these messages. In this way, they confine both themselves and their patients to the realm of conscious experience, far from the more powerful world of deep unconscious happenings and processes.

The extraction of implications from manifest contents tends to be an arbitrary, uncertain and biased effort, and interventions made on this basis do not obtain patients' *unconscious, narratively encoded validation* – the ultimate criterion of correct formulations and interpretations. This type of manifest therapeutic work tends to deal with relatively weak emotional issues and therefore to have a highly defensive function because trigger-decoded meanings are far more powerful and disturbing than directly communicated meanings. This applies to all weak adaptive forms of psychotherapy, which can be understood to be *conscious system modes of treatment*. This mode of therapy is dramatically different from those based on trigger decoding, which are *deep unconscious system modes of treatment*.

To sum up, the direct and implied meanings of all manifest messages are vehicles of expression that reflect the operations of the conscious system of the emotion–processing mind. Clinical research has shown that, on the whole, these messages tend to be only minimally charged with emotional impact, even when they involve the analysis of very damaging incidents like earthquakes and personal assaults. They tend to take shape as patients' highly intellectualized comments and analyses, or as the surface meanings of dreams and stories. These manifest and implied meanings tend to involve transparent conscious and unconscious psychodynamics that are easily brought into awareness. These features of manifest contents stand in sharp contrast to the encoded meanings of narratives, which tend to deal with far more disturbing issues, to be far from evident to the conscious mind, and to be much more difficult to ascertain.

Despite the limitations that accrue to work with manifest contents and their evident implications, studies based on the strong adaptive approach suggest that a great deal of psychotherapy, including those forms that are psychoanalytically–oriented, is conducted on the basis of this level of communication. Questions are asked and previously unstated thoughts and feelings are unearthed, and these are taken to reflect previously unconscious material. In circular fashion, this kind of therapeutic work is taken to support mind-centred, weak adaptive approaches to treatment and their focus on the minds of patients. Mental thoughts and feelings, viewed in isolation and on their own terms, are the sum and substance of these efforts. Should adaptation be considered, it's viewed in terms of conscious and manifest responses to manifestly experienced triggering events – notions of unrecognized triggers and unconscious perception and processing are not invoked.

A formal research study that was conducted on the basis of strong adaptive thinking (Langs *et al.*, 1996) provided unexpected tentative evidence that interventions of this kind are unconsciously designed to avoid or reduce the expression of patients' highly threatening deep unconscious perceptions – many of them related to errant and unconsciously harmful interventions made by their therapists. While this type of avoidance may bring temporary relief to both parties to therapy, it does so on the basis of avoidance and denial – costly forms

of redress at best. I'll have more to say about these difficult issues later
in the book.

Double-message units

As for dreams and stories, the conveyors of both manifest and latent
(in the sense of trigger-encoded) messages, it's well to first appreciate that weak adaptive, mind-oriented therapists do at times formulate and interpret disguised unconscious meanings that are thought
to be reflected in manifest dreams and fantasies. But in so doing,
they tend to treat the purported encoded image as a universal sym-
bol or as an isolated disguised content within the mind of the
patient. These readings of unconscious meaning revolve around
theories of the mind related to mental symbols and archetypes,
unconscious fantasies and unconscious memories. Thus, elongated
objects are seen to symbolize the phallus, while a rounded container
symbolizes the womb.

As is the case in extracting implications from manifest messages,
determining the symbolic meanings of dream elements and other
narratives is an extremely arbitrary, theory-driven endeavour. They
allow for an almost unlimited range of possibilities and interpretations. Thus, whatever grain of truth there is to these ideas, they
nevertheless reflect an incomplete, weak adaptive orientation in
which the mind is believed to operate relatively divorced from reality
and adaptation is given little or no consideration.

The strong adaptive approach takes a very different position in
regard to the nature and functions of storied messages. It stresses their
role as messengers from the deep unconscious system of the emotion-
processing mind and their essential connection to the unconsciously
perceived meanings of triggering events. Narratives are seen to
primarily reflect unconscious adaptations to actual events, although,
secondarily, they may also encode the fantasies and memories associated with these events.

Almost all of the triggers to which patients' deep unconscious systems are sensitive, involve the interventions of their therapists, verbal
and behavioural, and especially their impingements on and efforts to
manage the ground rules of treatment. This places therapists at the
very centre of their patients' deep unconscious (but not necessarily
conscious) adaptive struggles. Communicatively, this natural, evolved
tendency puts therapists in a unique position to experience and know
first-hand the nature of the triggers to which their patients are

responding deep-unconsciously – that is, the triggers are constituted by their own therapeutic efforts. And they affect the nature and flow of their patients' encoded narratives and adaptive preferences, as well as the extent to which they are inclined to narrate at all – all of it interacting with the patient's own inclinations. Indeed, every patient has a preferred style of expressing encoded themes – some do so extensively, while others do so sparingly. Almost always this trait is evident in the initial session, largely because it is inborn and virtually unmodifiable in the course of a therapy experience.

There are, then, two dialogues going on in every treatment situation, the first of which is an exchange of conscious, manifest messages loaded with detectable implications. The second dialogue, however, may take one of two forms: the first is an unwitting exchange of deep unconscious perceptions and experiences in which neither party to therapy becomes consciously aware of this level of transaction and its effects – a most unfortunate situation. But the second is a dialogue in which the patient expresses unconscious, encoded messages without being aware of their meanings, while the therapist trigger decodes their unconscious meanings and brings them into the patient's awareness – a most salutary circumstance.

As I have been emphasizing, the deep unconscious level of experience holds enormous power over the emotional lives of both healers and those whom they are trying to heal. Even when a therapy is centred on manifest contents and their implications, as seen in relational forms of therapy or cognitive retraining, the unconscious exchange of messages between patients and therapists will have a strong although unseen effect on both parties to the process. Therapists of all stripes are well-advised to tune into that second dialogue because it's exerting a profound influence on how the treatment is proceeding and on the lives of both participants – spill-over into everyday life is inevitable. As the following excerpt shows, even the smallest amount of attention to encoded themes and their evocative triggers can go a long way towards keeping any kind of treatment process and the lives of both participants on an even keel, and helping all concerned move towards improved adaptive functioning.

A clinical illustration

Mrs Kassen, an investment advisor, was undergoing cognitive retraining for a severe depression; her therapist was Ms Reed, a clinical social worker. The patient had made progress initially, but had then suffered a relapse. Ms Reed was at a loss to explain the regression, so she reviewed the case with her supervisor, Mrs Doran, who had some knowledge of the strong adaptive approach.

Inquiry by Mrs Doran came around to the ground rules and conditions of the treatment. The client was being seen in a clinic, and before each session she was required to pay the fee for the training session based on a bill given to her by the clinic secretary. It turned out that before each of the last two training sessions, the secretary had mistakenly given her a bill meant for another client – and had given the other client the patient's bill. Each time it happened, Mrs Kassen was delayed and was late to her session, and each time she had apologized for her lateness, while excusing the secretary's error as a result of her being new to the job.

When Mrs Doran suggested in supervision that these errors may have contributed to the recurrence of the patient's symptoms, Ms Reed suddenly was reminded that Mrs Kassen had told an odd story before they began to work on her exercises last hour. Ms Reed had forgotten the story, but bringing up the secretary's error had brought it back to her mind because it was about the patient's secretary at work. It seems that the secretary had made a serious blunder, a book-keeping error that involved depositing a large check, sent to her by one Mrs Kassen's clients, into the wrong account. The offended client had accused Mrs Kassen of stealing the money from him. But, worse still, as luck would have it the secretary had put the money into the account of the client's ex-wife. The client was enraged. He felt that his confidentiality had been seriously compromised – the last thing he wanted was for his ex-wife to know that he had some surplus cash. He took his account away from Mrs Kassen, who had been terribly depressed over the incident.

Because it was an event that had depressed her client, Ms Reed had briefly worked over the manifest narrative and tried to reassure Mrs Kassen that the error wasn't hers, that she had no cause for guilt, and that she would survive quite well without this client's business. Mrs Kassen had accepted the reassurance, but her depression continued unabated to a point where Ms Reed began to think of referring her to the clinic psychiatrist for anti-depressant medication.

Mrs Doran had another view of this material. The themes in the story of the secretary's error bridged over, and seemed connected to, the error made by the clinic secretary in two ways: first through the theme of a monetary error, and second through the theme of a third party inappropriately obtaining privileged information. The frame violations made by the secretary at the clinic involved both an error with the bill and having Mrs Kassen's name revealed to another client – as well as the other client's name being revealed to Mrs Kassen.

Mrs Doran trigger–decoded Mrs Kassen's story in light of the trigger of the clinic secretary's error – an intervention for which the client, unconsciously and justifiably, would hold Ms Reed fully responsible. The themes in the narrative about the incident at work indicates that while Mrs Kassen dismissed the incident consciously, on the deep unconscious level of experience she was infuriated by the billing error and the violation of her confidentiality – and her deep unconscious adaptive recommendation was to leave treatment.

As for Mrs Kassen's depression, it evidently stemmed from the hurt and rage at the clinic secretary and Ms Reed that she was experiencing deep-unconsciously, even as consciously she was denying any sense of harm. The damage was compounded by Ms Reed's failure to appreciate the importance of these frame violations and her deafness to the patient's encoded messages. As a result, the patient's unconscious perceptions and rage went uninterpreted and no effort was made to rectify and secure the frame by trying to prevent further mistakes of this kind.

To some extent, it seems likely that Mrs Kassen turned her anger at her counsellor against herself in the form of a heightening of her depression. At the same time, the symptom was a defeat for, and an attack against, Ms Reed's therapeutic efforts, thereby extracting a degree of revenge for the patient. These are typical consequences of therapists' failures to pay attention to deep unconscious experience and the encoded level of their patients' narratives.

It seems clear that once again, in the context of a non–dynamic treatment arrangement, a frame violation – that of the patient's privacy – evoked a naive, excuse-ridden, denial-based conscious response. But it has in addition triggered a narrative communication that encodes a very different and highly critical deep unconscious reaction to consciously unrecognized meanings of the same event. As a weak adaptive therapist, Ms Reed had all but forgotten the story and recalled it only because of her supervisor's exploration of the status of the ground rules of the therapy. It's quite easy for therapists who are unfamiliar with the adaptive approach to miss the communication of a narrative vehicle and thereby fail to realize that it's encoding a deep unconscious reaction to a triggering event that is deeply affecting the treatment experience and its outcome. Sensitivity to narrative communications is essential for detecting and formulating the vicissitudes of the deep unconscious dialogue between patient and therapist.

In weak adaptive forms of psychotherapy, it's not uncommon to find that therapists are unwittingly sending their patients mixed messages. On the one hand, they're trying manifestly and consciously to train or explain away or superficially interpret a patient's symptoms. But on the other, they or someone affiliated with them becomes involved in ground-rule or boundary infractions that are harmful to the patient and thereby unconsciously promote the very symptoms that they are trying to alleviate. Indeed, as we shall see, no matter how a therapist defines the ground rules of a therapy situation, the patient unconsciously seeks an ideal, universal set of ground rules that the deep unconscious mind inherently recognizes as the optimal conditions for treatment. Patients respond unconsciously to ground-rule management on the basis of these deep-unconsciously sought standards no matter how a therapy is structured.

Notice, too, that even though the therapy involved cognitive retraining, once the unconsciously sought frame was violated, the client found a way to tell a story. This is a psychobiological given: in response to infringements of ground rules and boundaries, humans find or create narrative vehicles with which to convey their deep unconscious experience of, and adaptive response to, the frame-related triggering event. This means that when patients narrate, therapists should pay attention to their stories, make note of the themes, and search for the interventional triggers to which the patient is responding. This is especially true for negatively toned stories because harmful themes almost always encode responses to harmful triggering events – they are a strong indication that the therapist has done something hurtful to the patient. Finding the provocative trigger – the erroneous comment or, more often, the frame violation – enables the offending therapist to understand what the patient is experiencing as damaging at a deep unconscious level and to set matters right through both interpretation and frame-securing efforts.

A therapist may wish to work with their patients' manifest material and make use of superficial interpretations, exercises and so on, but it's well to keep in mind that their interventions as healers, whatever they may be, have both conscious and deep unconscious effects. Many errant interventions that go unnoticed by patients, as well as many unregistered, anxiety-provoking meanings of interventions that patients allude to consciously, do register and are processed by the deep unconscious minds of everyone involved in the treatment situation. The unconsciously perceived harmful qualities of these interventions then have their damaging effects on both parties to the therapy. Keeping an ear open for narratives and their themes is vital to ascertaining their triggers and taking proper measures to bring a damaging style of intervening to a halt and offer the much needed interpretations and frame rectifications that will have a healing influence on both parties to therapy.

You can ignore nature, but you can't hide from its effects. And when it comes to psychotherapy, the most imposing experiences take place without conscious awareness. The trigger-evoked, encoded meanings of narratives hold the key to that realm. Therapists are well-advised to take hold of that key and to keep opening the doors to the deep unconscious domain to which it gives them – and their patients – access.

3

Models of the Mind

As a scientist steeped in biology, Freud appreciated the need for, and value of, models of the mind as a source of otherwise unavailable insights. He offered two such clinically-founded models: the two-system topographic model (Freud, 1900) which featured the systems UCS (unconscious) and PC–CS (preconscious–conscious), and the three-system structural model of ego, id and superego (Freud, 1923). While the structural model prevails to this day and is inherent to all weak adaptive approaches to psychotherapy, the strong adaptive model of the mind hearkens back to and is an extensively modified version of the topographic model. Let's turn now to these models of the mind to gain a sense of how the emotion-related mind is thought to be structured and to operate.

Freud's first model of the mind

In *The Interpretation of Dreams*, Freud (1900) proposed the first psychodynamic model of the mind (that is, the emotion-related mind) – his map or topographic model. His goal was to account for the development of neuroses in terms of unconscious conflict and warring systems of the mind, and his essential insight was that the unconscious structure of dreams is comparable to that of emotional symptoms. His quest was to study the nature of unconscious contents in order to discover how they are activated and find expression in dreams and symptoms.

In essence, Freud proposed that *the systems of the mind are defined by the status of their contents vis-à-vis awareness* – essentially, whether they're in awareness or potentially capable of entering awareness directly and undisguised, or are outside of awareness and capable of entering awareness only if sufficiently disguised. Those contents that are outside of awareness belong to the system UCS (unconscious), while those that are in awareness belong to the system CS (conscious) and those that can easily enter awareness directly and undisguised belong to the system PCS (preconscious), which is the gateway to the system CS. The defining feature of the systems of the mind was, then, whether its contents are conscious or unconscious, and on this basis Freud also defined a number of distinctive properties for each system – UCS and PCS–CS.

In developing this model, Freud described the operations of the mind in a somewhat adaptive vein by proposing a sequence of processes that begin with the *conscious perception* of an actual incident – the so-called *day's residue* of a dream, for example – and ends with some type of discharge, be it through a dream, action or neurotic symptom. Thus, the consciously experienced day's residue activates unconscious wishes and memories within the system UCS *and then falls to the wayside*. The aroused UCS wishes, which are mainly of a primitive, infantile, incestuous nature (aggressive wishes were added later on), seek discharge or expression. But the search for discharge is blocked by the censorship of the system PCS–CS, whose defences are activated by the conscience, which also belongs to this system. The result is a compromise such as a disguised manifest dream that satisfies or expresses both the wish and the defence. In this light, *repression* of the forbidden wishes is seen as the fundamental psychological defence. And the goal in analysing a dream is to undo the mechanisms of disguise (that is, displacement, symbolization and condensation) in order to identify the repressed, unconscious wish or memory camouflaged in the dream and bring it into awareness for conscious processing, renunciation and resolution.

In addition to formulating this sequence of processes, Freud proposed a set of properties that distinguished the operations of the two systems of the mind. Thus, the system UCS was said to operate according to the pleasure principle and the so-called *primary processes* that included the search for immediate discharge by the primitive, forbidden wishes within the system; an utter disregard for reality considerations (see however, Holt, 1967; Noy, 1969); the timelessness of its wishes; the absence of logic or rational thinking; and a fluidity of representations (one thing standing for another) through the mechanisms of symbolization, condensation and displacement.

In contrast, the system PCS–CS was said to operate with the so-called *secondary processes* that included a strong capacity to delay the discharge of its relatively mature wishes and needs; is in close contact with, and shows respect for, reality; is logical and sensible; and operates with direct representations of its thoughts and their meanings – an image or thought stands for itself alone.

Freud's model stressed the role of intrapsychic conflict between the two systems of the mind in both dreams and symptom formation – essentially, he postulated a battle between unconscious wishes and conscious sensibilities. Thus, a symptom was viewed as a compromise like a dream – it was seen as an emotional disturbance that unconsciously expressed or represented both the forbidden wishes of the system UCS and the defences of the system PCS–CS. The model is based on an inner mental, weak adaptive viewpoint, which, in turn, supports thinking along those very lines – the classical idea that theory drives observation and theory-driven observations drive the creation of models that are then used to sustain the theory. Breaking out of this vicious cycle is no easy matter.

Freud's structural model

Over the years that followed his creation of the topographic model of the mind, Freud discovered several seemingly intractable problems with his vision. His centrepiece for psychoanalytic theory was the concept of unconscious intrapsychic conflict, but he began to realize that his patients tended to be unaware of their resistances and of their use of psychological defences like repression. This meant that the defences of the system PCS–CS often operated outside awareness – that is, that they were part of the system UCS. It was inconceivable to Freud that both the forbidden wishes and the defences erected against their expression – the warring parties – could be in the same system and, thus, on the same side of the conflict.

Freud also discovered a critical problem with his view of the conscience, which he had located in the system CS. He became aware that a great deal of guilt is experienced unconsciously – that is, that his patients acted in self-punitive ways without realizing that they were doing so. So here too an element of his proposed system CS was also to be found in the system UCS.

All in all, then, Freud's conflict theory was at odds with his model of the mind. He became convinced that he had to abandon one or the other. He chose to preserve his conflict theory and give up topography

(Freud, 1923; Arlow and Brenner, 1964), and did so by introducing his structural model of the mind – the three-system configuration of ego, id and superego. In this model, neuroses and dream formation were conceived of primarily in terms of a conflict between the superego (conscience) and the id (forbidden instinctual drives), as mediated by the ego in light of reality considerations.

The hallmark of psychoanalysis – the existence of unconscious contents (and processes) – suffered badly from this change in models. The term *unconscious* was no longer the defining feature of the systems of the mind. Instead, it was reduced to a quality of mental contents and operations, which could be either conscious or unconscious. *The defining feature of a system of the mind was now the nature of its functions.* Thus, the ego was seen to be responsible for executive functions, relating, tension regulation, psychological defences, and so on; the id was the seat of the instinctual drives of sex and aggression; and the superego was seen as the conscience and ego ideal.

While the structural model has been the basis of advances in ego- and self-psychology, the study of object relations and much more, it also has significant drawbacks (Langs, 1992b). In particular, once 'the unconscious' lost its status as a system of the mind, it became a waste-basket term that had lost its clarity and explanatory powers. It was used to refer to anything that a patient seemed to be unaware of – be it a pattern of thinking or behaving, an opinion or need, a fantasy or memory, or a way of relating. In addition, many conscious com-munications from patients were treated as if they reflected uncon-scious contents and processes – that is, the concept became confounded. Also lost was the small adaptive element found in the topographic model – considerations of reality became a relatively minor function of the very busy ego. All in all, the new model spawned a variety of competing, weak adaptive, mind-centred theor-ies of neurosis, such as ego- and self-psychology, and relational, intersubjective and constructivistic theories, none of which is domin-ant today. The resultant contradictions in viewpoints and confusion speaks for problems in the basic model of the mind (see also Gedo and Goldberg, 1973; Goleman, 1985).

Comparing topographic models

Clinical observations made from the vantage-point of the strong adaptive approach speak for the greater utility of a two-system topo-graphic model of the mind in which the basic configuration is that of a conscious and deep unconscious system – the latter being so-called in order to distinguish it from Freud's view of the unconscious domain (Langs, 1986, 1987, 1995). Taking the formation of a dream as our framework, the adaptive model of the mind postulates that mental processing begins with a triggering event comparable to Freud's day's residues. However, in contrast to Freud's position that the event and its meanings may be innocuous and always consciously perceived, the adaptive model claims that *many of the most critical and anxiety-provoking aspects of the event are not perceived consciously, but unconsciously or subliminally.* (In a footnote added to *The Interpretation of Dreams* in 1919, Freud acknowledged the new researches of Potzl [1917] who had demonstrated the phenomenon of unconscious perception in the formation of dream images, but Freud never applied it to his dream theory.) Further, while Freud suggested that the day residue drops by the wayside and the aroused unconscious fantasies and memories take over the situation, the adaptive approach proposes that the day's residue, and especially its traumatic and unconsciously perceived aspects, continues to be processed by the emotion-processing mind – and that this processing activity is reflected, however disguised, in the resultant dream. Thus, where Freud detached the mind from reality and formulated an isolated intrapsychic process, the strong adaptive approach formulates a continuing tie to reality and an ongoing, inner mental processing of this reality as well.

This strongly adaptive position has a number of additional distinctive features that are missing from the Freudian topographic model. Unconscious adaptive processing requires the use of intelligence, and thus requires postulating the existence of a *deep unconscious wisdom system* – an attribute that is absent in Freudian thinking where the processing of unconscious wishes are matters of seeking discharge and expression. In addition, the adaptive model recognizes the ever-present use of unconscious perception in coping with emotionally-charged traumas. Thus, contrary to Freud's position that the system UCS is out of touch with and disregards reality, the adaptive view is that the deep unconscious system is exquisitely in touch with reality – far more so than the conscious mind. Indeed, it's the conscious system that's denial prone and out of touch with real events and many of their meanings – this too is the very opposite of Freud's thinking (see also Holt, 1967; Noy, 1969).

To continue, the Freudian picture of an illogical system UCS is revised by the adaptive approach into a system that engages in sound, logical and quite brilliant adaptive processing efforts. Once more, it's the conscious system that's seen as inclined towards illogic and false reasoning – it is strongly inclined to make use of denial and of rationalizations for aberrant behaviours. Similarly, while both models recognize the use of primary process mechanisms of disguise and encoding, the Freudian view applies these processes to unconscious wishes, while the strong adaptive approach applies them to unconscious perceptions. Thus, where Freud strives to decode unconscious fantasies, the adaptive therapist seeks to decode unconscious perceptions. Finally, it's well to note that the Freudian decoding of unconscious fantasies and memories is an arbitrary, theory-driven effort, while the decoding activities of the adaptive therapist pertain to and are organized by the nature of the unconsciously perceived trigger and therefore has more structure and definition than its forerunner.

All in all, the two views of the emotion-related mind and the principles of therapy derived from them are diametrically opposed. The Freudian model takes a therapist into an isolated inner mental world of unconscious memories and fantasies, while the adaptive approach takes him or her into a world in which traumatic events activate an inner mental world in which the adaptive unconscious processing of the most painful meanings of emotionally-charged events dominates the scene. The former is entirely mind-centred, while the latter sees the mind as actively coping with reality.

A clinical vignette

The following vignette illustrates the main differences between the ramifications of Freud's topographic model and the one developed by the strong adaptive approach:

Mr Arkin, a single man in his early thirties who is suffering from severe episodes of anxiety, is a salesman for a manufacturer of sporting equipment. He's in psychotherapy with Dr Gregory, who is a male psychologist.

About a year into the therapy, the patient enters Dr Gregory's consultation room, hands him a cheque, sits down in his (the patient's) chair, mumbles something about how annoying it is to have to spend so much money for therapy, and begins the session by saying that he'd had a dream the previous night. In the dream, he's in his boss's office at work and his boss, Harvey, is holding a gun to his head and robbing him of his wallet. Harvey pulls the trigger of the gun, but it doesn't fire. Mr Arkin awoke from the dream feeling extremely anxious.

Associating to the dream, the patient says that Harvey looks like his friend Ernie whom he ran into during lunch on the day of the dream. Ernie talked about how well he was doing in business. Somehow, Mr Arkin took umbrage over what he was saying and how he was saying it, and he felt annoyed. But that's one of his problems, isn't it, he's never at peace with other men. The fact that Ernie is a furniture salesman and Mr Arkin's father was in the furniture business must have something to do with it, but it shouldn't affect him like that. Harvey also is annoying; Mr Arkin has a tense relationship with him. Harvey's a lot like his father, very cheap and demanding, and ready to deduct an expense from Mr Arkin's salary at the drop of a hat. He's a crook.

Mr Arkin then pauses. Being robbed now brings to mind a nasty incident from his adolescence – something he hadn't thought about in years. His family was always under financial pressure, but he managed to get a job as a stock clerk in a supermarket and saved up his salary and some gift money until it came to over a thousand dollars. The money was in a joint savings account that had his father's name on it and, one day, he discovered that his father had withdrawn the money to pay some very pressing bills that were long overdue. Mr Arkin flew into a rage and confronted his father with his thievery and began to shake him. He never got the money back and he guesses that he never forgave him either.

To discuss the vignette to this point, the identified day's residue or trigger for the dream appears to be Mr Arkin's lunch with Ernie and his sense of annoyance at him. This is a relatively innocuous event and it lends itself to the Freudian theory of dream and symptom formation – it's a consciously experienced day's residue that seems to have prompted the creation of the dream of Harvey and being robbed of his wallet. The associations to the dream reveals the use of condensation (for example Harvey represents both himself, Ernie and Mr Arkin's father), displacement (for example the shift from the father to Harvey; from Mr Arkin's home to the boss's office at work; from the money taken by the father to the money in Mr Arkin's wallet), and symbolization (for example the gun may symbolize Mr Arkin's wish to murder his father; its failure to fire may symbolize Mr Arkin's helplessness in the situation with the father).

Everything seems to fall neatly into place. The incident with Ernie, which was registered consciously and is of little consequence, activates a series of memories and fantasies in Mr Arkin's system UCS and then falls to the wayside. The aroused memories and fantasies mainly involve being robbed by his father, having the fantasy of murdering him, and being helpless to do so. At the behest of his conscience, the defences of the system PCS–CS seem to have moved into action and insisted on forging a compromise. Instead of dreaming of being robbed by his father and then murdering him, Mr Arkin dreams of being robbed by his boss with a gun that fails to fire. The primary-process mechanisms of the system UCS and the defences of the system PCS–CS seem to have done their jobs.

It takes associating to the dream to discover the underlying fantasies and memories. They do, however, provide insight into Mr Arkin's relational problems with men – unconsciously, men are viewed as stand-ins for his much-hated father. This includes the therapist, Dr Gregory, so it's likely that Mr Arkin's annoyance at having to pay his fee is the tip of an iceberg, under which is the client's distorted belief that he's being robbed of his money by his therapist. The patient also seems to be entertaining the unconscious fantasy of murdering his therapist, as he once wished to do with his father. The past is distorting Mr Arkin's view of, and feelings towards, men in general and his therapist in particular.

We can see, too, that although the Freudian model works quite well, it does so only up to a point. The conscience does indeed seem to be acting unconsciously, as are the client's defenses. But rather than discarding the model on this basis, as Freud decided to do, the model could have been preserved by acknowledging that the conscience and psychological defences have both conscious and unconscious components – that they do indeed belong to both the system UCS and PCS–CS – and revising the model accordingly. Nevertheless, the model seems to work very well and the formulations could easily be restated in terms of the structural model by proposing that the patient's id wish to murder his father had evoked unconscious objections by his superego that activated his ego's mechanisms of defense to produce a dream that disguises this unconscious drama.

In this light, we may ask, once again, why there's a need for anything more? And, once again, the answer lies in a consciously denied, but deep-unconsciously registered trigger. To clarify this point, let's return to the vignette.

In the session, Dr Gregory offers an interpretation along the lines discussed above – about Mr Arkin's murderous wishes towards his father, how these wishes are affecting his relationships with men, and how they are coming into play 'in the transference'. Mr Arkin pauses, nods in agreement and then says that he has another association to his dream. Yesterday, which was the day of the dream, while reading the newspaper, he came across a story about a doctor who was found guilty of Medicare fraud in an amount close to half a million dollars. The weird thing about it is that his picture was in the newspaper and he looked a lot like Dr Gregory.

At first, Dr Gregory takes the emergence of this fresh material as supportive of his intervention. After all, the material has become more powerful and the distorted transference fantasy that has Mr Arkin believing that he's being robbed of money by his therapist has obtained a clearer representation in the disguised story about the doctor. But as he's mulling this over, he suddenly remembers something that he'd completely forgotten. During the previous month, he had called Mr Arkin at work in order to cancel one of his sessions because he (Dr Gregory) had developed an acute phlebitis of his leg and needed immediate medical care. When writing out Mr Arkin's bill, he'd forgotten about the cancelled hour and had charged his patient for the session. And he'd accepted Mr Arkin's cheque with the over-payment as well – his patient seemed to have also missed the error.

Recognition of this interventional triggering event sheds entirely new light on Mr Arkin's material in this session. Everything that was interpreted from the Freudian vantage point as unconscious fantasy must now be seen as unconscious perception. But even before we spell this out, we should realize that many therapists who work with weak adaptive approaches would not discover this missing trigger – they'd have no reason or motivation seek out a trigger of this kind and strong unconscious motives for not doing so. Indeed, in this situation both the therapist and patient had made use of denial and repression to obliterate the conscious registration of this triggering event. Dr Gregory over-billed his client, and for his part Mr Arkin accepted the error and over-paid the fee. If the imagery and themes of the story about the fraudulent doctor hadn't jarred Dr Gregory into suddenly realizing consciously that he'd made a mistake, it's entirely possible that the error would have been sustained and never consciously noticed by either party to this psychotherapy. The use of denial precludes the conscious recognition of this kind of trigger. Alertness to patients' themes in the context of thinking of them as conveying encoded perceptions of a triggering event, and searching for the evocative trigger, are the only known means by which this kind of shared denial can be uncovered and rectified.

As for trigger decoding this material, we need first to dismiss the Freudian theory of innocuous day's residues as the stimuli for dreams and realize that confining oneself to such events serves as a defence against consciously recognizing the existence of traumatic triggering events. We also must forgo thinking of these images and themes initially as disguised reflections of aroused fantasies. They are serving first and foremost as Mr Arkin's means of encoding his unconscious perceptions of a traumatic interventional trigger that did not register in his conscious awareness, although it did register deep-unconsciously. It's this trigger more than the lunch with Ernie that aroused the client's memory of his father's financial treachery – again, not as part of a string of fantasies and wishes, but as an expression of a past reality that was being relived again in the relationship with the therapist.

To be specific, Mr Arkin's dream of being robbed by his boss encodes his unconscious perception that he is, in fact, being robbed by his therapist. This is not a transference fantasy, but an accurate perception of the therapist's behaviour regarding his bill. It's a clear example of a patient's conscious system denial and obliteration accompanied by a sound unconscious perception. The error is also unconsciously perceived as an attempt to do violence to the patient – as an attempt at murder. In this light, the memory of being robbed by his father expresses Mr Arkin's deep unconscious experience that, by over-billing and robbing him, the therapist is repeating the exploitative act of theft that Mr Arkin's father had perpetrated on the patient when he was an adolescent.

When Dr Gregory offered a weak adaptive transference interpretation involving a purported unconscious source within Mr Arkin for his relational problems with men, the patient responded with a powerful story. But the responsive communication of power themes is not in and of itself a sign of validation – whether that is the case depends on the nature of the themes. Thus, positively-toned themes generally speak for validation, while negatively-toned themes, as is the case here, do not – they speak for an erroneous intervention. Thus, in serving as an unconscious commentary on the therapist's interpretation, the patient's unconscious message is that, in light of what he just said, Dr Gregory is robbing him of a lot of money. This unconscious response is very different from Mr Arkin's conscious reaction, which was to simply nod in agreement.

In this situation, the new story served a second function. It's another story of theft, but this time the images are far less disguised than they were in the stories about Mr Arkin's boss and father – they allude to a doctor who, in addition, is said to have looked like Dr Gregory. These representations of the therapist are called *close derivatives* – that is, is they are minimally disguised images. Thus, it seems likely that, quite unconsciously, the patient was making an unconscious attempt to get his therapist to consciously realize the existence of a critical triggering intervention by the therapist that he (the patient) was unable to bring into his own awareness. And the effort proved to be successful – the image did, indeed, enable Dr Gregory to forgo his use of his denial and repressive defences to the point where the missing trigger finally dawned on him. Remarkable encoded, trigger-evoked dramas of this kind go on in psychotherapy every single day – their recognition depends on how a therapist listens and formulates.

Summing up

I have in this chapter used Freud's topographic approach and his structural model of the mind as representatives of weak adaptive approaches. My aim was to show the logic of Freud's thinking and its seeming support in well-chosen clinical observations. But, in addition I have tried to show how this line of thought appears to serve conscious system denial because the focus on the conscious registration of relatively innocuous day's residues serves to obliterate and avoid the deep unconscious registration of far more powerful, emotionally disturbing triggering events. There's a strong, in-built tendency for therapists to ignore or obliterate compelling, anxiety-provoking triggers and to work with far lesser issues and meanings – and to do so in terms of fantasy formations and unconscious wishes. But, as the vignette shows, these seeming fantasies actually serve to express valid unconscious perceptions that are invisible to weak adaptive therapists. Recognizing this kind of unconscious experience as expressed through encoded narratives would take them and their patients to the dark side of human emotional life where issues of therapists' errors, unconscious guilt and needs for self-punishment, and life and death hold sway and unconsciously direct the course of our lives. It has been wisely said that doing adaptive psychotherapy asks a lot of the therapist – but it gives even more in return.

4

The Conscious System

We turn now to a detailed study of the emotion-processing mind, which is comprised of two operating systems – *the conscious and deep unconscious systems* – along with several supplementary systems. As I indicated in the first chapter, this mental module – that is, collection of mental faculties – is an evolved, biological organ of adaptation. As such, it has a set of inherent, universal features and capabilities shared by all humans; variations on this basic configuration depend on biological genetics/inherited factors, as well as life experiences – especially those that are death-related (Langs, 1995, 1997, 2002).

The conscious system, which is the main subject of this chapter, is that part of the emotion-processing mind with which we are familiar subjectively. It's the system that receives inputs of which we are directly aware and which we use each day to cope with consciously perceived emotionally-charged events and their meanings. Thus, it's the source of our conscious thoughts, feelings, coping strategies and behaviours. Nevertheless, the system operates under considerable unconscious influence which is of a different order from the deep unconscious, adaptive processing system that will be described in the following chapter. In addition, it is greatly affected by two supplementary systems that receive all emotionally relevant, incoming information and meaning before conscious registration takes place. Let's begin our study of the emotion-processing mind with a look as these two entities.

The synthesizing and message analysing centres

In order to fully understand the operations of the conscious system, we must take a closer look at the details of the architecture of the emotion-processing mind (Goleman, 1985; Langs, 1986, 1987, 1995). There are at least two unfamiliar postulated systems in this mental module that play a crucial role in what we, as humans, are and are not aware of in the emotional realm – and, thereby, in how we adapt to environmental impingements. In this regard, the first step in the mental processing of all types of emotionally-charged, sensory/perceptive experiences is carried out by a Synthesizing Centre (SC) which transforms raw sensory data – for example forms, shapes, sounds and so on – into meaningful components such as physical objects, living beings, words, and so forth. Even here, at the very moment of sensory impact, unconsciously determined errors may be made in the form of misperceptions and the like. Nevertheless, most incoming raw stimuli are faithfully and extremely rapidly transformed into meaningful elements for further processing. These elements are then forwarded to an extremely critical component of the emotion-processing mind called the Message Analysing Centre (MAC).

The MAC is an autonomous, psychological sorting system that operates automatically and unconsciously, again with great rapidity and under considerable unconscious influence (Langs, 1986, 1987, 1995). It is the 'choice point' of emotionally-charged human experience in that the system has the 'responsibility for deciding' which events and which meanings of events can enter awareness, and which cannot. It has a variety of evaluating capabilities that allow it to respond to emergency situations in one way, and non-emergencies in another. Thus, when faced with an immediate threat to life or limb for which prompt action is called for – for example being attacked by someone wielding a knife – the MAC passes on to awareness many meanings of the situation that, under less threatening conditions, it would bar from consciousness. In essence, then, the recognition of an immediate threat lowers the MAC's threshold for the entry of information and meaning into the conscious system – denial is reduced to a minimum.

In situations without a present threat to one's life, the MAC unconsciously receives and recognizes both an emotionally-charged trigger in its entirety, and all of its detectable universal and personal meanings and implications – that is, it determines incoming meanings in context. It then responds to this concatenation of events and meanings on the basis of a complex gradient that measures the potential of each of these incoming elements to activate feelings of anxiety and depression, and their likelihood of disrupting conscious-system functioning – an assessment that is measured against the sensory intensity and significance of the elements themselves. In this way, the MAC 'decides' which events, and which of their meanings, can move on to conscious registration and which are to be shunted to the deep unconscious system for unconscious registration and processing – all of this in nanoseconds of time.

Surprisingly, the decisions made by the MAC appear to involve mutually exclusive choices. Events and meanings of events are forwarded to only one of the two systems of the emotion-processing mind – conscious or deep unconscious. As a rule, then, some meanings of an emotionally-charged triggering event will be sent on for conscious registration, while other meanings will be barred from awareness and passed on to the deep unconscious system for registration there. The remaining adaptive processing efforts are carried out by the two receiving systems without crossover from one system to the other – that is, relatively independently.

The processing activities of the MAC indicate that when we speak of conscious registration, we are describing a second-order mental event and are referring to contents whose ramifications have been evaluated by the MAC and allowed to enter awareness. And when we speak of conscious-system defensiveness and denial, including perceptual denial, we are actually alluding to the protective shield and defensive activities of the MAC as it bars access of contents to awareness. Similarly, when we speak of unconscious or subliminal perception, we are referring to events and meanings that have, throughout, been perceived and processed in the absence of awareness – at first, by the MAC and then by the deep unconscious system.

The MAC is by no means a simple cognitive apparatus. Its activities and screening choices are governed by the nature of incoming reality events, as well as complex unconscious, psychodynamic processes and anxiety and other gradients. Sound nurturance and positive emotional experiences tend to have salutary effects on the operations of the MAC and help to keep its thresholds of anxiety low. Under these conditions, the appearance of conscious-system denial is kept to a minimal level and many anxiety-provoking events and meanings are allowed to enter awareness and to be processed consciously. On the other hand, clinical evidence shows that significant traumatic experiences, especially those that evoke intense levels of death anxiety, lead to an increase in the MAC's threshold for the entry of contents into awareness and thereby increase the mind's use of perceptual defences and conscious system denial. This type of increased conscious system defensiveness, which interferes with effective emotional adaptation, is often difficult to modify clinically.

There are two basic types of emotionally-charged events – *emergency and non-emergency experiences* – and the MAC is designed to handle each class in a different manner. *Emergency-related perceptions* involve immediate dangers to life and limb. Under these circumstances, no matter how painful and anxiety-provoking the triggering event may be, the perceived danger is almost always directed to conscious awareness for a rapid response. In the more usual, *non-emergency* type of perceptive situation, the process described above – the MAC's default position, so to speak – prevails.

As noted, the processing activities of the MAC take place at an incredibly rapid rate so it can deal with the continuous and unrelenting flow of unfolding events and shifting meanings that we, as humans, experience each day. But these screening activities are vital to survival because they spare the conscious mind an enormous amount of distressing information and meaning that might otherwise lead to system overload and cause serious dysfunctions and maladaptations. Nevertheless, the resultant conscious-system denial and obliteration have many detrimental consequences: they deprive us of a great deal of critical information and meaning about ourselves and our environments, limit our knowledge-base for adaptive responsiveness, restrict the development of our adaptive capabilities, and stultify our emotional growth and development. The operations of the MAC appear to reflect an evolutionary trade-off in which the protection afforded by conscious-system denial and ignorance is pitted against unrestricted vision and knowledge. Indications are, however, that natural selection has favoured the use of denial and our consequent ignorance over perceptiveness and understanding, which is a most unusual outcome in the evolutionary history of living entities.

The 'decision' as to which events and meanings are 'allowed' to reach awareness and which are barred from doing so is a complex one. Some enormously painful aspects of traumatic events do enter awareness, but others do not. The nature of the trauma and its meanings, the ability of a given individual's conscious system to tolerate disruptive inputs, and his or her prior emotional history, especially as it pertains to death-related traumas, all play a role. Nevertheless, in all cases *unconscious perception precedes conscious perception* – this is an inherent and universal property of the human emotion-processing mind. In situations where conscious registration is bypassed entirely, the result is termed *perceptual denial*, the basic human form of denial and obliteration. This type of denial is supported by behavioural forms of denial, actions that interfere with conscious perceptions of traumatic events, and by mental forms of denial that are applied to repressed contents that are thereby blocked from reentering awareness.

Some key features of the conscious system

Mode of expression

Turning now to the conscious system, clinical study has shown that while its operations are under unconscious influence, much of it related to death anxiety and deep unconscious guilt, its operations as an adaptive system are quite apart and different from those of its counterpart – the deep unconscious adaptive system. Communicative expressions from this system come forth as manifest, directly stated messages that are generally without disguise. The conscious system's perceptions, processing activities and adaptive preferences are conveyed through two kinds of communications: single-message intellectualizations and the surface or manifest contents of double-message narratives. Manifest contents that are not in awareness at any given moment, but are potentially or easily made conscious – so-called preconscious contents – also belong to the conscious system.

Quite apart from the deep unconscious system, then, the conscious system has its own unconscious reservoir of memories, thoughts and feelings which we call the *superficial unconscious subsystem of the conscious system*. This subsystem houses two kinds of thoughts, fantasies, perceptions, memories and the like: those that are easily brought into awareness in total – that is, manifestly and directly, without disguise; and those that are dynamically repressed within the conscious system and that are allowed into awareness in thinly disguised form. The hallmark of these repressed, superficial unconscious contents is the simplicity of their encoded representation and the ease with which the image is decoded – their disguised meanings are relatively transparent. Such unconscious contents are relatively unempowered – they do not deal with the most compelling triggers and the most anxiety-provoking aspects of emotional life. That role belongs to the more heavily disguised, encoded messages that are emitted by the deep unconscious system. To offer a simple illustration of conscious-system disguise, following a moment when a male therapist became annoyed

with his female patient and spoke harshly to her, an incident came to
the patient's mind. It was a situation in which one of her male teach-
ers suddenly became unreasonably annoyed with a question she asked
in class and nastily put her off. The trigger and disguised meaning of
the image is relatively transparent and easily decoded.

Many of the present-day versions of psychoanalysis, as well as all
non-analytic forms of treatment, appear to be *conscious-system forms of
therapy*. Their practitioners deal with patients' manifest material and,
at times, their seeming unconscious implications, extracting hidden
meanings from manifest themes and interpreting easily decoded
disguised images. They do not, as a rule, engage in the strong adaptive
process of trigger decoding themes and images in light of their evocative triggering events which often involve their own interventions.
This means that their therapeutic endeavours are confined to
relatively weak conscious-system issues and that they have no means
of realizing the existence of, and dealing with, the far more powerful
and difficult to negotiate realm of deep unconscious experience and
conflict. This kind of therapy is limited by its unavoidable acceptance
of patients' conscious-system denial and obliteration, features that are
inherent to the system with which they work.

A basic commitment to defence

While the conscious system has a wide range of capabilities that enables
us to negotiate the difficult waters of emotional life, a second basic
feature of this system of the emotion-processing mind is *its overriding
commitment in the emotional domain to adapt to emotionally-charged triggering
events primarily by means of psychological defences*. In this connection,
exploratory research has shown that, in all likelihood, natural selection
has orchestrated the evolution of the conscious system on the basis of a
template or set of selection pressures that are comparable to those that
served for the design of the immune system (Langs, 1996). This is of
importance because it supports the thesis that the immune system
has evolved to deal defensively with microscopic predators, while the
conscious system of the emotion-processing mind has evolved to deal
defensively with large predators, primarily other humans. Defence
against threat is the main shared feature of the two systems.

Because the conscious system is basically designed to adapt to perceived events in the external world, and to some extent the inner
world as well, the fundamental mental defences used by humans are
denial and *obliteration*. These are our primary reality-directed defences,

much as *repression* is our main inner-directed defence against the conscious realization of unconscious fantasies and memories. As noted above, the means by which these fundamental reality-obliterating defences are effected is through the screening activities of the MAC, and thus a great of denial takes place on the perceptual level. This is an expensive defence and the source of considerable emotional pain, largely because denial prevents us from dealing with events and individuals who are causing us harm – we are simply unaware that this is the case. In addition, we have no conscious means of realizing that we're making use of denial – that is, we cannot be aware of what we're not aware of. The use of this defence can, however, be detected by searching for and finding encoded themes that suggest the existence of an unrecognized trigger and using the themes as a guide in searching for the obliterated trigger event that has evoked them – for example stories of someone who is nude in a public setting which suggests that the therapist has revealed something personal about himself to the patient. Short of that, an individual needs a well-informed observer to detect the use of this mechanism.

The psychotherapy situation is an ideal place in which to detect the use of denial and obliteration by patients – and for the careful adaptive listener, the therapist as well. This arises because therapists' interventions are, as a rule, the triggers for the adaptive responses of the deep unconscious systems of their patients' emotion-processing minds. It follows, then, that therapists who keep track of their interventions and are fully cognizant of their implications are in a position to identify when a patient has or has not alluded directly and consciously to a strong triggering intervention. In order to do this, therapists themselves cannot make use of denial, lest they too fail to consciously recognize a traumatic trigger that they have created for a given patient. This is by no means an easy task because adaptation-oriented clinical observations reveal that conscious-system denial is far more pervasive than is generally recognized.

In the vignette offered in the previous chapter, the patient, Mr Arkin, seemed to make use of a combination of perceptual denial and repression, in that he knew that a session had been cancelled, but did not see or realize consciously that he'd been overcharged for the month. He did, however, perceive the error unconsciously, as witnessed by his encoded themes. For his part, Dr Gregory knew of his absence from a scheduled session, but had obliterated its memory while writing his patient's bill – here, too, both repression and denial appear to have played a role in the failure to recall.

Denial is a costly defence. It reduces a person's information about the world, about him or herself, and about one's own inner state of mind and body. The events and meanings that we obliterate are not available for conscious processing, a problem that is made all the more difficult by our not having an easy means of being able to realize that we're making use of these obliterating defences. Indeed, it's only by consistently attending to the themes in one's own stories and maintaining a vigilance for triggers to which these themes may apply that a patient or therapist has any chance of discovering what he or she has denied and obliterated. The conscious mind is, however, not inclined to engage in activities that involve the search for denied events and meanings. It seldom, if ever, will examine narrative themes in a search for a missing and therefore denied triggering event, much as it is disinclined to engage in trigger-decoding and accessing deep unconscious experiences and processes. As a result, the conscious mind tends to operate in a vast, generally unrecognized sea of ignorance – taking us along with it. Reducing a patient's use of denial and obliteration is one of the healing goals of psychotherapy and, with severely traumatized patients, this is no easy task.

The nature of unconscious influences on the conscious system

Clinical study indicates that the conscious system is impervious to certain, largely constructive, unconscious influences, yet strongly affected by unconscious motives that are seemingly disadvantageous and self-defeating. Thus, the extremely profound and wise wisdom of the deep unconscious system does *not*, by and large, affect conscious-system adaptations. This arrangement evidently arises because deep unconscious intelligence is built around triggers and perceptions that are unbearable to awareness when experienced, and thus all output communications from that system enter awareness in encoded form. Decoding these messages in light of their evocative triggers is the only means through which the conscious mind can take advantage of deep unconscious intelligence – it is not accessible through any direct means. This point is also illustrated in the vignette offered in the previous chapter, where we saw that Mr Arkin's conscious system was unaffected by the perceptiveness, knowledge and sound adaptive recommendations of his deep unconscious mind regarding his therapist's overcharge. Deep unconscious perceptions and adaptive processing activities are not intuited by the conscious mind, nor do they break through in complete form into awareness, while their encoded representation in narrative vehicles does not allow for conscious usage. This is another unfortunate consequence of the denial-prone design of the conscious system of the emotion-processing mind.

On the other hand, there appear to be two major sources of unconscious influence on the adaptive operations of the conscious system: death anxiety and deep unconscious morality and ethics. The former has mixed effects in that predatory death anxiety – the fear of being harmed by others – tends to mobilize conscious-system resources, but it also may activate denial mechanisms when the offending party is someone on whom one is dependent. Existential death anxiety – the fear of the inevitability of personal demise – tends to solely promote the conscious system's use of denial mechanisms. The third form of death anxiety, predator death anxiety – the fear of being harmed in response to having harmed others – is connected with deep unconscious guilt and needs for punishment. It affects the conscious system by orchestrating self-defeating decisions and self-harmful actions. The sole positive note in this regard is the finding that helpful acts are also perceived by the deep unconscious system of morality and ethics and create unconscious motives that support adaptive functioning and making wise decisions.

Attitudes towards ground rules and boundaries

Rules, frames and boundaries play a crucial role in emotional life and in the process of psychotherapy (Langs, 1998b). The position taken by the two processing systems of the emotion-processing mind on this aspect of the human condition tend to be radically different and often diametrically opposed. The deep unconscious system is centred on this dimension of everyday life and psychotherapy, and through its encoded messages, it advocates and supports an ideal and universal set of ground rules that hold us well, are inherently healing, and enhance emotional adaptations. In contrast, the conscious system tends to be insensitive to this dimension of human experience and to be inclined towards departures from the ideal frame – that is, to favour frame modifications which it supports with a wide variety of justifications and rationalizations. Thus, in psychotherapy, conscious minds tend to accept or prefer alterations in ground rules such as changes in the time of sessions, reductions in fees, and violations of privacy and con-fidentiality – even though these rule infractions tend to be highly maladaptive and emotionally harmful. This preference is partially explained by the finding that frame violations are action forms of denial and that they are, as well, typically self-harmful – that is, they satisfy unconsciously driven, conscious-system needs for punishment.

When it comes to the ground rules of psychotherapy, then, the natural proclivities of the conscious mind render it a very unreliable if not treacherous source of guidelines. Nevertheless, weak adaptive forms of therapy tend to be constructed on the basis of the conscious-system thinking of both patients and their therapists. Doing so puts both parties to therapy at risk with little or no way of appreciating the harm that's being done by accepting conscious-system frame preferences. This is one more reason that psychotherapists of all kinds should seriously consider the framework findings derived from strong adaptive clinical studies. They would do well to appreciate the frame preferences of the far more reliable and constructive deep unconscious system – a subject to which we now turn.

5

The Deep Unconscious System

The world experienced by the deep unconscious system of the emotion-processing mind is very different from the world experienced by the conscious system. There are notable differences in the events and meanings of events encountered by each system, much as they differ in needs, defensive alignment, adaptive preferences, intelligence and moral position. Indeed, the world of deep unconscious experience is quite unfamiliar to the conscious mind. Therapists who trigger-decode the remarkable messages emanating from the deep system consistently are impressed by the beauty, purity, creativity and inordinate wisdom possessed by this entirely unconscious, adaptive system of the mind. Most striking is the finding that while the conscious system often acts against our best interests, the deep unconscious system is unfailing in its efforts to heal our emotional wounds and to point to the most optimal adaptive solutions to our emotionally-charged environmental challenges and traumas. In a true sense, the deep system has many of the attributes of a loving, caring inner God.

As noted in the previous chapter, the deep unconscious system is the receptor site for all events and meanings that are deemed by the MAC to be too potentially disruptive to be experienced consciously. These emotionally powerful contents therefore never enter awareness directly – they're unconsciously perceived, registered and processed adaptively without the least conscious sense that these experiences and processes are taking place (Dixon, 1971, 1981; Smith, 1991; Langs,

51

1995, 1996; Haskell, 1999). Thus, the deep unconscious system silently copes with some of the most painful and forbidding emotional experiences with which we, as humans, are compelled to deal. And it does so using its two basic subsystems – one devoted to evaluating and adaptively responding to environmental impingements, and the other devoted to assessing and responding to issues of morality and ethics. The operations of each of these subsystems are based on a mixture of evolved, naturally selected design features, personal heredity, and personal conscious and, more importantly, unconscious experiences and learning.

Deep unconscious wisdom

The *deep unconscious wisdom system or subsystem* is the knowledge-based, adaptive processing component of the deep unconscious mind – a superb operational intelligence that carries out its functions without awareness interceding. This subsystem is living proof that intelligence and adaptation are activities that do not depend on awareness. But, in addition, studies have shown that deep unconscious intelligence is far superior to conscious intelligence, indicating that in respect to emotionally-charged events, we cope better in the absence of awareness than we do in its presence – unconscious perceptions are far better informed than conscious perceptions, which are restricted by the extensive use of MAC-based denial.

The operations of the deep unconscious wisdom system are logical and highly sensible, and based on a large number of considerations that involve past, present and future events. The system also tunes in on and evaluates the implications of the multiple meanings of a given triggering event, weighs the pros and cons of various possible adaptive responses, and arrives at the best possible adaptive solution to each environmental challenge or traumatic trigger. And once, all things considered, an adaptive solution has been reached, the entire process from unconscious perception to adaptive recommendations are encoded in a dream or story – there's no direct access to these transactions. As a result, access to deep unconscious adaptive activities can be made solely by trigger-decoding communicated narrative themes in light of their evocative triggering events. This is the only known means that we have at present to bring the world of deep unconscious experience into the conscious realm.

The deep unconscious wisdom system operates on the basis of perceptions that are undistorted and quite accurate. The particular meanings of events that are perceived and processed unconsciously by a given individual are selected from the universal meanings of the event in the context of personal sensitivities. These meanings are experienced in frank and raw terms, with an incisive understanding of the many implications of each triggering event. The knowledge-based pool of memories available as perspectives and the level of comprehension of the wisdom system far exceeds the capabilities of the conscious system in these areas – our UQ (unconscious intelligence quotient) is much higher than our IQ (conscious intelligence quotient). In addition, deep unconscious adaptive preferences reflect a total basic devotion to the emotional healing and best interests of the individual. The main exception to the incisiveness and lucidity of the system is seen in some instances of extreme trauma, during which *deep unconscious denial* holds sway. This defence, which tends to be short-lived, is seen when a patient responds to a blatantly harmful triggering event with positive narrative themes. In time, these themes give way to those that are devastatingly damaging, reflections of the true nature of the triggering event.

While the conscious system looks at many aspects of human experience, deep unconscious intelligence is sharply focused on three areas, a finding that is most clearly visible in the psychotherapy situation. For both patients and therapists, the most intense concentration is on the therapist's impingements on and management of the rules, frames and boundaries of the treatment situation – and on the patient's frame-related preferences and activities as well. Patients' deep unconscious wisdom systems monitor the level of listening and intervening that a therapist adopts, and along different but related lines their systems accurately assess the validity of each intervention made by a therapist – behaviourally and verbally. In this regard, the deep unconscious wisdom system consistently validates the offer and enforcement of an ideal set of secured ground rules and boundaries for the treatment experience, supports therapists' listening to the encoded level of communication, and endorses trigger-decoded interpretations. The system universally disconfirms – subjects to non-validation – all departures from the ideal frame and all interventions made on the level of manifest contents and their implications.

In the vignette presented in Chapter 3, Mr Arkin's deep unconscious system generated two encoded narratives – his dream and his associations to the dream. Each story conveyed aspects of his unconscious perceptions of his counsellor, Dr Gregory, in light of the consciously denied, but unconsciously recognized overcharge that the therapist had made. Together, the stories reflect a raw, accurate, undefended picture of the therapist in light of the triggering event – the overcharge – as someone who had committed fraud and was stealing money from his patient and who deserved to be punished for his crime (the contribution of the deep unconscious moral system). There's no distortion here and no sign of denial, only a frank and incisive encoded unconscious view of the triggering event and its perpetrator.

Deep unconscious morality and ethics

The deep unconscious subsystem of morality and ethics evaluates every thought we think, word we say, and deed we perform, and it does so on the basis of a very strict, ideally suitable, universal moral code. The system also has enormous powers of enforcement in the form of unconsciously orchestrated rewards and punishments. These issues come to the fore in psychotherapy largely because clinical studies of thematic responses to modifying and securing the frame have shown that *on the deep unconscious level, the ground rules of psychotherapy are experienced as ethical and moral precepts by both parties to treatment.* Thus the nature of the frame conditions that a therapist offers to a patient speaks for the therapist's moral position and his or her integrity – or its lack. Much the same applies to the patient – the ground rules that he or she accepts or rejects, or tries to modify unilaterally, speak for his or her moral position as well.

While conscious-system morality is highly individualized, variable among and within individuals, and easily corrupted, deep unconscious morality is based on a universal set of standards that speak for compassion and caring for others and for personal integrity as well. Similarly, there's an ideal set of deep-unconsciously sought ground rules and boundaries for all forms of psychotherapy – a ground-rule archetype, if you will. Adherence to these rules – for example establishing a set fee, time and place for the therapy, and maintaining total privacy and confidentiality – provides a patient with a strong sense of safety, holding, and a positive sense of the moral turpitude of the therapist, whom it also holds and heals. On the other hand, departures from these optimal ground rules are unconsciously experienced as immoral and harmful to both participants to treatment, and as compromising the safety and holding qualities of the therapeutic relationship. In principle, then, all ground-rule transactions and interpretations raise moral issues that are unconsciously processed by the deep unconscious system of morality and ethics with the aid of deep unconscious wisdom.

In addition to responding to the vicissitudes of the ground rules of therapy, the deep unconscious system of morality and ethics is activated whenever a therapist offers an erroneous intervention – one that is not validated unconsciously by the patient. Most of these interventions cause harm to the patient and evoke unconscious perceptions in both parties to therapy related to what is experienced unconsciously as the immorality of the hurtful healer. Given the fact that most therapists offer their patients modified frames and interventions that fail to obtain unconscious confirmation, we can appreciate that unconscious guilt is the primary occupational hazard of weak adaptive psychotherapists.

Similar moral issues arise when patients work over situations in which they have harmed others – at times the therapist, but most often people outside of treatment. To cite one such example, patients who have been involved in elective abortions tend to show strong resistances against exploring their deep unconscious reactions to such events, much of it based on predator death anxiety. When these resistances diminish and the related unconscious issues emerge in sessions, themes of guilt and suicide tend to emerge – reflections of the demands of the deep unconscious system of morality and ethics for self-punishment for a deed that is unconsciously experienced as murder. It takes a great deal of working through and repentance before this persistent moral system shows indications of forgiveness.

As noted, therapists who work on the basis of weak adaptive principles and who tend to offer modified frame conditions and non-validated interventions to their patients are well-advised to be mindful of these issues. Such interventions, which unconsciously are experienced as harmful predatory acts, tend to create predatory death anxiety in the patient and are often an unconsciously mediated way of providing patients who are guilt-ridden with a measure of the punishment that they are unwittingly seeking. The therapist in turn will unconsciously experience him or herself as predatory to the patient, suffer from predator death anxiety and deep unconscious guilt, and engage in self-punitive behaviours. As a result, both parties to therapy suffer unknowingly. Securing the frame and making unconsciously validated, strong adaptive interventions is, as far as I know, the only known antidote to these harmful situations.

Comparing the conscious and deep unconscious systems

The two systems of the emotion-processing mind, conscious and deep unconscious, operate on the basis of very different perceptions, premises, needs, adaptive preferences, intelligence, and so on. The following sums up the differences between the two systems:

1 Deep unconscious adaptive processing is, as a rule, undefended and unencumbered. In contrast, conscious efforts to cope are greatly hampered by the continuous use of the defence mechanisms of denial and obliteration which limit the adaptive choices available to the system.
2 The knowledge-base for deep unconscious processing, which is not restricted by denial, is far superior to that used by the conscious system. Adhering to encoded, deep unconscious choices is far more salutary than adhering to choices made by the denial-prone conscious mind.
3 Deep unconscious processing is fully committed to sound adaptive choices, reasonable consideration for others, and self-healing. Conscious processing, which is compromised by the influence of death anxiety and deep unconscious guilt, often leads to self-harmful choices and behaviours.
4 Deep unconscious processing is based on incisive moral and ethical evaluations and the system's choices are always morally strong. Conscious processing often neglects such considerations and the system's choices are often morally compromised.
5 Deep unconscious processing is highly focused and concentrates primarily on frame impingments, the validity of a therapist's interventions, and the level at which he or she listens and intervenes. In contrast, conscious processing entails an exploration of many different dimensions of life and the therapeutic process, many of them of little emotional consequence. It also tends to avoid ground-rule issues, to refrain from examining emotionally-charged triggering events in depth, and to steer clear of trigger-decoding.
6 The results of deep unconscious processing reach awareness solely through encoded narratives, while the outcome of conscious processing is conveyed through manifest contents and their implications.
7 In regard to responses to interventions, encoded forms of validation – for example the emergence of positive narrative themes – tend to offer highly reliable guidelines in respect to an intervention's accuracy and healing effects. In contrast, conscious support for an intervention may, or as is more often the case, may not be reliable and therefore may speak for a patient's need for errant and harmful therapeutic work. To be considered valid, a conscious affirmation of an intervention must be accompanied by encoded support as well.

As humans, then, we experience and adapt to the world of emotional impingements with minds that are naturally and deeply divided. The lives we lead and the therapies we conduct are dramatically different depending on which system we listen to and take as our guide for understanding and intervening. While deep unconscious wisdom is wiser, more trustworthy and more healing than conscious wisdom, the human mind is not naturally inclined to seek and heed it's advice and directives. The principles of the strong adaptive approach can take therapists a long way towards rectifying the disadvantages that nature has wrought in naturally selecting many defensive and self-defeating features for the conscious system of the emotion-processing mind.

Deep unconscious sensitivity to therapeutic interventions

With the sole exception of rare, extremely severe outside traumas, once a patient enters psychotherapy, his or her deep unconscious perceptions and processing activities are focused on their therapists' interventions. This is, of course, another difference from the conscious system which will address events both outside and within therapy, most often the former. In addition, patients in therapy tend to process outside traumatic events consciously rather than deep-unconsciously – the experienced unconscious ramifications of these events tend to be superficial rather than deep.

This finding indicates that most trigger-decoded interpretations will, of necessity, pertain to a therapist's own interventions, broadly defined to include everything of significance that a therapist does and does not do. The illumination of the unconscious meanings of emotional problems and symptoms in the everyday life of the patient is carried out by exploring these within treatment issues. This work is supplemented by discovering connections between a patient's deep unconscious responses to a therapist-evoked triggering event and the patient's symptoms and behavioural problems outside of therapy.

Among the evident reasons for this deep unconscious focus by patients on the efforts of their healers is the innate tendency of living beings to concentrate their adaptive efforts on immediate adaptive challenges – for patients in therapy, then, these are their therapists' interventions. The deep unconscious system carries forward this biological tradition in virtually all instances, while the conscious system does so only intermittently. In addition, this deep unconscious concentration seems to be based on the role of the psychotherapist as a healer of human suffering, much like shamans, priests, ministers, rabbis and physicians. Finally, therapists are responsible for establishing the conditions of a therapy situation, including its rules, frames and boundaries, and for intervening in this regard as well. These are fundamental aspects of relatedness and efforts at healing that have enormous effects on patients and greatly influence the course of their therapies and their lives. Patients' deep unconscious systems therefore quite wisely pay careful attention to their therapists' words and deeds, while in general the conscious minds of patients are inclined to deny the pervasive effects that their therapists have on them and tend to look elsewhere for such authority.

The output centre

Having considered the intake and operating systems of the emotion-processing mind, a few words are in order regarding its Output Centre (OC) – the unconscious system that receives all incoming information and meaning and their adaptive processing, and 'decides' on what is to be suppressed and what is to be expressed – and how this is to be done (Langs, 1986, 1987). The OC receives both conscious and deep unconscious impressions, evaluations, links to past experiences and adaptive responses, and then organizes them into a unity. It also has access to a wide variety of output modes of expression – affects, conscious thoughts, vehicles of encoded communication like dreams and stories, physical and psychological symptoms, and behaviours – many of them, like gross behavioural resistances in the form of frame violations, directed at the therapist and therapy.

All in all, the OC amasses an enormous amount of information and meaning and then 'chooses' an expressive response to each incoming emotional stimulus or trigger – especially those that are perceived and processed deep-unconsciously. Perhaps the most basic consideration involves the choice between a verbal or behavioural response – that is, a conscious thought or comment, or an encoded narrative message on the one hand, or a physical reaction such as a bodily healing or ill-ness or a behavioural response on the other.

Factors in making these choices include the patient's preferred mode of output response – mainly, whether it's bodily or via action versus the use of verbalized messages and imagery; the nature of the triggering event to which the patient is responding – mainly, whether the therapist has intervened by acting out though frame violations or has secured the frame and is also making use of verbal-affective interventions like interpretations; the power of the interventional triggers in respect to their death–related connections and other sources of anxiety; the conditions of the therapy – mainly, whether they favour acting out versus verbal expression; and the overall status of the patient's psychological resources. The role that the therapist plays in the patient's choice of output vehicle is of great importance.

An illustrative vignette

Mr Turner was driving his car when he inadvertently went through a stop sign and was hit by another car. On impact, his 10 year-old son, Martin, who was in the passenger seat, struck his head against the side of the car and suffered a fractured skull. He was comatose briefly, but eventually recovered, although there was some minor residual brain damage.

In his psychotherapy with Dr Sparks, a male psychiatrist, it was discovered that following the accident, Mr Turner repeatedly made poor business decisions and suffered from many seemingly 'bad breaks'. His marriage inexplicably turned sour and his wife divorced him; a promising business venture in which he had invested heavily somehow failed.

With the frame well-secured for several years, themes of harming others and of accidental murder began to emerge in Mr Turner's material. Almost always, they were accompanied by themes of self-harm and suicide. Repeated interpretations were made to the effect that Mr Turner's unconscious view of his having damaged his son was that he had, in effect, murdered him. Also interpreted was his conscious and unconscious guilt over the incident, and his inner wish to punish himself in kind by taking his own life or by finding ways to suffer socially and in business. Encoded, unconscious validation usually followed these interpretations, but it took many years of therapy before the imagery became less punitive and more forgiving, and Mr Turner was able to straighten out his life.

This vignette illustrates the powerful effects of predator death anxiety and deep unconscious guilt on conscious decisions and behaviours. Morality and ethics are often matters of life and death – in and outside of psychotherapy.

6

Ground Rules and Boundaries

Clinical studies within the framework of the strong adaptive approach have made it unmistakably clear that the management and status of the ground rules, boundaries and physical setting of psychotherapy – its *frame or framework* – are highly complicated and critical aspects of the treatment experience and important factors in its outcome (Langs, 1982, 1997, 1998b; Smith, 1991; Gabbard and Lester, 1995). This aspect of therapy affects the nature and meanings of the communications exchanged between patient and therapist, and in addition has a large number of psychological meanings and behavioural effects.

The main reason that these ideas are unfamiliar to weak adaptive therapists lies with the finding that the conscious system with which they work is frame-insensitive. Indeed, the deep unconscious system alone shows a profound appreciation for this dimension of treatment and life itself. And it's solely through trigger-decoding patients' responses to therapists' frame-related interventions – for example their managing the ground rules and interpreting their implications for patients – and thereby gaining access to the relevant deep unconscious experiences and frame preferences of the deep unconscious system that the importance and range of effects of this dimension of therapy can be appreciated. These ideas find ready support as soon as a therapist begins to attend to his or her patients' encoded responses to frame-related efforts. With utmost regularity, one finds validation for frame-securing interventions (that is, adhering to the set of deep-unconsciously sought, ideal ground rules) and non-validation for frame modifying endeavours (that is, departures from these ideals).

Unlike the highly variable frame-related attitudes of the conscious system, the deep unconscious system is extremely consistent in this regard.

Two approaches to the functions of frames

The clinical propositions and beliefs that therapists develop about a given aspect of psychotherapy depend entirely on the means by which they listen to, formulate and validate (if at all) the meanings that they ascribe to patients' behaviours and communicated material. There are, then, two basic approaches to formulating the functions of the setting, ground rules and boundaries of psychotherapy, and they lead to very different viewpoints on this subject.

The first is called the *conscious-system approach* – the exploration of the manifest thoughts and communications from patients and their therapists. On this level, we find that conscious minds vary greatly in respect to their attitudes towards rules, frames and boundaries, and that they tend to ignore this dimension of therapy and lean towards loosely defined frames that are replete with departures from deep-unconsciously sought ideals. The handling of ground rules is generally thought of as a matter of personal choice, open to all types of opinions and possibilities, without clear underlying principles, and as having minimal and unpredictable effects on the treatment experience. These attitudes appear to be accounted for by the two primary unconscious influences on conscious thinking – death anxiety and guilt. This is the case largely because departures from the ideal frame unconsciously tend to function as ways of offering maladaptive and often self-punitive protection against the entrapping, existential death anxieties and conflicts that arise under secured frame conditions (see also below).

The second type of perspective on the ground rules is called the *deep unconscious system approach*. This type of listening and formulating is based on trigger-decoding patients' narrative themes in response to frame-related triggering events – for example the set of ground rules that therapists propose for therapy in the initial session, frame lapses by therapists, as seen when they begin a session late or make an error in billing. Clinical studies have shown that the deep unconscious minds that are reflected in the encoded responses have remarkably uniform attitudes towards frame conditions, with little or no variation among patients. The encoded narratives consistently support and speak for a *deep-unconsciously sought set of ideal ground rules*, and just as consistently reject as inappropriate and harmful all departures from these ideals. This uniformity speaks for an evolved, archetypal, universal set of unconsciously preferred, deeply needed and healing, rules, frames and boundaries – a significant finding that is quite alien to conscious thinking. Indeed, trigger-decoding also confirms that the management of the ground rules of treatment has extensive effects on virtually every aspect of the therapy experience.

The basic ground rules

Years of clinical study have enabled adaptive therapists to define a basic set of unconsciously validated, ideal ground rules and boundaries that pertain to the deep unconscious needs of all patients and therapists. These rules demarcate so-called *secured frames* and *secured frame therapies*, while treatment situations that are structured without one or more of these ideal precepts are called *deviant* or *modified frame therapies*.

Adhering to the ideal or optimal ground rules is the means by which both participants to a treatment situation are afforded safety, holding, caring and inherent support. A therapist's ability to hold to this frame also has unconsciously mediated healing powers. Conforming to theses rules also helps to set limits on the extent of damage that one party to therapy can cause the other party. Thus, these codes of behaviour tend to preclude or minimize patients' conscious and unconscious inclinations to do psychological damage to their therapists, and, likewise, therapists' inclinations to psychologically damage their patients. There's a measure of harm for all concerned in every frame modification, no matter how necessary. That said, it's also important to realize that, nevertheless, it's quite feasible to do effective psychotherapy under frame-modified conditions. This is especially true when the departures from ideal conditions are an utter necessity, although much of the success depends on the use of proper techniques.

The tried and tested ideal framework of psychotherapy includes:

1   A single, professional locale with a suite that is used by the therapist alone and that has a sound-proofed consultation room.
2   A group of relatively stable ground rules including a single, set fee, and a set time, length and frequency of sessions – the so-called *fixed frame*.
3   Full responsibility for both parties to be present for all scheduled sessions.

4   The patient's fiscal responsibility for the time and, therefore, for all scheduled sessions.

5   The therapist's prerogative and responsibility to take occasional vacations that are announced well in advance.

6   Total privacy, with no access to the therapy in any form by outside (third) parties.

7   Total confidentiality, with no note-taking or recording of the transactions of sessions by either party and no release of information of any kind.

8   The relative anonymity of the therapist, with no deliberate self-revelations, advice, opinions, directives, extraneous comments, and so on.

9   The fundamental rule of *free association*, with the patient directed to say whatever comes to mind, generally supplemented with the rule of *guided associations* that advises patients to communicate dreams and other forms of narrative expression, and to seek narrative associations to these so-called *origination narratives*.

10   The therapist's obligation to intervene as called for by the patient's communications and behaviours, basing interventions entirely on the material from the immediate session.

11   The therapist's offer of (neutral) interventions that are likely to obtain encoded, deep unconscious validation – in effect, the use of appropriate silences, trigger-decoded interpretations, and efforts to secure the ideal conditions of treatment at the behest of the patient's encoded narrative material.

12   The absence of physical contact between the two parties to the therapy.

13   Confinement of the contact between the patient and therapist to the time and place of the sessions.

14   A group of less well-defined, implicit rules such as the therapist's full dedication to the therapeutic needs of the patient.

It's quite evident that in today's world of psychotherapy, very few therapists offer, or indeed are able to offer, their patients these ideal conditions for treatment. While there is, as noted, a measure of harm meted out to both patient and therapist under these circumstances, both parties also have an unconscious perspective as to the necessity for frame modifications when such is the case – for example patients whose finances are such that they can be seen only if there are third-party payers, and patients who can only afford a clinic-type therapy. In addition, strong curative interventions are feasible under deviant conditions because patients tend to repeatedly encode their deep unconscious perceptions of the implications of the modified frame elements. In response, then, therapists can offer trigger–decoded interpretations that, if properly formulated and unconsciously validated, provide patients with healing insights and often lead to the rectification of those aspects of the ground rules than can be secured.

In addition to social and financial necessities, there are many reasons for the almost universal laxity in therapists' approaches to the framework of psychotherapy. Much of it stems from the aforementioned effects of death anxiety and guilt that unconsciously motivate the turn to modified frames. Another factor is the natural preference of conscious minds for denial–based defences, a tendency that is well-served by modified frames – violations of ground rules serve to unconsciously convince participants that they also are exceptions to the existential ground rule that life is inevitably followed by death. To support these denial–based tendencies, conscious minds tend to prefer relatively unprincipled approaches to therapy, loosely defined frame conditions, and the use of intuitive interventions that lack support from unconscious validation. These trends are buttressed with highly defensive, essentially misguided conscious–system criticisms of more defined, adaptive approaches to psychotherapy as unduly rigid and insensitive to patients' therapeutic needs. The alternative deep unconscious view is quite to the contrary in that it's been clinically found that unconsciously validated, circumscribed precepts of technique and well-defined prescriptions for the frameworks of therapy not only serve patients' deep therapeutic needs, but also enhance a therapist's sensitivity to the implications and meanings of patients' material. Well-articulated, strong adaptive precepts also facilitate sound empathic responsiveness, safeguard the effectiveness of a therapist's interventions, and inherently protect the patient from the unintentional harm caused by most undisciplined, so-called intuitive interventions.

As for the role of economic factors in the neglect of frame conditions, there are motives in both patients and therapists that fuel wishes for modified frames and the denial of their detrimental qualities. There are, of course, many patients who cannot afford the standard fees charged by psychotherapists. These individuals must therefore be seen for reduced fees, find insurance coverage, or be treated in low-cost treatment settings like clinics. In most of these situations, however, unneeded frame violations abound, and with them, the potential for unnecessary harm to the patient and deep unconscious guilt in the therapist. The attempt to deny this guilt motivates therapists to consciously deny the harmful consequences of modified conditions for treatment, even as they unwittingly punish themselves for their frame violations. In addition, financial pressures prompt therapists to sanction and offer patients all manner of frame violations so they can collect fees from third parties like insurance companies. Money corrupts, even in psychotherapy.

Along different lines, the existential death anxieties of therapists evoked by secured frames unconsciously motivates them to ignore frame conditions and to prefer to work in modified frames. The ideal, secured frame is temporally limiting and, in a sense, creates an entrapping closed space, much as human life goes on for a limited time and is confined to our planet. Death looms unconsciously in both situations, thereby evoking unconscious anxieties that are in need of processing and resolution. Doing psychotherapy in deviant frames is a way of acting out the denial of death – rules, including those about death following life, do not apply to all concerned. Typically, frame breaks are invoked to gain temporary but costly relief from underlying anxieties in lieu of searching for their insightful resolution.

In addition, for most therapists their own therapeutic experience is or was based on a conscious-system, weak adaptive approach and was therefore likely to have been replete with departures from the ideal ground rules. Such therapists have not personally experienced frame-related interventions, secured frame conditions, or trigger-decoded interpretations of their deep unconscious perceptions of frame conditions. In addition, because of their natural tendencies to identify with their own therapists, these practitioners are inclined to offer ground-rule conditions that are similar to those that had been offered to them by their own therapists. In this way, their therapists' frame-related denials and avoidances become their own frame-related denials and avoidances – a vicious circle that's very difficult to interrupt.

Frame-related interventions

Insight-oriented therapists are accustomed to think of themselves as offering a variety of verbalized interventions that are ultimately designed to offer patients insights into various unconscious aspects of their personal psychology – interpretations of meaning and of genetic connections between the present and the past chief among them. Frame-related interventions, which are seldom considered, are however of a different order than the usual verbal efforts of a therapist.

While they may involve interpretations of meaning, there is in addition a second, very distinctive component to these efforts – the actual management of the rules that define the conditions of treatment and the behaviours of the participants. When a frame issue arises, therapists are obliged to not only interpret the relevant encoded material, they must also take a position: they have no choice but to either sustain the use of the ground rule in question or to not do so.

In conscious-system forms of therapy, this decision is left to the therapist and is arbitrarily defined as a matter of his or her 'good judgment'. In deep unconscious system forms of therapy, however, the decision is made by the patient's deep unconscious wisdom system and imparted in encoded form to the therapist for his or her use. Thus, it's been found clinically that whenever a ground-rule issue arises, patients virtually always encode the proper response that should be adopted by the therapist – *and it's always in the direction of securing the frame.* In principle, then, the ground rules of therapy are managed by adaptive therapists at the behest of patients' encoded, frame-securing directives. While these needs exist in the deep unconscious minds of both participants to treatment, the patient serves as the guide to how and when to intervene because he or she is obliged to free associate and narrate. Properly trigger-decoded, these narratives and the deep unconscious wisdom that they embody and disguise are the most reliable healing force in the psychotherapy experience.

All in all, frame-related interventions are unique in a number of ways. Their action component – the actual position that the therapist takes – is in and of itself a message to the patient, one that is far more powerful than the therapist's verbal comments. In general, however, there's a tendency for therapists who offer insightful trigger-decoded interpretations to also be inclined towards frame-securing attitudes and interventions, while those who tend to use interventions based on manifest contents and their implications generally lean towards frame-modifying therapeutic choices. The importance of a therapist's position on these matters is seen in the finding that frame-related attitudes unconsciously reflect the therapist's moral code and, in addition, speaks for his or her preferred mode of adapting to emotion-related events and anxieties: deep understanding and frame securing is one choice, and the lack of deep insight and the use of frame violations, and thereby acting out, is the other.

While patients and therapist generally are not consciously mindful of these distinctions, they are very sensitive to them at the deep unconscious level. Thus, even when financial need requires that a patient be in a low-fee therapy or in one covered by insurance, these frame-deviant conditions activate strong unconsciously-driven tendencies in both parties to the therapy to act out and modify frames far beyond the necessary minimum. Patients often tend to be late to these therapy sessions, to arbitrarily miss sessions, to fail to pay their fees, and to frequently request changes in the time of their hours. For their part, these conditions prompt therapists to be inclined to make frame-violating 'deals' with their patients that are designed either to help the patient avoid their coinsurance responsibilities, or to earn a larger than the contracted fee for themselves. They also tend to go along with most of their patients' requests for additional frame modifications and introduce many unnecessary frame changes themselves. For the conscious system of the emotion-processing mind, deviation begets deviation and it becomes not only an unhelpful way of doing therapy, it is soon an unhelpful way of living one's life. A shift by the therapist towards securing the frame to the greatest extent feasible, and his or her ability to process and interpret patients' requests to alter the frame, are the best antidotes to these inclinations.

To cite a brief example, when all options are open, securing a ground rule or alternatively modifying it are very different ways of coping with secured-frame, existential death anxieties – successfully in the first case and unsuccessfully in the other. A therapist who unnecessarily advocates or invokes a frame modification unwittingly speaks for his or her own unresolved, unconscious existential death anxieties and for coping by means of frame-deviant acts rather than through holding frames secured and seeking deep insight. In addition, these frame modifications are harmful to all concerned, and therapists who gratuitously offer less than ideal conditions for treatment are expressing their unconscious need to damage their patients – and themselves as well. No amount of words can undo these telling, enacted messages from therapists to their patients, nor can words lessen the impact of their acts. Technically, this means that proper frame management is a top priority in psychotherapy. It should entail the offer of sound trigger-decoded interpretations of patients' unconscious perceptions of secured and modified frames (the meaning aspect); and in the case of rectifiable ground-rule deviations, the interpretive effort should be accompanied by actual, frame-securing efforts (the action aspect).

Another unique feature of frame-related interventions is that their management and interpretation influences all other transactions between the parties to the treatment situation. This includes the mode of communicative exchange, the meanings of what is expressed, the unconscious perceptions that each party to the therapy has of the other party, and the prevailing mode of 'cure' or symptom relief – be it through frame modifications that bring temporary but costly emotional relief to the patient (frame modifications always cause a measure of emotional harm), or through the healing powers of the secured frame and the deep adaptive insights that can be developed under those conditions.

It needs to be stressed that while the conscious minds of the participants in a treatment experience may or may not be mindful of ground-rule conditions, the deep unconscious mind continuously monitors and responds to this dimension of the situation. Thus, even in therapy settings where the ground rules are entirely neglected, loosely constructed or subjected to continual change, the deep unconscious system's need for a secured frame persists in both parties to treatment and they are adversely affected by the deviant aspects of the frame conditions. Patients – and often their therapists as well – may develop new symptoms because of their unconscious perceptions of being harmed by their therapists' frame modifications. They may also become quite resistant to their therapists' ministrations and begin to act out in frame-deviant ways themselves – both within the therapy and in their outside lives.

Despite the belief of most conscious minds that therapists are in a position to define any reasonable set of ground rules that they deem advisable, the deep unconscious system does not accept arbitrary rules as the best possible conditions for the treatment experience – it sustains its insistence for a more ideal set of ground rules for the therapy. The deep unconscious system has a fixed blueprint in mind and it assesses the conditions of every therapy and every life situation accordingly, much as it takes the measure of all concerned in light of the frame conditions that they propose, accept or reject. The conscious mind must be reminded again and again of the deep unconscious need for, and belief in, a single set of ground rules – an ideal frame for a therapy experience. It's an unchanging requisite for emotional health that's quite alien to conscious thinking.

In this light, we can see why it's incumbent upon all therapists to be aware of the existence of this dimension of therapy and to develop a sense of the ideal frame. It's also of value to learn how to work well in both secured and modified frames (the latter is especially challenging) and to develop the ability to listen to the communications from patients for encoded frame-related messages. Most importantly, it's important for therapists to mistrust their own and their patients' conscious opinions in respect to rules and boundaries, and to have a strong sense of the unconscious ramifications of both secured and modified frame conditions. With the goal of fostering the development of these skills and insights, let's look more closely at the ideal, deep-unconsciously sought frame.

Secured frames

Therapies in which the ideal ground rules are offered and adhered to in their entirety are called *secured-frame therapies*. In addition, in treatment situations in which the basic ground rules include departures from the ideal frame, there may be *secured-frame moments*. These are interludes in which a modified ground rule is challenged by a patient, usually through a request to further alter the rule, and the therapist, using the patient's encoded directives, adheres to the ground rule in question. To cite a brief example:

Mr Adams, a low-fee clinic patient, asks his therapist, Mr Bell, for a fee reduction because he (the patient) has taken on some extra debt. When the therapist encourages him to continue to say whatever is coming to mind, the patient then tells a story about his mother's over-indulgence of him with food and money, which sent him down the path to drug abuse – she should have known better than to have done that.

  With the narrative in hand, the therapist interprets that if he were to reduce his fee, the patient would unconsciously perceive him as over-indulgent and inviting him to become addicted again to drugs. His comment that his mother should have known better than to do that kind of thing clearly advises the therapist to know better and not offer a fee reduction. The patient responds by recalling the only business customer he ever worked with who refused to get involved with him in a kick-back scheme he had dreamt up. He then adds that it feels stuffy in the therapist's office today.

This last segment contains an encoded, unconsciously validating image (the customer's refusal to violate the law), as well as an indication of secured-frame anxieties (the stuffiness of the office). A similar sequence is seen in private psychotherapy when circumstances change so as to permit the therapist to secure a deviant ground rule – for example, when it proves possible to eliminate insurance coverage for treatment because a patient has developed the financial means to pay for treatment on his own. The rectification of the frame is followed with the patient's encoded, validating imagery and then indications of secured-frame anxieties tend to emerge.

Secured frames have, then, two opposite basic effects on both parties to a therapy situation. On the one hand they create a sense of safety, support and tolerance, and are deeply holding and healing, but on the other they evoke severe forms of existential death anxiety – much of it because of the limits that they set on the patient's – and therapist's – behaviours and options, and the feelings of restraint and entrapment that they evoke. This combination of healing and unconsciously mediated, terrifying existential death anxieties is reminiscent of life itself in that the gift of life comes wrapped in the package of death. Thus, the paradox for all forms of psychotherapy is that the conditions of treatment that are most ideally healing are the very conditions that evoke the most frightening forms of existential death anxieties in both parties to therapy. Communicatively and adaptively, then, secured-frame conditions evoke a striking mixture of positive encoded themes of care-taking, safety, reliability, strength, devotion and, at the same time, negative themes of entrapment and annihilation.

It's been found that, in principle, efforts at therapy that are intended to be deeply healing should include one or more secured-frame moments. Patients need to experience, process and resolve their existential death anxieties to have a fully effective, insightful cure. This is needed because these anxieties exist in all humans and their unconscious component tends to be unresolved and to disrupt their lives. Although as humans we are all aware of the inevitability and finality of personal death, we have little conscious faith in our ability to cope with the deep unconscious anxieties and the unconscious conflicts with which they are connected. There is, then, a strong conscious-system preference to avoid secured frames despite their unmatched healing qualities. Rather than confronting and processing their existential death anxieties towards personal insight and resolution, both patients and therapists prefer to deal with these issues through denial mechanisms. Violations of the ideal ground rules serve this function because, as noted, they are action forms of the denial of death.

Another disturbing feature of secured frames is that they are the conditions under which a patient's own predatory acts and deep unconscious guilt are most vividly activated and reexperienced. Modified frames place the therapist in the role of the primary predator, thereby enabling the patient to cover over and avoid expressions of his or her own predatory history. But this is not the case with a secured frame because the therapist is not, in fact, behaving in predatory fashion – conditions under which the patient's predatory acts and issues come to the fore. As a result, patients with predator death anxiety and deep unconscious guilt have mixed reactions to secured frames. On the one hand they unconsciously experience these frames as offering them a unique opportunity to process and work through their devastating deep unconscious guilt, but on the other hand the activation of this guilt and, with it, fresh demands from the deep unconscious system of morality and ethics for self-punishment that typically reach suicidal proportions make these patients enormously fearful of such conditions for therapy. They experience a strong unconscious dread of self-harm and entertain the unconscious belief that their therapists, in pursuing these issues in light of their encoded material, are trying to murder them. This creates powerful unconsciously driven resistances against the treatment experience and verbal assaults on the therapist are not uncommon – even as these patients continue in therapy with an unconscious appreciation of what the therapist is actually trying to help them accomplish. Carefully-dosed trigger-decoded interpretations often enable this group of patients to work through their resistances and make their peace with their existential and predator death anxieties.

Finally, we may note that under secured-frame conditions, patients generally work over all three types of death-related anxieties and experiences – predatory (fears of being harmed by others), predator (fears connected with having done damage to others), and existential (fears linked to the inevitability of personal demise). This means that patients with histories of highly traumatic death-related incidents, such as the loss of loved ones or being ill or injured themselves, suffer from especially severe forms of secured-frame death anxieties. They tend to avoid ideal frames and make repeated attempts to modify the secured frame when it's offered to them. They're also inclined to flee secured-frame therapies soon after entering them, an inclination that challenges a therapist's frame management and interpretive skills. Keeping these fragile and anxious patients in therapy is crucial for their future lives because they tend to get involved in self-punitive and death-denying forms of acting out and to live severely constricted and disappointing lives which they naively accept as their fate. Consciously, they have no awareness of the deep unconscious, death-related motives that account for their plight. Consistent use of adaptive principles of listening and intervening is the best means of enabling these long-suffering individuals to remain in and benefit from the frame-securing, insightful therapies that they so sorely need.

Deviant frames

A deviant- or modified-frame psychotherapy situation is one in which one or more of the ideal ground rules are not offered to the patient. All such therapies have a set of shared features, and in addition there are effects that are specific to the particular rule or rules that have not been invoked. Examples include therapies in which a low fee is set, there's a cancellation policy that forgives the patient's fee for a given session, make-up sessions are offered when a patient misses an hour, insurance forms are completed – the list is almost endless.

In principle, deviant frames offer a trade-off with uninsightful, denial-based protection from existential death and other anxieties on one side, and unconsciously mediated psychological damage on the other. Thus, for both patients and their therapists, the modified frame, no matter how necessary, is experienced deeply unconsciously as a predatory act by the therapist, one that is psychologically harmful and exploitative, and at times inappropriately seductive. These frame modifications are important interventions – that is triggering events – to which the deep unconscious system is exceedingly sensitive. Patients will, from time to time, allude to them directly or in encoded fashion, and offer narratives that encode their deep unconscious experience of the deviations in the frame. Therapists have the responsibility to interpret this thematic imagery in light of the frame-related triggers that have evoked them, and, at the behest of the patient's encoded directives, secure any modified ground rule that can be rectified. Being on the alert for this kind of material from patients is essential, largely because, on the conscious level, both patient and therapist tend to accept modified frame conditions for treatment with little direct thought. In contrast, the deep unconscious system consistently addresses these frame issues and incessantly encodes frame-related and frame-securing messages – often in the form of early memories in which family and other frames were less than ideal and needed securing.

These early memories do not, however, reflect unconscious sources of distorted pictures of the therapeutic situation or mistaken views of the therapist – that is, they do not indicate that the past is confounding the present as an unconscious form of transference. Instead, they are indications that the past is actually being repeated in some form in the present – that is, that the frame-deviant behaviour of the therapist is a repetition in some way of past acts of frame-deviant harm suffered by the patient in the past, often at the hands of his or her parents. While it is unconsciously mediated, the harm, which may be psychological or physical in nature, is quite real and has damaging effects on both parties to treatment. Indeed, frame violations often lead to emotionally-founded, somatic symptoms and harmful forms of acting out by both patients and their therapists – both within and outside of the therapy.

Whenever a therapist offers a patient an altered frame, the conscious experience of both parties to the therapy tends to be naive and bland, and very much denial-based. But the deep unconscious experience of all concerned is that the therapist is acting in a predatory fashion and the patient has taken the role of the willing victim of his or her predation. Thus, the frame-modifying therapist deeply unconsciously perceives that he or she has acted in predatory fashion, suffers from deep unconscious predator death anxiety and guilt, and is unconsciously driven to act in a self-punitive fashion. So despite the fact that most frame violations are sanctioned consciously by the various weak adaptive approaches to psychotherapy, the unconsciously mediated, untoward consequences of these acts of predation make doing psychotherapy and counselling personally hazardous for the uninsightful but well-meaning healer.

Why, then, does the conscious mind tend to prefer modified to secured frames? The basic answer is that deviant frames enable both parties to a therapeutic situation to avoid secured frames and the existential and other forms of death anxiety that they evoke. As noted, modified frames also create an unconscious illusion or delusion of invincibility against death – the rule-breaker unconsciously believes that breaking a rule of any kind implies that he or she can also defy the existential rule that death follows life. Clearly, as humans we tend to prefer deviant to secured frame conditions. That is, we'd either rather be victimized, harmed and suffer from predatory death anxieties, or be predators and suffer from predator death anxieties and deep unconscious guilt, than deal with and resolve our existential death anxieties – an opportunity that is possible only in secured frames.

A clinical excerpt

Let us turn now to a clinical vignette that will help to clarify some of the points made in this chapter:

Ms Benson is in psychotherapy with Dr Wall, a woman psychologist, because of her poor relationships with men. Referred to Dr Wall by her internist, in the consultation session Ms Benson, who's an editor for a trade magazine, brings up the fact that she has insurance coverage for 50 per cent of the fee for her sessions. She offers Dr Wall the form that must be completed in order to initiate coverage for the therapy, but the therapist suggests that the patient hold on to it until they have time to explore its meanings for her. She then advises Ms Benson to continue to say whatever comes to her mind.

Ms Benson explains that she has no problem with using the insurance, even though it means that the financial people at work will know about her being in therapy – and who knows who else. Money isn't the issue, she earns enough to pay for the therapy. It's that she paid dearly to have the coverage and she wants to use it.

Dr Wall remains silent and the patient goes on to talk about the doctors who have been treating her various physical ills, especially her recent, recurrent bouts of diarrhea. Most of them seem to have no idea how to treat her illness, but she now thinks of one who did. He medicated her and spent time talking to her about her problems, and her symptoms had disappeared. But when he suddenly died, her symptoms recurred and she still suffers with them from time to time.

An incident from her childhood, from around age 12, comes to mind. She'd fallen ill with a fever one Sunday afternoon in the middle of a family gathering. Her mother called their doctor who came to the house to see the patient. She was lying on the couch in the living room and the doctor decided to examine her there, in front of everyone. She was utterly humiliated when he began to undress her and she became furious with the doctor and refused to cooperate. When he persisted, she vowed to never see him again.

Dr Wall intervenes. She points out that the patient's story is about being examined in front of others by a doctor. It (the story) seems to be connected to her (Ms Benson's) request that she (Dr Wall) fill out the patient's insurance form which would, as the patient said, bring the financial people and others into her therapy. The story indicates that, while consciously, she (Ms Benson) wants the insurance form to be completed, unconsciously she would experience her (Dr Wall's) doing so as exposing Ms Benson to others in an inappropriate way that would be utterly humiliating to her. Ms Benson would be furious with her for doing it and would not want to come back for further treatment.

To comment briefly, this is a trigger–decoded, frame–securing intervention that begins by alluding to a theme that bridges from the narrative of the incident in the past to the therapy situation in the present – that of public exposure. The trigger–decoding effort is centred around the patient's deep unconscious perceptions of the anticipated trigger of the therapist completing the insurance form and then attempts to secure the frame – that is eliminate the third–party coverage – at the behest of the patient's encoded themes. To continue the vignette:

Ms Benson pauses for a while, and then recalls that she actually did see that doctor again – the one who tried to expose her – once, at his office. She insisted that she be seen by his associate who was a kindly, elderly woman physician who was able to understand her being so upset over having been treated so badly. She was someone whom the patient could trust.

Dr Wall points out that this last story seems to be saying that her last intervention shows that she understands the issue with insurance coverage and that she (the patient) feels that she can trust her (the therapist). Ms Benson responds that this doctor also died on her, so what's the point of trusting someone? So despite her stories and what they're saying, she still wants to use her insurance. She isn't going to continue to see Dr Wall unless she agrees to take the form and fill it out.

With time running out, Dr Wall agrees to do as her patient asks, with the proviso that she (Ms Benson) continue to explore the meanings of her (Dr Wall) doing so. She then spells out the other ground rules of the therapy – that it would be once weekly at this time and in this office for 50 minutes; that their contact would be restricted to this time and place; that the time was set aside for the patient, who had to assume full responsibility for her part of the fee, which should be paid for each month's sessions in the first session of the following month; that the patient had to assume full responsibility for the fee if she missed a session since the insurance did not cover missed sessions; that for now at least, other than her (the therapist's) reports to the insurance company, which the patient would be given to read, the therapy would be confidential and private; and that the patient should do as she did this session, continue to say whatever comes to mind and that she (the therapist) would comment from time to time when it seemed advisable to do so. Ms Benson accepts these conditions for treatment, makes a few nondescript comments, and the session comes to a close.

To comment further, Dr Wall usually structured a new therapy situation about half-way through a consultation hour. She delayed doing so until late in this session because she wanted to see if the proposed frame-modifying trigger of her completing the insurance form would evoke narrative imagery that would lend itself to interpretation and to likely rectification – the patient's decision to forgo the insurance coverage. At issue were the ground rules related to the total privacy and confidentiality of the therapy and the patient's assumption of the full responsibility for the fee. As we saw, the themes did coalesce around the frame violation of confidentiality and privacy, and they did indeed point to the need to secure the frame. Dr Wall then offered a trigger-decoded interpretation along these lines and the intervention obtained encoded, interpersonal validation through the story of the trustworthy elderly woman physician. When this was pointed out to her, the patient nonetheless refused to accept the secured frame. She was therefore taken into therapy under frame-modified conditions.

This is a generally workable arrangement that enables the patient to enter treatment and offers her the opportunity to explore and understand the deep unconscious meanings of her conscious need for a third party presence. The deep unconscious system is focused on such issues and we can be quite certain – it's a psychobiological given – that from time to time the patient will encode narratives that reveal the unconscious sources of the patient's need for the frame modification – and with them will come themes that will also again call for frame rectification. Properly interpreted, these fresh interventions could provide the patient with insights that would enable her conscious mind to support the secured frame sought by her deep unconscious system.

Even when a patient can't afford therapy on their own, defensive and self-punitive deep unconscious needs of some kind are usually served by a deviation of this kind. In Ms Benson's case, financial need was not at issue consciously , but the unconscious sources of her secured-frame anxieties – that is, the early trauma or traumas that prompted her conscious rejection of the secured frame – did not emerge in her manifest material. The only hint of deep need was the allusions to the deaths of two care-giving physicians, but Dr Wall was unable to decode these themes in light of the deviant frame trigger of completing the insurance form, nor was she able to use these themes in her interventions.

Technically, however, it's well to note that Dr Wall nevertheless should have mentioned these two powerful themes – power themes should always be alluded to in intervening. For example, she could have indicated that the patient's need for the presence of third parties to her therapy seems to have something to do with death and loss, noting that the patient had alluded to the death of a doctor twice in the session. An intervention of that kind, which is called a *playback of encoded themes*, would have implicitly encouraged the patient to express additional encoded images related to the underlying basis for this frame-modifying, *gross behaviour resistance* (engaging in a frame deviation is an act of resistance because it is a substitute for and interferes with work directed towards deep insight). Fresh encoded themes from the patient might have enabled Dr Wall to interpret the traumatic, unconscious, genetic basis for the patient's deviant need. (It's advisable to think that the therapist's avoidance of the death–related themes was based on her own unresolved death anxieties – a thesis that I won't pursue here except to note that death–related issues are not only difficult for patients to process, they also are problematic for therapists as well.)

As for the material of the session, we see again the naivety, proneness to denial, seemingly self-harmful proclivities, and preference for modified frames that are so characteristic of the conscious system. The patient consciously denies any problem with using the insurance, but then encodes a story in which the presence of third parties to a treatment situation is humiliating and infuriating, and reason to stop seeing a doctor. At the very moment that the patient's conscious mind is saying that therapy can continue only if there's inappropriate exposure of the patient to third parties, her deep unconscious mind is saying these conditions are hurtful and reason to not see this therapist again. And in typical fashion, the patient heeds her conscious adaptive choice, which seems to be self-defeating, and is quite unable to follow her own, far wiser, deep unconscious counsel to the contrary. Even when the patient's deep unconscious advice is interpreted to her, she refuses to accept it consciously. Once more we see that the emotion-processing mind has evolved in a seemingly dysfunctional and self-defeating manner.

The watershed session, which occurred some three months into the therapy, was triggered by a request from the insurance company that Dr Wall forward a detailed description of the treatment experience and present an elaborate treatment plan. Dr Wall informed the patient of these requests and indicated that she would not respond to them until Ms Benson had ample time to explore the meanings and consequences that this would have for her.

Ms Benson begins the session following this announcement with a dream in which she's in her childhood home, lying in bed with her mother. A man with a knife breaks into the room and her mother slips away, leaving the patient unprotected. The man calls the patient a murderer and begins to stab her in the chest and abdomen. She begins to bleed heavily; she's convinced that she's going to die. She woke up frightened and in a sweat.

She's been having trouble sleeping at night. The request for information from the insurance company was bothering her, but she still doesn't want to give up the coverage. Being in bed with her mother brings to mind something she hasn't mentioned before. She had an older sister named Kim and they slept in the same room. When Kim was seven and the patient five, Kim fell ill with meningitis and died. Their mother blamed the doctor for her death because initially, he had missed the diagnosis and didn't give her the antibiotics she needed to survive. Her parents had worried that the patient would also become ill and she was treated with prophylactic antibiotics. Being the only child left, her parents also began to worry about losing her and took her into their bedroom to sleep with them at night. The patient became fearful of close relationships, withdrew from her friends and became a loner. When she did make friends, it was always in pairs. Somehow that doesn't work with men, so she's not been close to a man in years.

Dr Wall interprets that the dream portrays how the patient would see her (the therapist) if she were to comply with the request from the insurance company. Like her mother in the dream, she'd be seen as abandoning the patient to a murderous assault by the intruding insurers. Complying would also be seen as making a mistake – as missing the diagnosis and not offering the proper curative measure – and as harming the patient in some fatal manner. These themes speak unmistakably to the harm that would be done by sending further material to the insurance company – harm that would unconsciously be experienced as killing the patient much as the family doctor was felt to have murdered her sister.

Ms Benson pauses for a while, then laughs and says that it sure as hell looks like the time has come to stop using her insurance to pay for her therapy. Dr Wall goes on to say that the patient's dread of being alone and her fear of losing someone close to her are based on a belief that she won't survive such situations – that she'll be murdered. It's also evident that she tries to protect herself from losing others by having two friends at any given time, so if one died, she'd have the other one left. This dread of loss, which was based on the death of her sister, must be behind her need for the insurance company's presence in the therapy. These same anxieties are one reason that she doesn't get involved with men: her dread of loss – the fear of a repetition of the loss of her sister – has prompted her to avoid these relationships. And, finally, the accusation made by the man in the dream – that the patient is a murderer – indicates that the patient somehow feels responsible for her sister's death and has an unconscious need to be punished in kind. Her insistence on having a murderous third party involved in her therapy was in the service of these self-punitive needs.

Ms Benson pauses again and then thinks about Al, a man at work who's been showing an interest in her lately. He's attractive, but she's been keeping him at bay. Now that she thinks of it, she was very provocative towards him this week: she'd talked to people he knew about his weaknesses and when he found out about it, he was very angry with her. She had also failed to pass a memo on to him and her oversight had put him in a bad light. Maybe that's similar to what she did with Dr Wall – had she completed the insurance forms so she (the patient) could feel alienated from her (the therapist). She sure overdoes the protection from loss stuff. Then, almost as an after-thought, she mentions that as far back as she can remember, she wished that she would die, but she never knew why. In the years after her sister's death, she had had many bouts of illness. She had fallen ill with a cold the week before her sister contracted her fatal meningitis – does she feel responsible for her death? With that, the session came to an end – as did the insurance coverage for this therapy.

Technically, the material following Dr Wall's trigger–decoded inter-pretations and efforts to secure the frame is a good illustration of *cognitive validation* – affirmation through the emergence of fresh material that significantly adds to the insights that have just been offered. As for our discussion of the ground rules of psychotherapy, the violence done by frame violations is well-portrayed in the dream of being stabbed to death by an intruder. While the patient's conscious mind entertained the idea of giving more information to the insurance carrier, her deep unconscious mind was telling the patient that she was arranging for her own destruction – her own self-punishing murder. The insurance people – and the therapist in joining in with them – were both the patient's protectors from loss and her punitive executioners, the latter in response to her deep unconscious guilt over the unconscious belief that she had caused the death of her sister. Deeply unconsciously, then, there was both a need for protection from loss and a need for punishment – the modified frame satisfied both of these pathological needs, albeit at great cost to the patient. A history of an early death-related experience and loss is common among patients who unnecessarily insist on third-party coverage – it often is indeed a costly unconscious effort to protect against further loss. So goes the unconscious ramifications of frame-related issues and behaviours – and the reasons why therapists need to pay attention to the ground rules of psychotherapy.

7

Death Anxiety and the Evolution of the Mind

By adopting a new way of listening and formulating the material of the therapeutic interaction, the strong adaptive approach has come upon a vast array of new clinical and theoretical findings and ideas that hold great promise to advance both the theory and practice of psychotherapy. Notwithstanding these advances, adaptive therapists also came upon a number of seemingly inexplicable or unsolved clinical puzzles (Kuhn, 1962) which engendered theoretical and therapeutic uncertainties that challenged the tenets of the approach. While this was a frustrating state of affairs, we also took our ability to recognize our limitations and uncertainties as a sign of the viability of the adaptive position. And because the solution to these puzzles did not emerge with repeated clinical investigations, it proved necessary to turn to new avenues of study in the hope of resolving these dilemmas using ideas drawn from, developed outside of, the therapeutic arena. As we shall see, these ventures proved to be quite rewarding.

Some unsolved puzzles

Clinically, perhaps the most daunting problem was the finding that some patients who were offered an ideal, secured set of ground rules for their psychotherapies, and who unconsciously validated and confirmed the positive holding and healing qualities of these frames, nonetheless abruptly terminated their treatments. Interpretation of their underlying secured-frame anxieties, most of them death-related, obtained unconscious validation, yet the resultant insights did not enable them to remain in therapy. The mystery lay with why these patients abandoned a therapy that they so strongly validated at the deep unconscious level. Efforts to find the answer clinically failed to provide a satisfactory answer.

Still another set of unsolved puzzles arose from the clinically-derived insights that were unfolding in respect to the architecture and operations of the emotion-processing mind. Why, for one, does the emotion-processing mind appear to be organized in a way that locates our wisest and most adaptive emotional intelligence in a deep unconscious system whose adaptive recommendations are not available to conscious awareness and adaptive use? And why are both patients and therapists reluctant to decode the invaluable encoded messages sent forth from this deep system? The consequent loss of adaptive capabilities is staggering.

There was more. Why is it that we have an unconscious component in the emotion-processing mind in the first place? Why don't we adapt emotionally entirely within awareness, as so many of our evolutionary predecessors appear to do? Why, too, do we have a deep unconscious system of morality and ethics with such pristine values and an unconsciously mediated enforcement policy that is so strict and unrelenting? Why aren't conscious morals sufficient standards and constraints for human behaviour – and why are conscious values so easily compromised? And, finally, why have we been saddled with a conscious mind that is so strongly protected by – so bent on – the use of denial and obliteration? Why have humans evolved an adaptive system in which knowledge reduction – a diminution of contact with and sensitivity to the environment – plays such a significant role? This attribute runs counter to the usual evolutionary history of living species for whom the trend has been to evolve organ systems that are capable of greater rather than lesser contact with, and knowledge of, environmental conditions, stimuli and events. Why has this trend been reversed in humans? There was a lot that needed explaining.

Searching far and wide for answers

The unanswered questions raised by adaptive theory and practice seemed to be intractable despite extensive clinical efforts over many years. This vacuum motivated a turn to science and biology that, after many blind alleys, eventually led to the development of a formal science of psychoanalysis based on the quantitative study of emotion-ally-charged communication within psychotherapy and, later on, in everyday life (Langs 1992a, 1999b, Langs *et al.*, 1996). This work, which was based on the distinction between the narrative (double-message) and non-narrative (single-message) modes of expression, produced many significant findings. Chief among them was the dis-covery of a series of well-defined, universal, biological, laws of com-munication – laws of the mind, if you will – that are to be found in all humans, and in chimpanzees as well. These research studies differ-entiated the strong adaptive approach from other approaches to psy-chotherapy on many different measures, with findings that put the adaptive position in a highly favourable light. The work also generated a series of clinically meaningful quantitative results, including several apparent quantitative indicators of countertransference problems in the therapist.

Despite the richness of these findings, they did not help to resolve any of the clinical and theoretical dilemmas that had initiated this journey into science. Yet the research did make clear that the emo-tion-processing mind has universal features and is a lawful biological entity – our findings generalized across all cases studied. And, in time, this led to the realization that, as such, this mental module must have an evolutionary history, especially in respect to its adaptive prefer-ences – and its evident failings. This insight prompted a turn to the science of biology and its most fundamental subscience, *evolutionary biology* – the study of the present-day adaptations of living organisms and of the long-term histories of these adaptive capabilities as they pertain to the history of the living beings that have populated and still populate this earth.

With good reason, evolutionary biologists claim that it's not possible to fathom the nature of a biological entity without a full knowledge of its adaptations and their evolutionary story. Nevertheless, with few exceptions (Glantz and Pearce, 1989; Lloyd, 1990; Nesse, 1990a, b; Nesse and Lloyd, 1992; Slavin and Kriegman, 1992; Badcock, 1994) psychotherapists have seen little reason to turn to the science of evo-lution for insight – much of it because their models and understand-ing of the emotion-related mind do not lend themselves to such pursuits. In contrast, the adaptive approach's emphasis on emotional adaptation, and its formulations regarding the mental module with which this is accomplished, seem to establish a natural pathway that led directly to evolutionary thinking and research – it was simply a matter of realizing that the path was there, ready to be traversed. Studying the current adaptations of the emotion-processing mind and their evolutionary history seemed, then, to be a promising way of shedding new light on the clinical quandaries confronting the strong adaptive approach. These efforts did not disappoint.

Key factors in evolution

In brief, present-day evolutionary theory, so-called neo-Darwinism, states that living organisms naturally compete for the limited amounts of available space, supplies of nutrients, and opportunities to reproduce found on our planet. As they do so, they naturally undergo random mutations which are passed on to their offspring, thereby altering their ongoing gene pool and adaptive resources. In the face of threats caused by drastic changes in environmental conditions – caused by nature and/or by other living entities – those organisms whose natural mutations enhance their adaptations to these new dangers tend to survive best and to be favourably reproduced. Other, less suited competing organisms eventually become extinct, which has been the fate of over 98 per cent of the organisms that have populated this planet (Dawkins, 1976; Slavin and Kriegman, 1992; Plotkin, 1994; Dennett, 1995; Langs, 1996; Rose, 1997).

Environmental conditions that test organisms' adaptive resources are called *selection pressures*, and they implicitly determine whose adaptive resources and random genetic alterations fit best with the new situation and thereby survive and are favourably reproduced. Selection pressures include adverse changes in the physical environment, as well as modifications in predators that enhance their deadliness and thus more seriously challenge the physical defences of their prey – the so-called evolutionary predator–prey battle for survival. Then, too, the acquisition of especially favourable faculties by other organisms – and at times by an organism itself – may affect the survival of all of the entities within a given ecosystem and affect reproductive success for all concerned.

As part of living nature, the emotion-processing mind has inevitably evolved in response to a variety of selection pressures. Identifying these factors and understanding how they affected the development of this mental module and led to the natural selection of its present architecture promised to take us a long way towards understanding the present-day features of this adaptive entity and the clinical dilemmas that they were causing.

Language acquisition

The hominid species, of which we, as *homo sapiens sapiens*, are a member, is about six million years old. In its struggle for survival, hominids have had to face both powerful predators and stark, life-endangering environmental conditions. These threats and selection factors have led to the natural selection of spontaneous mutations that facilitated the favourable reproduction of abilities like the upright stance, opposable thumbs, long-distance vision, and the expansion of brain size which sponsored the development of new brain structures and mental capabilities.

Supported by changes in the structure of the pharynx that facilitated the use of sounds that allow for the spoken word (Lieberman, 1991), about 100,000 to 150,000 years ago, advances in the size and configuration of the hominid brain eventually led to the acquisition of language capabilities. This ability, which evidently was built from mimetic forms of communication, developed slowly but surely and may well be the single most fateful event in the evolutionary history of living beings. Indeed, language acquisition has had countless consequences for humans, as well as for the earth's ecosystem and all life on this planet – many of them favourable, some of them enormously unfavourable. Everything from philosophy and science to toxic gases, from antibiotics to atom bombs, from child-rearing practices to social structures, and from morality to abstract thinking, has come from language acquisition. This achievement was also a watershed accomplishment for the emotional side of human existence and for the development of the emotion-processing mind (Bickerton, 1990, 1995; Corballis, 1991; Pinker, 1994).

Among the many developments that appear to have been fuelled by the attainment of language capabilities in humans was the ability to represent and process events within their minds, thereby creating the capacity to work over danger situations and traumas mentally while away from the scene of an untoward incident. Other animals, including apes, are confined to event-perception and can work over traumatic events only when approaching or present at the scene of former or pending harm. These new human mental adaptive processing efforts appear to have been carried out entirely within awareness, but over time and under the influence of strongly traumatic selection pressures, the ability to engage in unconscious processing was also developed and favourably selected (Donald, 1991; Mithen, 1996).

Language usage also facilitated the development of a strong sense of personal identity as distinct from other living beings, and in addition led to an ability to think about and develop expectations regarding the future. This in turn led to the realization of the inevitability of death for all humans, and to the explicit recognition that death implies non-existence and that it may arise from harm caused by others as well as by one's own body and mind – as in suicide. Thus, language capabilities created an unprecedented set of capabilities, but also a unique set of dangers and unusual threats to survival – selection factors – many of them configured mentally.

Another uniquely human, language-based problem can be seen in the fact that other living species have, by and large, had to deal solely with physical predatory threats from other living beings and to some extent within their own bodies. But in addition to these physical threats, humans are also called on to deal with psychological dangers caused by others – for example, forms of mental torture and ways people drive other people crazy or to suicide – as well as dangers that arise from their own disturbing thoughts and fantasies which may involve harming others and/or themselves in the past, present and/or future. The most serious of these inner mental dangers takes the form of thoughts of, and intentions to commit, suicide or murder.

A fateful human form of mentally experienced danger involves the anticipation of the death of others and especially of oneself. For most humans, the specific source and cause of this inevitability is uncertain for much of their lives. Death may come from within one's own body, from the mental decision to commit suicide, or from mental processes that so weaken the body as to cause it to deteriorate and die. Death may also stem from external causes in the form of deadly actions by other humans, devastation caused by other living organisms – for example, animals and microscopic predators like viruses and bacteria – and from accidents or natural disasters. Above all, it appears that the awareness of the certainty of personal death has been one of the most critical selection factors for the evolved architecture of the emotion-processing mind. That is, minds that were able to cope successfully with the actual threat of the eventuality of personal demise, with its future certainty, and with the death anxieties that these realizations evoked, tended to survive better than those who did not cope as well with these threats and tended to be favourably reproduced.

The three forms of death anxiety

Evolution, with its stress on adaptation and survival, and on life and death, brought with it serious considerations of the problem of death and death anxiety – issues that held the key to solving our unsolved mysteries. There are three basic forms of death anxiety (Langs, 1997, in press); each has had a profound and distinctive effect on the evolution of the emotion-processing mind, and each affects its present-day operations in major ways. And while some of these concerns occupy the conscious mind, it's been found clinically that most of the anxieties caused by the threat of death operate outside of awareness, as does most of their effects. Thus, death anxiety tends to have a profound unconscious influence on human adaptations and it appears to be the basic underlying source of all emotional maladaptations – and of all human creativity as well. With this in mind, let's examine the three forms taken by human death anxieties.

Predatory death anxiety

Predatory death anxiety (broadly defined as responsiveness to a threat of harm) is almost as old as living organisms – it emerged as soon as organisms found it necessary to compete for living space and nourishment. All living entities possess some type of capability with which to detect external dangers and mobilize defensive responses. In the earliest unicellular organisms, reactions to threat took the form of flight, while later-developed organisms were also able to react by freezing or fighting (LeDoux, 1996). Over the eons, there was also a broad shift from total organismic responses to predatory threats to the development of well-defined organ systems, like the immune system, whose main defined function was to cope with such threats – a shift from non-specific to specific modes of adaptation (Beck and Habicht, 1996). In time, with the development of brains and then minds, the mental registration of danger and ways of coping psychologically were added to these physical alerting and responding systems. Fear responses in complex organisms played a notable role in this regard (LeDoux, 1996; Langs, 1999b).

Over millions of years, as part of the arms races between predators and preys, the level of predatory threat escalated, while the means of coping with such dangers became more and more sophisticated and effective. Thus, on the one hand humans have experienced an increasing number of predatory threats to life, limb and mind, but on the other hand they have developed increasingly effective means of detecting and responding to these dangers. The latter include the creation of elaborate fear and anxiety signals of danger – fear as a response to physical threat and anxiety as a response to emotional threat. Both signals promote the rapid development and use of effective physical and mental reactions to predatory threats.

Predatory death anxiety is, then, a response that arises in humans by virtue of the presentation of a danger situation and through our ever-present knowledge of death itself – that is, existential death anxiety is a special class of predatory death anxiety. Any event that presents a threat to the life or integrity of an individual, whether it takes a physical or psychological form, is treated emotionally as a predatory danger and dealing with predatory threat is one of the main specific adaptive functions of the emotion-processing mind – it is a danger-oriented organ of coping.

Predatory danger situations have also served as selection factors in the evolution of the emotion-processing mind. Environmental threats – for example, natural disasters and living predators – appear to have created selection pressures that favoured individuals whose minds were linked to and capable of strong perceptive capabilities and had high levels of conscious-system intelligence. These threats also selected for minds that could mobilize a variety of effective bodily responses to external dangers – activities that involved the brain and nervous system, as well as the hormonal, immune and muscular systems. The ability to rapidly mobilize mental and physical resources was, then, the key to surviving *predatory physical dangers*.

The effects of *predatory psychological dangers*, which are uniquely human threats, are, however, somewhat more complicated than those that arise from physical threats. On the one hand, in a manner similar to dealing with physical threats, survival in the face of psychological dangers is favoured by conscious minds with effective perceptual abilities – that is, minimal use of conscious-system denial and obliteration – along with a high degree of conscious emotion-related intelligence. High levels of these endowments enable individuals to consciously assess the extent of the danger at hand and to minimize its potentially disruptive psychological and physical consequences.

But, on the other hand, there are indications that psychological predatory threats also selectively favoured the reproduction of minds that use perceptual denial and the related capacities for unconscious perception and deep unconscious processing. Denial is needed because many of the psychological threats experienced by humans are created by people on whom the predatory victim is dependent for survival.

It is dangerous and mentally disruptive to experience murderous impulses from people who provide care, nurturance and other vital forms of support, as seen with the parents of infants and children. In order to maintain these life-sustaining relationships and avoid states of anxiety and panic over their rage and threats of abandonment – situations that would add to the threat of survival – aspects of the danger situations created by these predators need to be obliterated and therefore relegated by the MAC to unconscious perception and processing. However costly in loss of knowledge of the environment and in the impairment of effective, conscious coping skills, this use of denial would actually enhance rather than diminish chances of survival. This is not the case, however, with threats of bodily harm, where conscious registration and the full use of consciously mobilized resources is vital to surviving the threat.

The contradictory selection pressures created by psychological danger situations help to account for some of the more puzzling and seemingly disadvantageous features of the emotion-processing mind. They include the extensive human use of conscious-system denial as a means of protecting the individual from anxiety-provoking conscious perceptions of their caretakers at moments in which they behave in predatory fashion. And these opposing pressures also help to account for the evolution of unconscious perception and deep unconscious wisdom – possibly as ways of storing threatening information from the environment for future access.

Predation death anxiety

Predation death anxiety arises when an individual causes physical and/or psychological harm to others. The extent and power of this anxiety is proportional to the amount of harm caused to the victim. In all instances, however, predatory acts directed against others, whether psychological or physical, are unconsciously experienced as acts of murderous violence. Thus, predation death anxiety is both the anxiety caused by having, in some real or imagined sense, killed another person, and also the fear of death as punishment in kind for the harm done to other living beings.

Causing harm to others may, at times, be recognized consciously and the sense of guilt it evokes may also be in awareness, along with conscious fears of retribution. But most often some or all of the harm is denied consciously and, instead, registers deep-unconsciously. There, the deep unconscious system of morality and ethics recognizes the full measure of the damage done to the other person and metes out punishments for the deed through a series of unconsciously orchestrated self-punitive decision and actions that are the result of deep unconscious guilt. In situations where extreme harm has been caused, themes of suicide are the rule. The guilt and self-punishing acts of self-harm tend to persist for many years, although processing these events in an adaptive psychotherapy may, with extended working through, eventually lead to repentance and deep unconscious forgiveness – and a diminution of the self-punitive behaviours. Nevertheless, the activation of this constellation, which most often takes place under secured-frame conditions, is extremely anxiety-provoking for patients and it evokes strong resistances that are difficult to resolve.

As with predatory death anxiety, predator death anxieties are anchored in reality – in causing actual physical and psychological harm to others. The power of the deep unconscious mind over emotional life does not lie with wishful fantasies of a sexual or aggressive nature. Instead, it lies with actual moments of destruction and with the memories of these events.

The natural selection of minds capable of experiencing deep unconscious guilt and of unconsciously orchestrating acts of physical and psychological self-harm as punishment are major consequences of predator death anxiety. While at first glance this arrangement seems to work against personal survival, further thought suggests that having both conscious and unconscious deterrents to harming others actually favours individual survival – and the survival of our species. These deep unconscious pressures are likely to motivate individuals to refrain from future acts of violence against others. That said, there are many indications that these evolved and selected deep unconscious restraints have not fulfilled their mission very well – violence against others is the world's most devastating problem today.

The human need to do violence to others seems to have played a significant role as a selection pressure that favoured the development of conscious and deep unconscious guilt and self-punitive tendencies. The urge to act violently has many sources, such as being physically harmed by others; insufficiencies of food, shelter and/or space; being subjected to narcissistic and other psychological wounds; emotional deprivations; jealousy and envy of others; efforts to magically deny the inevitability of personal death – and much more. Effective restraints against violence towards other humans have been, and still are, sorely needed.

But here, too, design problems arose because on the one hand conscious knowledge of the wish or intention to harm or murder another human being may serve as a vital deterrent, but on the other hand conscious awareness of this urge can disrupt conscious-system functioning because of the guilt it evokes. Here, too, natural selection was pulled in opposite directions – both for and against the conscious registration of acts of harm against others. This seems to have been another factor in the development of the deep unconscious system – the need to be unaware of one's own violent intentions and acts, especially those that are psychologically harmful, as a way of avoiding the experience of conscious guilt. This inner-directed denial is also a form of knowledge reduction that has proven costly to human life.

All in all, natural selection has not been able to solve the problem of human violence; neither conscious nor deep unconscious deterrents seem to have curtailed these urges. The denial of psychologically damaging acts has proven to be costly in the long run because it causes considerable harm to both the perpetrator (via deep unconscious guilt) and the victim (via the harm that he or she suffers). A case in point is the consciously unappreciated finding that every violation of a ground rule or boundary in a relationship, including that between patients and therapists, is experienced at the deep unconscious level as an act of predation. When enacted by a psychotherapist, the patient suffers emotional damage and the therapist must endure deep unconscious guilt and self-punishing behaviours. The use of interventions that are unwittingly harmful to patients, and the deep unconscious guilt and self-punitive inclinations they orchestrate, stand as one of the most insidious occupational hazards of being a psychotherapist.

Existential death anxiety

The third form of death anxiety is existential – the dread of the inevitability of death for all living humans, especially oneself, and for other multi-cellular creatures. Existential death anxiety is a severe form of dread of non-existence and evolution has favoured minds inclined towards but one mechanism in dealing with this form of anxiety – *denial in its many forms and incarnations* (Becker, 1973; Langs, 1997; Liechty, 2002). This automatic use of denial is an evolved, fixed feature of the conscious system – a basic defence that is, as noted in Chapter 4, a consequence of the evolved sorting preferences of the MAC. The explicit, conscious awareness and anticipation of personal death which resulted from language acquisition was therefore a significant selection factor for the design of the emotion-processing mind. And it fostered the selection of minds that not only made extensive use of conscious-system denial, but also possessed deep unconscious systems so that death-related issues could be processed mentally without conscious awareness and without disrupting conscious-system, adaptive functioning.

The intensity of existential death anxiety and the concomitant need for an abundance of responsive denial mechanisms seems to be based on a number of factors. For one, there's the awareness that, religious beliefs aside, death is the end of life and the termination of an individual's existence. *The basic existential ground rule of life states that it ends in death.* And this rule is the prototype and deepest unconscious meaning of all secured ground rules and boundaries. Thus, all frame-securing events remind us, however unconsciously, of this basic rule of life and death. It's largely for this reason that most conscious minds tend to favour denial-serving rule violations over adhering to ground rules. Unconsciously, frame modifications are efforts to establish the claim – the illusion or delusion – that the person who defies or violates a single ground rule thereby becomes an individual who is an exception to all rules, the existential ground rule in particular.

Another factor that renders this form of anxiety especially unbearable is that most humans do not know when and how the final blow will come – be it from one's own body or from an outside event such as a natural disaster, an accident, or an attack by another living being. It is this uncertain yet certain expectation of eventual harm that renders existential death anxiety a special case of predatory death anxiety. Another notable reason for the intensity of this anxiety is the fact that, in the end, there's absolutely nothing we can do to overcome this danger – we cannot defeat it; it will always defeat us. We can fight predators and win; we can control our inclination to predate others, and be successful at it; we can struggle against illness and adverse environmental conditions – but, at best, all we can do is postpone the inevitability of our demise. In this light we can appreciate why, in dealing with existential death anxiety, nature has favoured minds that use denial in one form or another – it's all we have available to us to maintain a relatively peaceful state of mind. And, as is the case with frame violations, most forms of denial operate unconsciously and are not appreciated for what they are. Regardless of other considerations, all religious belief systems are denial-based, as are extremes of celebrations, the distractions of sports and most other forms of entertainment, manic states, the urge to accumulate excessive amounts of money and to gain extremes of power, acts of violence directed against others ('they die and I live'), and similar behaviours.

All in all, the explicit, conscious awareness of the inevitability of personal death has the potential to destabilize conscious-system functioning. Thus, within limits, the denial of death safeguards our conscious adaptive capabilities. Nevertheless, because existential death anxieties are so discombobulating, we tend to overuse denial mechanisms to an extent that significantly reduces the availability of much-needed information about our environments and the threats that they often pose to our lives – for example denial of illness and of harmful sadomasochistic relationships. Paradoxically, then, the denial of death generally both protects and harms the denier. This principle applies not only to everyday life, but to the psychotherapy situation as well.

The unconsciously mediated effects of death anxiety

It needs to be emphasized that most of the effects of the three forms of death anxiety are mediated outside of awareness. We are not usually cognizant of the role that these anxieties play in our lives and in psychotherapy, and in the development of emotional maladaptations. Indeed, only adaptive forms of psychotherapy have been able to track the sources and define the consequences of these anxieties – in extended forms of adaptive psychotherapy, death-related issues appear in virtually every session. One or another form of death anxiety is a factor and an unconscious motivating force in virtually every important decision we make – including, for us as therapists, our preferred way of doing therapy – and these anxieties also underlie virtually all symptomatic disturbances experienced by ourselves and our patients.

Predatory death anxieties unconsciously motivate defensive assaults against others, unexplained moments of fight or flight, other kinds of untoward belligerent acts, and, in regard to psychotherapy, a preference for confrontational and assaultive modes of treatment. Predator death anxieties unconsciously motivate uncalled for self-destructive decisions and actions, masochistic types of surrender to the harmful acts of others, inexplicable forms of depression, suicidal thoughts and acts, and a preference for manipulative, highly exploitative forms of treatment. Finally, existential death anxieties unconsciously motivate many dysfunctional behaviours that serve conscious-system denial, such as extreme violence against others, frame violations of all kinds, maniacal quests for power and wealth, a wide range of religious beliefs, and therapies that are extreme in their obliteration of psychological factors.

That said, these death anxieties may also, paradoxically, motivate human creativity and, in rare individuals, a deep need to fathom deep unconscious experience – to know, instead of deny and not know.

The principles of technique advocated by the strong adaptive approach enable therapists to detect and track the unconsciously mediated effects of these three forms of death anxiety. Thus, therapists should be on the alert for allusions to death-related traumas and to death-related themes in patients' material. Once recognized, the themes can be explored and interpreted in terms of, first, their triggers within the therapy as created by the therapist's interventions, mainly in regard to frame management efforts, and, second, the early death-related experiences that are being activated by these triggers.

For example, when the frame is secured, the patient's images are likely to involve themes of entrapment – for example being trapped in an overturned automobile or in a room that's on fire. In these cases, existential death anxieties are at issue. In contrast, when a ground rule has been modified by the therapist, themes of violence and murder tend to appear in the narrative material – a reflection of the patient's predatory death anxieties. At the same time, the frame-modifying therapist will find him or herself dreaming about people who harm others and who act in self-destructive fashion. For them, predator death anxiety has reared its guilt-ridden, self-punitive head.

Death anxiety casts a shadow over every emotional moment of our lives. From time to time it is visible and conscious, and a moderate cause for concern. But in the face of powerful death-related triggering events, it may cause panic or extremes of denial as seen in experiences of derealization. At other times, the effects of death anxiety operate outside of awareness in ways that are so telling that it is incumbent on every therapist to identify the encoded expressions of this mighty force, interpret their sources and nature, and manage the framework of treatment towards its securement as guided by patients' encoded directives.

Solving the unsolved puzzles

The scenario that was postulated for the evolutionary history of the emotion-processing mind and the discovery of the likely death-related selection pressures that shaped its design took the adaptive approach a long way towards solving its unsolved mysteries. It became clear, for example, that patients who flee secured-frame therapies which they validate unconsciously tend to have suffered significant death-related traumas at some point in their lives. Examples include the early loss of a parent or other family member, the suicide of a family member or loved one at any time in their lives, and personal experiences with severe illness and injury that brought them close to death. As a result, these patients are especially sensitive to, and terrified of, entrapping frames no matter how healing they may be. Because of these anxieties, a therapist should move slowly but surely towards securing the frame with these patients. Tolerance of one or more modified ground rules is quite necessary, but if the therapist maintains his or her sense of reserve, the patient will, when ready for a secured-frame moment, encode the necessary directives to accomplish this change. Supplemented with trigger-decoded interpretations of the existential death anxieties and their unconscious sources, these efforts enable many of these patients to remain in treatment – much to their personal benefit.

Patients who cling to deviant frame therapies that are unconsciously perceived as harmful and predatory, and therapists who unnecessarily offer such conditions for treatment, tend to do so because they're attempting to defend themselves against the experience of secured-frame, existential death anxieties. Deviant frames are also embraced by patients with deep unconscious needs for punishment caused by their own prior acts of predation. At times, the deviant-frame therapist may provide enough unconsciously mediated suffering for a patient that he or she experiences temporary relief from their deep unconscious guilt. But such 'misalliance cures' are temporary and they inherently encourage the patient to seek emotional relief through further punishments in their daily lives.

As for the architecture of the emotion-processing mind, the various forms of death anxiety seem to have created competing and contradictory pressures regarding the ideal design of this mental module. Predatory death anxiety leads mainly to a favouring of highly perceptive and effective conscious systems, with minimal use of denial and deep unconscious processing. In stark contrast, existential death anxiety seems to have favoured minds steeped in conscious-system denial and able to process severe traumas deeply unconsciously, entirely without awareness. Finally, predator death anxiety may well have biased natural selection towards denial-based conscious minds that were also capable of experiencing deep unconscious guilt and evoking self-punishments. All in all, in response to these competing selection pressures, natural selection seems to have favourably reproduced minds that lean towards knowledge reduction *vis-à-vis* the environment, far more than sharp perceptiveness. In addition, it has favoured conscious minds that use denial more rather than reasonably limiting its use. This design feature is supported by avoidance forms of psychotherapy, while adaptive forms run counter to these natural inclinations.

The unavailability of deep unconscious wisdom for conscious-system coping, and the requisite that all communications from the deep unconscious system emerge in encoded form, seem to be accounted for by the fact that deep unconscious wisdom deals with extremely anxiety-provoking, death-related unconscious perceptions. Thus, awareness of the activated wisdom requires an awareness of the very experiences and meanings that were deemed by the MAC to be too disruptive to enter awareness in the first place. These same factors also account for the evolutionary development of encoded messages. Finally, the strong influence exerted by deep unconscious guilt on conscious–system adaptations is accounted for by the need to deter humans from harming other humans.

★   ★   ★

Humans are unique in having to continue to deal with the competing selection pressures that have made the rendering of an ideal evolved design of the emotion-processing mind all but impossible. With environmental conditions, including a host of language-based developments, pressing the mind towards contradictory configurations, it's small wonder that the emotion-processing mind is in a state that promotes maladaptations as much as, or more often than, sound coping responses when it comes to emotionally charged triggering events. For good reasons, then, this mental module is one of nature's most compromised creations; and this is why humans suffer so much emotional pain and so many psychologyically-based dysfunctions. It's also why we, as therapists, must find the means to deeply and accurately understand the evolutionary history and present design of the emotion-processing mind, so we can do as much as possible to undo and rectify the mental chaos and psychological pain that nature and natural selection have wrought.

PART II

Clinical Technique

8

Indicators: Symptoms and Resistances

While many schools of psychotherapy advocate a loose, intuitive approach to doing therapy (see for example, Kohut, 1971; Mitchell, 1988), the strong adaptive approach has found that clear-cut principles of technique are an absolute necessity for a sound, deeply insightful therapeutic experience and outcome. These contrasting viewpoints stem largely from the differences between the conscious and deep unconscious systems and the contrasting ideas about how to do therapy.

The adaptive approach has discovered clinically that left to its own devices, the conscious mind of a therapist will naturally adopt a conscious-system approach, one that deals with superficialities rather than more powerful, deep unconscious issues, and will offer a therapy that is conducted in a frame-deviant context. Given the great variability of conscious-system thinking in the emotional realm, these forms of therapy are inevitably quite variable in their techniques and they tend to lack well-defined principles of listening and intervening. The additional absence of a sound means of testing the reliability of interventions makes it all but impossible for conscious-system modes of therapy to come up with definitive rules of technique. In addition, as I've tried to show, the conscious choices that a therapist makes regarding his or her approach to psychotherapy are greatly influenced by unconsciously driven conscious-system needs for punishment, denial and other interfering defences – forces that move treatment away from ideal forms of healing. The natural aversion of the conscious mind to trigger-decoding also severely limits the scope and healing powers of these types of therapy. All in all, the absence of unconsciously validated guidelines renders conscious-system forms of treatment very risky undertakings. Yet these are problems that conscious-system therapists have no way of recognizing and correcting.

In contrast, the deep unconscious system is highly organized and operates on the basis of well-defined, universal rules and processes. The system is quite consistent in its approach to psychotherapy and the therapeutic frame, and is a reliable guide to healing interventions – verbal and frame-related. Gaining access to the contents and operations of this most important system therefore requires a highly organized approach to treatment. This is possible because, with remarkable regularity, the system emits encoded messages that validate well-structured, definable, therapeutic work and fails to support work that is loosely structured – work it sees as harmful not only to the patient, but to the therapist as well. Highly principled forms of technique are the only answer to the potential damage that less consistent approaches may – and often do – cause.

In this light, it's well for us to pause and question the basis for seemingly favourable therapeutic outcomes of vaguely defined, weak adaptive psychotherapies (Langs, 1985). While deep insight clearly cannot play a role in these results, therapists' support for their patients' denial-based defences may be one way that these treatments bring a measure of relief to patients, doing so by helping them to avoid issues they dread to explore. The same denial mechanisms may also prompt the parties to therapy to overlook the hurtful consequences of errant interventions, and unconscious idealizations of the therapist may prompt the patient to report a favourable outcome of treatment without alluding to residual difficulties.

Along different lines, paradoxical positive reactions to damaging interventions are not uncommon, as is gaining a measure of temporary symptom relief on the basis of focusing on highly intellectualized, relatively unimportant material and the lesser emotional issues to which they pertain. Then, too, some relief may come from non-validated frame modifications that enable all concerned to avoid secured-frame, existential death anxieties. Other maladaptive forms of relief come from interpretations that unwittingly sanction patients' inclinations toward action-oriented, frame-violating means of discharging emotional tensions, and from unprincipled interventions that unknowingly punish guilt-ridden patients, thereby temporarily reducing their super-ego pressures.

Some weak adaptive therapies appear to bring relief to patients by overriding deep unconscious influences and training the conscious mind to think or behave in a manner that enables patients to unlearn particular symptoms, like phobias. But, as a rule, there are hidden costs in overlooked, untouched symptoms and personality disturbances that tend to be denied by all concerned. Then, too, there are unconsciously mediated means of relief such as a process called *cure through nefarious comparison* (Langs, 1985), which alludes to a patient's unconscious realization that his or her therapist is behaving in a dysfunctional manner, an insight that reassures the patient that he or she is far less disturbed than their therapist. Similar unconscious mechanisms underlie relief through bountiful gratifications (for example providing patients with food and/or drink, gifts, job leads, helpers, and so on), therapists' sanctions of inappropriate acts and maladaptive forms of sexual and aggressive satisfactions (such as, inappropriate affairs, and attacks on others), the offer of punitive interventions (overt criticisms and other assaultive comments), and the like (see Langs, 1985, for details).

All in all, given the intricacies of the emotion-processing mind, it's fair to say that evident symptom relief in a patient reveals little or nothing about the *unconsciously mediated* means by which this relief was achieved, nor does it in any manner stand as testimony to the validity of a therapeutic approach or the theory on which is it based. In contrast, encoded validation creates a viable framework within which insights into modes of cure can be soundly assessed and usefully developed. With this in mind, let's turn now to the clinical arena and to the development of sound principles of listening, formulating, intervening and validating all manner of offered interventions. We begin by exploring the kinds of information that we can obtain by attending to the manifest contents of patients' communications.

The manifest level of listening

The listening process developed by the strong adaptive approach considers the implications and meanings of both the conscious-manifest and deep unconscious-encoded messages from patients. Broadly speaking, the manifest level of communication is assessed for indications of a patient's current emotional status, adaptive preferences, conscious thinking about the therapy experience, the extent of his or her conscious integration of the therapist's interpretations and frame-management efforts, and the presence of surface resistances. Thus, therapists should, from session to session, consistently monitor the status of a patient's *symptoms* – a term that I shall use all-inclusively to allude to all emotionally and psychologically founded disturbances of behaviour and affect, interpersonal and relating difficulties, certain physical disorders, and other emotionally-founded maladaptions and dysfunctions. Also in need of monitoring is the status of a patient's *resistances* or obstacles to therapeutic progress, including negatively-toned attitudes towards the therapist and treatment. These two areas – symptoms and resistances – are the ultimate targets of therapists' trigger-decoded interpretations and frame rectifications. The overall goal is to explain their immediate basis in both conscious and deep unconscious experience, and their past sources as well. Because they constitute cause for a therapist to intervene, disturbances in these areas are called *indicators* – that is, they are indications that a patient is in need of a frame-rectifying and/or trigger-decoded interpretation in the session at hand.

Symptomatic indicators

Psychotherapy is an informed effort to favourably modify patients' emotionally-founded maladaptations. These disturbances take two basic forms: symptoms and resistances. In psychodynamic, insight-oriented therapies they are the target of efforts to illuminate the deep unconscious basis for patients' maladaptations.

Symptomatic emotional problems take a wide range of forms, including disorders of affect (such as excessive anxiety and depression), behaviour (compulsions, addictions, excessive acts of sexuality or violence, and so on), relating (for example withdrawal, excessive dependency, provocativeness, masochistic submission), personality (for example character disorders), style of living (withdrawal, constriction, excessive involvement with others), contact with reality (the psychoses, for example), and bodily functioning (for example psychosomatic disorders). A manifest allusion to a particular symptom in a given session is a patient's way of presenting a maladaptive problem as an indicator – that is, as a target for intervening.

The adaptive approach has shown that once a person enters psychotherapy, the *deep unconscious basis* for the continuation of a patient's symptomatic complaints and for the development of a fresh symptom is a product of the bipersonal, interactive field created by each patient and therapist. In general, these disturbances in patients are responses to errant interventions by their therapists, although occasionally they may follow an unconsciously validated interpretation or frame-securing

effort – secured-frame existential death anxieties and deep unconscious guilt play a role in these responses which tend to be short-lived.
Thus, while factors outside of therapy may contribute to symptom
formation, the illumination of the deep unconscious structure of
patients' emotional problems must, of necessity, be made through
trigger-decoded interpretations developed around their therapists'
interventions – frame-related and otherwise.

The key principle is that patients' symptoms are interactional products of the bipersonal therapeutic field (Baranger and Baranger, 1966),
and that their interpretation should be interactional as well – that is,
should be organized around patients' unconscious perceptions of their
therapists' interventions (Langs, 1976, 1999a). The main exceptions to
this rule are found, first, at times of extremely traumatic external
events like major disasters, and, second, in long-standing secured-
frame therapies in which the patient's early-life, death-related traumas
– especially incidents in which he or she behaved in predatory fashion – are activated by the backdrop of security. In these situations, the
death anxieties that are fuelling the patient's symptoms are either
externally or intrapsychically evoked, and the triggers created by the
therapist play a secondary role. Nevertheless, these are unusual
moments in therapy; at all other times, the happenings within treatment are the deep unconscious motivating factors in the patient's
dysfunctions.

All in all, then, emotional problems are triggered by real events, and
once a patient enters psychotherapy, except for major disasters, these
events are constituted as the interventions of their therapists – mostly in
the realm of managing the setting, ground rules and boundaries of the
therapy. Responses to errant interventions are, then, the most common
unconscious basis for the activation or sustenance of a patient's symptom. This means that a therapist's interpretation of the deep unconscious sources of an active symptom will, as a rule, begin by alluding to
the patient's unconscious perceptions of the relevant triggering event
and then address the patient's particular symptomatic ways of dealing
with that trigger. If genetic material is also present in some form, the
connection to past life events also is delineated.

Resistance indicators

Resistances in psychotherapy are broadly defined as any obstacle to
therapeutic progress manifested by a patient. They, too, are interactional
phenomena, products of the bipersonal field (Baranger and Baranger,

1966; Langs, 1976) in which both patient and therapist play a role. Thus, resistances are triggered by therapists' interventions and their unconscious basis must be understood and interpreted in that light. Of note, too, is the realization that resistances are defined and identified within the framework of a given theory and practice of psychotherapy. Thus, there are many situations in which a patient would be seen by a weak adaptive psychotherapist as resisting therapy, while a strong adaptive therapist would disagree – and vice versa. For example, a patient who intellectualizes about a subject introduced by a therapist would be seen as cooperating by the weak adaptive therapist, but as communicatively resistant (that is, not encoding as needed) by the strong adaptive therapist. Because the approaches of these two basic schools of psychotherapy are so different, there are countless examples of this kind.

Gross behavioural resistances

As understood and defined by the adaptive approach, there are three forms of resistance seen in psychotherapy situations. The first type is called *gross behavioural resistances* – actions taken by patients that interfere with the forward movement of the treatment. These acts tend to involve departures from the ideal framework of therapy – that is, they are violations of the ideal therapeutic contract. Examples include a patient's lateness to a session, leaving the session before time is up, extended silences and premature terminations. Whenever these resistances appear, the therapist is obliged to attend to the patient's material in order to identify the interventional trigger that has evoked the enacted resistance. Most often the trigger is some type of frame violation, although on rare occasions it may be an unconsciously validated interpretation or a frame-securing effort. These paradoxical responses are identified by the nature of the activating trigger, the patient's encoded themes which tend to reflect secured-frame death anxieties, and by their generally rapid resolution.

Technically, gross behavioural resistances are directly observed by the therapist and the key problems lie, first, with verifying that the observed behaviour is truly an obstacle to therapeutic progress, and, second, with identifying the contributing trigger. Resistances are not confronted or thought of as solely the patient's responsibility. Instead, they are interpreted in light of activating triggers and the decoding of the patient's narrative themes in order to ascertain the patient's unconscious perceptions of the therapist that are the deep unconscious source of the enacted resistance. When a frame modification is a contributing unconscious source of a resistance, frame rectification, if at all possible, should also be carried out using the patient's encoded directives to do so.

It is, however, crucial to appreciate that while most gross behavioural resistances reflect maladaptive responses to therapists' interventional errors and frame modifications, some of these seeming resistances are quite appropriate and adaptively sound in light of a therapist's interventional efforts. In simple terms, some therapeutic work is harmful to patients — for example unneeded frame violations and erroneous, assaultive or seductive verbal interventions. It is, then, actually maladaptive for patients to continue in therapy with therapists who intervene in this manner — that is, the absence of resistance is a sign of disturbance in the patient. On the other hand, leaving a therapy of this kind is adaptive, so that the apparent resistance is actually appropriate and healthy. Nevertheless, in almost all instances, extended silences during, and lateness for, sessions are maladaptive resistances because even a therapist's errant ways should be explored in therapy rather than handled through frame violations.

In sum, the assessment of the adaptive and maladaptive aspects of a gross behavioural resistance depends on a full appreciation of the nature of the interventional triggers that have evoked the seemingly resistant response in the patient.

Communicative resistances

The second class of obstacles to therapy are called *communicative resistances* — a type of resistance whose definition is built around adaptive understanding of the role and nature of manifest and encoded communication in psychotherapy. These resistances take two forms. The first are *patients' silences*, which are gross disruptions in communicating; and the second involves *a patient's failure, in the presence of a disturbing intervention by a therapist, to generate an interpretable and, if need be, frame-rectifying encoded communicative network*. In brief, in the face of an activating trigger, communicative resistance is seen when the patient fails to generate the material needed for sound intervening by the therapist.

Patients' extended silences are both gross behavioural resistances — violations of the fundamental rule of free association — and a form of communicative resistance. On the other hand, the failure to generate a complete communicative network is solely a communicative resistance.

Its definition is based on the strong adaptive finding that there is an ideal, resistance-free communicative network that fulfils what's called the *recipe for intervening* – the ingredients needed by a therapist in order to offer a trigger-decoded interpretation or engage in a frame-securing effort when such is called for. Ideally, this recipe includes the following ingredients or elements:

- First, a manifest allusion to an active triggering event – that is, a direct mention of a critical and recent intervention made by the therapist.
- And, second, a rich pool of encoded themes, replete with two ingredients: *bridging themes* that connect the disguised narratives to the triggering event – for example a story about exposure that deals with a therapist's personal self-revelation, and *power themes*, which are allusions to violence, illness, injury, death and so on. The latter are essential because the deep unconscious system deals solely with the most anxiety-provoking and traumatic aspects of emotionally-charged triggers – it's domain is that of powerful issues.

Communicative resistances take a variety of forms. The triggering event may obtain encoded rather than manifest representation – for example a therapist's reducing a patient's fee may be represented in a story about a patient's friend who voluntarily agreed to a salary cut. A more severe form of this resistance is seen when an active trigger is not represented in any detectable form. Along different lines, the pool of themes may be lacking in bridging themes and/or power. As always, these communicative resistances need to be understood and eventually interpreted in light of active triggers – they are interactional products. Technically, in the presence of communicative resistances, the therapist must refrain from intervening in the expectation that, eventually, the patient will generate an interpretable network. At times, a playback of the available themes related to an unmentioned trigger will facilitate the patient's doing so.

Most often, communicative resistances are unconsciously activated by non-validated, harmful therapeutic interventions such as frame modifications and erroneous or irrelevant verbal comments. But on occasion the resistance is a response to unconsciously validated efforts at frame securing and interpreting – that is, they are the result of secured-frame death anxieties. These resistances may also arise because an unconsciously validated interpretation or frame-securing intervention has activated painful, anxiety-provoking and guilt-promoting genetic material which often pertains to a patient's past predatory acts and is a consequence of his or her predator death anxiety. It is essential, then, that a therapist keep track of his or her recent interventions and the patient's deep unconscious issues, death anxieties and traumatic early life experiences. This kind of deep understanding is helpful in enabling the therapist to wait patiently for the emergence of the material that he or she needs to intervene. It also fosters therapists' tolerance of extended communicative resistances, which patients need to sustain until they can gather the strength to offer the therapist an interpretable communicative network of trigger and themes related to terribly painful deep unconscious memories and issues.

The conscious refutation of unconsciously validated interventions

The third class of communicative resistances emerge after an unconsciously validated interpretation – that is, after the patient has generated positive encoded images in response to the therapist's intervention. These resistances reflect an extreme, defensive split between the conscious and deep unconscious systems in that the patient deep-unconsciously supports the therapist's intervention, recognizes the encoded confirmation in his or her material, but nevertheless consciously refutes the insights so generated.

As noted, the conscious mind is naturally unaware of deep unconscious contents and processes, and the anxiety-provoking meanings so contained. When such meanings are interpreted to a patient, he or she will, as a rule, consciously accept and work over these fresh insights. In so doing, however, the trend is for the conscious mind to rapidly repress its awareness of the meanings involved. While sporadic conscious working through may occur in subsequent sessions, most of the healing that is activated by these interpretations tends to continue on the unconscious level alone. It's not uncommon to find that this week's trigger-decoded insight is no longer in the patient's awareness in the following week's session. This is a major reason for the need for an extended working over and working through of deep unconscious experiences and their implications for a patient's symptoms. All in all, then, this phenomenon, which has resistance attributes, is so universal that it may be thought of as a resistance caused by the architecture of the emotion-processing mind.

In certain patients, however, there's a different kind of resistance response which, as noted, takes the form of an immediate conscious rejection of the very interpretation that a patient has just moments earlier unconsciously validated. This rejection often extends to the therapy itself in that, despite abundant unconsciously validated interventions, both interpretive and frame-securing in nature, these patients repeatedly insist that nothing has happened in their treatments. Strikingly, this belief does not obtain encoded support – the deep unconscious system continues to validate the therapeutic work whose existence is being denied by the conscious system. This deep unconscious support is the main reason why, despite their unending conscious protests, these patients tend to remain in treatment for long periods of time. Most often the unconscious motive for this type of defence, in which the therapist is repeatedly subjected to verbal attacks and abuse, appears to be predator death anxiety and unbearable deep unconscious guilt for past predatory acts. These issues cause these patients to dread the experience of deep unconscious meaning and insight, and meaningful therapy – the confrontation with the harm that they've caused and the conscious experience of guilt – is horribly painful for them.

Some additional aspects of resistances

Implicit to this discussion is the realization that *resistances are conscious-system phenomena* – albeit, under considerable unconscious influence. Throughout treatment – and life – the deep unconscious system speaks only for open communication, insight, healing and adaptation to extremely painful events and inner thoughts and impulses. It is solely the conscious system that speaks for denial, falsifications of reality and inner wishes, untoward actions such as unreasonably harming others and/or oneself, the use of inappropriate defence and resistances, and the like. And the unconscious needs and motives that drive these tendencies stem from a *deep unconscious influencing system* – a system that largely favours the use of denial *vis-à-vis* sources of unconsciously experienced death anxieties, and sustains the unconscious need for punishment caused by deep unconscious guilt. Under these influences, the conscious system is the main source of human suffering and the main enemy of the self and its best interests, while the deep unconscious system is the main source of inner emotional healing.

A special class of resistances involve patients' wishes to modify or sustain unneeded alterations in the ideal ground rules or boundaries of the therapy situation. Such behaviours are unconsciously motivated as ways of avoiding secured frames and secured-frame moments, and the existential death anxieties that they arouse. And while these resistances produce a measure of temporary relief, they do so at great cost in that these psychologically damaging frame modifications are likely to become a patient's preferred mode of coping with, and defending against, secured-frame death anxieties. In addition, because of the nature of the resistance, the patient who persists in these efforts is deprived of the chance to discover and work through the deep uncon-scious basis of these anxieties – an essential part of the healing process. Here, too, triggers – contributions from the therapist – must be con-sidered. Quite often patients' frame-modifying resistances are modelled on the frame-modifying, counter-resistance-based behaviours of their therapists. On rare occasions, a frame-modifying resistance arises as a response to a sound intervention that threatens to activate the patient's most disturbing unconscious issues, but these resistances tend to be linked to images reflecting secured-frame, existential death anxieties and they are quickly resolved.

Along different lines, it's well to realize that while patients vary in the extent to which they show gross behavioural resistances, commu-nicative resistances are inevitable – what varies is the form that they take. They, too, are the result of the evolved design of the emotion-processing mind and stem from conscious-system needs for defence – that is, denial and obliteration – because of the system's inherent dread of deep unconscious experiences and meaning. Every patient has a favoured means of obstructing access to these deep unconscious experiences, and their style of resistance is so inbuilt that it seldom lends itself to modification despite all efforts by therapists to confront the resistance and interpret its unconscious motives. Thus, some patients will consistently fail to generate powerful encoded themes, others will almost never manifestly represent an active trigger. Still others avoid engaging in trigger-decoding, while others will tend to ruminate intellectually rather than report dreams or tell stories. As noted above, a most trying group of patients will generate a full com-municative network with representations of triggers and abundant, powerful themes that enable a therapist to offer a trigger-decoded interpretation. They will then deep-unconsciously validate the interpretation (or frame rectification), but will quickly repudiate consciously the therapeutic effort in its entirety.

In response to these various forms of communicative resistance, the therapist should wait for illuminating, trigger-evoked encoded imagery before pointing out the nature of the patient's communica-tive resistance and interpreting its deep unconscious basis. Because these communicative-style resistances reflect the patient's preferred mode of defence against both deep-unconsciously derived insights and secured frames, they create valuable opportunities for patients to appreciate the very design and operations of their emotion-processing minds and to grasp the nature of the psychological defences that they invoke to avoid deep unconscious meaning.

Another valuable principle of technique requires that the therapist gauge the strength of a patient's symptomatic and resistance indicators in each session in order to determine the extent to which the patient is in need of an intervention. The strongest symptomatic indicators are suicidal and murderous thoughts and impulses and acutely distressing emotionally-founded symptoms, while thoughts of terminating therapy and the request for ground-rule modifications head the list of gross behavioural resistance-indicators. The strength of the indicators is then measured against the extent to which the patient's material fulfils the recipe for intervening. In the presence of very strong indicators, the therapist is obliged to make the best available trigger-decoded interpretation and/or frame rectification effort possible, even in the presence of a poorly represented trigger or weak network of encoded themes. On the other hand, when the indicators are weak, the decision to intervene largely depends on the extent to which the patient has fulfilled the recipe for intervening. In adaptive forms of therapy, working with patients' resistances occupies the bulk of the time in sessions. The processing of the deep unconscious meanings of a patient's core emotional problems is a rare and fleeting event. Fortunately, the interpretation of the unconscious sources of resistances is itself a meaningful and healing part of the therapeutic experience.

Conscious thoughts about the therapist and the therapy

Another reason for observing a patient's conscious thinking and behaviour is to determine his or her feelings about and view of the therapist, and the extent to which the patient has absorbed, accepted and consciously processed the trigger-decoded, deep unconscious insights and frame-related interventions that have been offered to him or her. A notable part of these efforts involves comparing the patient's deep unconscious insights and frame-related attitudes with his or her conscious position on these same matters. These conscious attitudes range from patients' openness to, and tendency to accept, deep unconscious insights and to incorporate them into their conscious understanding, to those patients who, as noted above, are continually critical of unconsciously validated therapeutic work.

It is, however, incumbent on a therapist to assess the validity of conscious criticisms of his or her interventions, although in this regard the deep unconscious system is far more reliable than the conscious system, which often fully accepts harmful therapeutic work and not infrequently rejects unconsciously validated therapeutic efforts. Valid conscious criticisms of a therapist's efforts are supported by deep unconscious, encoded criticisms as well. In the absence of such support, the patient's conscious reproaches may be taken to be conscious-system resistances whose triggers and unconscious motives need to be determined.

Further perspectives

To sum up, there are many notable unconscious motives for resisting therapeutic progress. They include the unconscious dread of the secured frame and the activation of secured-frame, existential death anxieties; deep unconscious predator death anxieties and the wish for punishment; the wish for uninsightful, frame-deviant, action-oriented relief from deep anxieties; and the dread of deep unconscious meaning and of repressed memories of traumatic events. Virtually every patient has suffered from death-related experiences in his or her childhood or later life. The activation of the memory and meanings of these events is the source of enormous amounts of death anxiety – which is why these events and meanings have been obliterated and repressed in the first place. Both gross behavioural and communicative resistances are evoked to preclude the emergence of these painful repressed and denied incidents and their meanings. Nevertheless, it must be stressed again that the processing and interpretation of these resistances reflect the patient's usual modes of defence, so that the interpretation of their deep unconscious sources is highly therapeutic. In addition, the analyses and momentary resolution of resistances clear the way for the occasional watershed session in which the unconscious core of a patient's symptoms is expressed meaningfully around a triggering event and is available for interpretation and working through.

Along different lines, it's well to appreciate that at the core of every symptom and resistance is a death-related trauma and issue. This may involve the death, serious injury or illness of someone close to the patient, which arouses predatory and existential death anxieties. Or it may stem from the death of or harm to someone close to the patient for which the patient bears some responsibility and which evokes predator death anxiety and deep unconscious guilt. Along different lines, it may involve harm suffered by the patient at the hands of others, as seen with congenital defects or illnesses, as well as later-life harmful incidents that involve serious injury, illness, damage caused by others, or natural disasters – events that evoke both predatory and existential death anxieties. Given both the pervasiveness and scope of the death-related threats with which humans must deal and the dysfunctional design features of the emotion-processing mind, we can appreciate why virtually every human walking this earth experiences a measure of emotional dysfunction and why every patient who has entered a psychotherapy situation shows some form of resistance – much as every therapist who offers this treatment must deal with his or her own symptoms and counter-resistances as well. Such is human nature – and life itself.

A clinical illustration

To illustrate aspects of this discussion, let's look now at a clinical excerpt:

Mr Arp, a man in his late twenties, recently began once-weekly psychotherapy with Dr Wren, a psychiatrist, for problems in relating to women and controlling his anger. He begins his third session by saying that he has to go to an out-of-town business meeting the following week and that he won't be able to make his session. He then asks Dr Wren if he could see him on a different day so he wouldn't miss a week of therapy.

To comment, Mr Arp's intention to miss a session is a frame-violating, gross behavioural resistance because it interferes with the progress of the therapy and violates the ground rule that the patient should be present at all scheduled sessions. No matter how seemingly necessary, most plans of this kind are either driven by or satisfy deep unconscious needs that involve both a triggering intervention of the therapist's and the patient's deep unconscious responses to the trigger. Thus, all intended or actual absences should be seen as psychologically-determined resistances until proven otherwise.

There is, in addition, another gross behavioural, frame-violating resistance here, namely the patient's request for a make-up session. This appeal asks the therapist to respond to the patient's frame break with a frame break of his own – that is, to violate the ground rule that pertains to the specified, agreed-upon, fixed time of the patient's sessions. Indeed, even when a school or job change makes it mandatory to change the time of a patient's sessions – a move that always should be made on a permanent basis – the alteration in the schedule is a frame modification. Thus, even though the change must be effected in order to ensure the continuation of the therapy – and therefore is also a way of securing the frame – the frame-violating aspect will register unconsciously and evoke encoded responses. Themes pertaining to the mixed nature of this trigger – breaking the frame to secure it – will emerge.

While on this subject, let's be clear that changes in the time of a single session, no matter what the reason and who initiates the change, is an unjustifiable frame violation. Patients who need to miss an hour must be allowed to have a secured-frame experience in this context, and not be made exceptions to the rules of therapy – and, by inference, of life itself. Similarly, the therapist who must, of utter necessity, cancel a session should not offer make-up hours to his or her patients – this, too, is a violation of the basic ground rules of treatment and an indication of unresolved secured-frame, existential death anxieties in the healer.

Returning to our discussion of the case material, we can see that technically, Dr Wren has no choice but to respond to his patient's frame-modifying request. Eventually, he must either comply or not do so. Even saying nothing is a meaningful response because it implies not changing the time of the session. Whatever the decision, though, it should be based on the directives contained in the patient's subsequent encoded themes and not made unilaterally or arbitrarily. Thus, if the therapist were to deny outright Mr Arp's request, doing so would be improper technique. This is the case, firstly, because he would be answering the patient's question directly, and thereby addressing manifest contents and implicitly encouraging the patient to avoid encoded messages; secondly, he would interfere with the patient's communication of the trigger and related encoded themes that account unconsciously for this frame-modifying request; and, thirdly, he would have failed to wait for encoded directives with which to fashion his frame-securing intervention (which is what the encoded themes inevitably would express) – a response that violates his neutrality because the intervention does not rely on the patient's material in the session at hand.

The ideal response, then, is to not answer the patient's question when asked and to wait for subsequent material. If the patient does not continue to free associate, the therapist could simply remind him of the fundamental rule and indicate that he should continue to say whatever is coming to mind. The therapist can be quite certain that the patient will then encode a directive to hold the frame secured by not changing the time of the session. The universal secured-frame needs of the deep unconscious system virtually guarantees that encoded themes of this ilk will be forthcoming.

Dr Wren asks Mr Arp to continue to say whatever comes to mind, and with some annoyance, the patient does so. He says that his job has become a burden for him, that he's been there only a year and already there's more pressure than he can tolerate. His trip involves seeing a major buyer of their products and, if the sale falls flat, he'll be in a lot of trouble. But that's how his life has gone lately – he'll catch a break and then something will screw it up. Maybe he's masochistic, maybe he likes to suffer. In his childhood, he was always the one who was blamed for everything that went wrong. It's like he's suffering from a repetition compulsion – wasn't that what Freud called it?

To pause for further discussion, we may note that this material is intellectualized and without the specific narratives that are the means by which the deep unconscious system expresses itself. It's ruminative, lacking in detailed story-telling or the report of a dream, and is laced with self-interpretations. They are typical of the offerings made by the conscious system, in that they are non-narrative and allude to tendencies and conflicts within the patient without an allusion to a trigger or an adaptive cast. They're reminders that many therapists believe that their patients are as good at interpreting their material as they are – that interpretations cannot be the source of 'cure'. This is certainly the case with so-called interpretations of manifest contents and their implications, but far from the case when it comes to forging interpretations that are trigger-decoded – an effort patients rarely, if ever, engage in.

Mr Arp is, then, showing strong communicative resistances. At least one of his active triggers has been manifestly represented – the *anticipated trigger* (that is, the expectation) that Dr Wren will comply with his request and change the time of his session. Undoubtedly, there are other active triggers, including those that have unconsciously motivated Mr Arp's request for a frame modification in the first place – and possibly his planned, frame-violating absence as well.

It's well to appreciate that changing the time of a session is a frame violation, regardless of whether the therapist has explicitly established the ground rule that specifies that the time and day of all sessions is fixed and should not be modified. This precept is one of the basic, healing and holding ideal ground rules of therapy that is sought for and supported by the deep unconscious system of the emotion-processing mind — it's a rule that is set and enforced by its system of morality and ethics. Thus, the deep unconscious mind sets the ground rules of treatment — the conscious mind may or may not agree or comply, but deep unconscious standards and needs should prevail.

In any case, before the therapist can get to and deal with any other active trigger, he must obtain the encoded imagery that will direct his immediate frame-management activities — that will, without question, advise him to hold the frame secured. Once he has secured the frame based on his patient's encoded themes, two things are likely to happen. First, the patient may be expected to encode his deep unconscious response to the frame-securing intervention — and we have every reason to expect that it will be validating in nature and arouse existential death anxieties. Second, the patient is likely to bring up — manifestly or in encoded form — the other triggers that he's processing at a deep unconscious level, the unconscious sources of his frame-deviant request for a make-up session. If this is the case, he will also encode fresh themes that pertain to his deep unconscious perceptions of these additional interventions and indicate how they are motivating his request to modify the framework of his therapy.

All in all, we're looking at a situation in which both gross behavioural (the planned absence and request for a make-up session) and communicative resistances (the absence of bridging and power themes) have surfaced. The immediate goal, then, is to discover the deep unconscious, trigger-related stimuli for these resistances, and to be in a position to interpret the deep unconscious needs and historical factors that are shaping Mr Arp's resistances and his choice of obstacles. Patient waiting is the therapist's best resource in this regard.

To be clear about the communicative resistances, we need to look at the communicative network for encoded reactions to the anticipated trigger and for clues to the background or unknown trigger — the earlier intervention — that prompted these gross behavioural and communicative resistances. Recall that the communicative need is for a workable representation of the triggers — manifestly or in thinly disguised (encoded) form — and for a strong pool of themes — or as it's called, a *full and powerful derivative network* — that would reflect the patient's unconscious perceptions and processing of the triggers in question. To this point in the session, then, the patient has given the anticipated trigger a manifest representation in his request for a make-up session, but he has not as yet generated a strong and meaningful pool of themes related to that expected trigger. As for the background or unknown trigger, as far as we can tell the patient has not given it a manifest or workable encoded representation and the weakness of the thematic pool applies to that trigger as well.

Communicative resistances abound. One reason for this may be that, for the moment, instead of working over the two triggers at issue with encoded communications that would lend themselves to interpretation, they are being dealt with through the patient's own planned modification of the ground rules (his intended absence) and by means of his request that the therapist further deviate as well (by offering a make-up session). Maladaptive actions of this kind relieve underlying anxieties and often substitute for and impede verbal-communicative processing activities.

The patient's frame-modifying act and request are therefore resistances in two ways. First, a missed session precludes therapeutic work, and second the frame modifications are being used as an action-based, maladaptive means of attaining relief from the patient's underlying, trigger-evoked anxieties and conflicts – an act that, as an alternative pathway to relief, bypasses the mental and verbal processing of the issues involved. Were Dr Wren to support these resistances in any manner, he would be unwittingly supporting the patient's frame-modifying, pathological mode of symptom relief, be encouraging the avoidance of deep insight and also promoting further acting out by his patient.

All in all, then, Dr Wren's silence – his intervention at the moment – seems to be appropriate and wise. The silence is an implicit way of letting Mr Arp know that he (Dr Wren) does not intend to engage in making manifest content-oriented, intellectualized interventions and that before he can intervene properly, the patient must communicate more meaningful material, including powerful encoded themes – an example of the complex implications of a simple listening attitude by a therapist. Dr Wren is, then, waiting for his patient to spontaneously forgo his communicative defences and turn to the encoded, narrative mode of expression – a highly likely prospect in light of the formal research finding that patients do indeed spontaneouly cycle in and out of this mode of communication (Langs *et al.*, 1996). Should this not occur, the therapist could point out the lack of narrative material as a way of confronting the patient's communicative resistances and implicitly encouraging, or explicitly asking, the patient to generate encoded thematic material. Returning to the vignette:

Dr Wren decides to intervene and points out that something is prompting Mr Arp to ruminate instead of telling stories – his material is quite flat. The patient then says that, well, he did have a dream the previous night. In the dream, he was in a high-school classroom, taking an examination. He felt panicky because he was unprepared for the exam.

The dream brings to mind his growing up in a poor neighbourhood in New York City. But his father's manufacturing business did well and he sent the patient to a private high school. Mr Arp felt out of place there and insisted that he be transferred to the public high school in his neighbourhood, even though he was in the middle of the term and the kids in the public school were known to be nasty and dangerous. His parents agreed to his request and on the first day that he attended classes there, he lost one of his textbooks and stole a copy from a classmate. The boy found out about the theft and beat him so badly he had to be hospitalized for a week. He really regretted changing schools. His parents never should have acceded to his stupid wishes.

Dr Wren intervenes again and points out that at the beginning of the session, the patient had requested that he (Dr Wren) also change something for him (the patient). The story about changing high schools seems to be connected to his request that he (Dr Wren) change the time of his (Mr Arp's) session the following week. But the story indicates that making the change would be against his (Mr Arp's) best interests, that in some way it would do violence to him. And his comment that his parents shouldn't have agreed to do it clearly indi-cates that he too (Dr Wren) should not accede to the patient's request. In keeping with his (Mr Arp's) advice, he (Dr Wren) will keep the time of his sessions as arranged and not offer a different time for the session next week.

Mr Arp pauses for a moment and remembers that his sister was the only one in his family who was against his leaving the private school. She had predicted that he'd be attacked in the public school. She had a good head on her shoulders; she wasn't like his parents, she had sound judgment and she was the only one in his family whom he could trust. It suddenly occurs to Mr Arp that he was in the private high school when his brother died. The anniversary of his death happens to be next Thursday, the day of his scheduled session. He really should be with his parents that day because they took his brother's death so hard. It occurs to him now that he probably can change the day of his out-of-town meeting to the following Monday. He must have been running from the whole sordid scene with his parents in making the appointment on the same day as the anniversary of his brother's death. 'And from me', Dr Wren, points out, 'You were running from me too'. 'Yes, from you too', agrees the patient, who then adds that he'll be able to make his session as scheduled.

With time running out, Mr Arp now recalls that Dr Wren had suggested in the previous session that some kind of dark memory seemed to be encoded in the dream he had reported in that hour. All he could remember about the dream at the moment was that his brother was in it and there was a twisted steel structure of some kind. The dream must have had something to do with the anniversary of the death of his brother. He and his brother were in a car that his brother was driving when he lost control of the car and it slid into a ditch and turned over. His brother wasn't wearing a seat belt and was killed; the patient had noticed it, but hadn't said anything even though he had his own belt on. The twisted steel reminds him of the horrors that confronted him when he regained consciousness after being knocked unconscious by the accident. With that the session came to an end.

To comment again, the patient's report of his dream – the turning point in the session – emerged only after the therapist did not join the patient in his intellectualizations, which were weak and trivial, and eventually pointed out the absence of narrative material. The dream and associations, which yielded a bridging theme to the anticipated trigger and many power themes, including the death of the patient's brother, led to the clarification of the unconscious basis for the patient's gross behavioural and communicative resistances. The deep unconscious motives behind these resistances appear to have been, in part, the patient's secured-frame death anxieties – essentially, the fear of dying in a closed or secured space, much as his brother had died and as the patient had nearly died in the car accident. There also seems to be a wish to be harmed by the therapist as punishment for his deep unconscious guilt over his belief that he had contributed to the death of his brother by not insisting that he use his safety belt – a wish encoded in the story of being severely beaten when he committed the crime of stealing the book at school.

The session aptly demonstrates the emotional weakness of manifest ruminations when compared to the death-related traumas that were related to the patient's dream and his storied associations – this is typical of the difference between the emotional world accessed by the weak and strong adaptive approaches. There is as well a vast difference in emotional impact when a patient ruminates about the loss of a sibling as compared to when the loss is worked over in the context of a patient's deep unconscious experience of that loss.

Additional motives for the patient's resistances evidently include the wish to avoid the arousal of manifest memories of the death of his brother in a setting where the deep unconscious conflicts caused by his loss were likely to materialize. Thus, the triggers for the patient's gross behavioural and communicative resistances were, first, the secured frame, and, second, the interpretive interventions by the therapist which were moving the patient towards images that were connected with his conscious and deep unconscious processing of the death of his brother. Notice, too, that eventually it was revealed that the patient did not need the frame change because he was in a position to change the day of the conflicting out-of-town appointment. In many situations of this kind, it does indeed turn out that a frame-modifying request is frivolous and not the result of events beyond the control of the patient.

In respect to technique, the therapist correctly maintained the secured frame – the agreed-upon time of the following session – on the basis of the patient's directive as reflected in his encoded themes. In response, he obtained encoded, deep unconscious, interpersonal validation from the patient through the story of the patient's sister who wisely spoke out against the change in schools and could be trusted. In addition, cognitive validation appeared through the emergence of fresh material, mainly about the death of the patient's brother, that illuminated aspects of the patient's resistances not previously communicated.

All in all, then, given the design of the emotion-processing mind, the processing of resistances is bound to occupy the bulk of psychotherapeutic work, and serve as the source of many frustrations and yet profound insights for both patients and their therapists. There is no other gateway to accessing the deep unconscious core of a patient's symptoms and therefore to lasting, insightful symptom relief. Therapists need to be patient with these obstacles to effective treatment and to maintain their therapeutic stance despite the assaultive effects of these momentary barriers. Doing so is richly rewarding for all concerned.

9

Triggers and Themes

As we have seen, the emotion–processing mind is an adaptive module geared primarily to coping with traumatic environmental events, broadly defined. These adaptive efforts are carried out by both the conscious and deep unconscious systems, and they are evoked by triggering events. On the deep unconscious level, the result is the generation of narrative themes that reflect the events and meanings that have been perceived and processed deep-unconsciously. Thus, triggers and themes – the subject of this chapter – are the key to understanding and interpreting the powerful emotional issues that we, as humans, process outside of awareness and that lie at the heart of patients' emotionally-founded symptoms and resistances. Reduced to its basics, then, the optimal intervention that can be fashioned in order to reach into the deep unconscious realm and obtain deep-unconscious encoded validation involves, first, correctly identifying the trigger to which the patient is responding deep-unconsciously and, second, decoding the narrative themes in light of that trigger. This is done by relocating or transposing the themes from their manifest context in a dream or story into the situation with the triggering event, and treating the resultant imagery as reflecting the patient's valid, unconscious perceptions of the meanings and implications of the triggering event.

To cite a brief illustration:

With the permission of his adolescent patient, Frank, Dr Hall, a male psychologist, has a session with Frank's mother in which they discuss some of her issues and problems with her son. In the session after the contact with the mother, Frank asks about the therapist's meeting with his mother, is told about it in broad terms by Dr Hall, and then Frank tells his therapist that his seeing her seems to have been helpful – his mother settled down after the meeting. He then tells a story about his best friend, Walter, whose mother has been listening in on his telephone conversations with his friends. When Walter complained to his father about what his mother was doing, the father sided with the mother, saying that they didn't trust Walter's friends. It was a dumb thing for him to say. The fact is that Walter is the one who can't trust his parents. The other day Frank and Walter laughingly plotted to kill Walter's parents with rat poison so Walter could have a life.

The trigger here is the therapist's session with the patient's mother. Even with the patient's permission, this is a violation of the deep-unconsciously sought ideal ground rules pertaining to total privacy and confidentiality. Typically, the patient consciously sanctions the frame violation, but objects vigorously at the deep unconscious level.

The trigger is alluded to manifestly. The story of Walter's mother's eavesdropping is the first encoded narrative theme. We lift the theme from the story and recognize that it's a frame violation – an invasion of privacy – that bridges over – is analogous – to the trigger of Dr Hall's talking to Frank's mother, an intervention that invited her to listen in on Frank's therapy sessions. So we bring the theme to the triggering intervention and use it to tell the story of Frank's unconscious perception of the trigger. The read-out is that Dr Hall had invited Frank's mother to violate the privacy of her son's therapy – to eavesdrop. This is a personally selected, valid perception of a universal meaning of such a contact – there's no sign of distortion or misperception.

The theme of sanction by Walter's father is also lifted from the narrative and transposed into the triggering situation. In translation, it says that the mother's request to see Dr Hall was based on a mistrust of her son and that Dr Hall's agreeing to see her, and thereby supporting her request to eavesdrop on her son, was a dumb thing for him to do – and, through the mechanism of condensation, the same applies to Frank's giving her permission as well.

As for the two boys plotting to murder Walter's parents, we lift that theme from the manifest story and bring it to the triggering situation. This narrative also allows for two translations. First, it seems to express Frank's deep unconscious rage at both his mother and therapist for having had an eavesdropping session together. And, second, it may also convey the unconscious perception that the session in some way murdered or did violence to both Frank and Dr Hall – that is, that it destroyed the therapy. In addition, the storied theme of Walter's not being able to trust his parents is transposed into the therapy as a valid deep unconscious response to Dr Hall's session with the mother – it has destroyed Frank's trust of his therapist.

Triggers and transposed, decoded themes are at the heart of every strong adaptive formulation of deep unconscious experience and of every unconsciously validated trigger-decoded interpretation and frame management effort.

The search for triggers

It seems evident that sound formulations of patients' material begin with the identification of the most powerful triggers or meanings of triggering events that are active in a given therapy session. As noted, these triggers are usually the interventions of therapists, or, more rarely, extremely traumatic outside events that have evoked the adaptive activities of patients' emotion-processing minds and their deep unconscious systems in particular. While the existence and some meanings of a given trigger may be perceived and registered consciously, the most critical triggers and/or meanings are perceived unconsciously and processed by the deep unconscious system. It's these experiences that are the unconscious roots of both symptoms and resistances, and they often take the form of an intervention that seems innocuous consciously, yet has a profound deep unconscious impact on the patient – and therapist as well.

Consciously registered triggers and meanings of triggers evoke conscious adaptive responses. They may involve the interventions of therapists, but, most often, they pertain to all manner of events outside of the therapy, and as such they are relatively unempowered *vis-à-vis* a patient's symptoms and/or resistances. It is important to appreciate that, as a rule, the most anxiety-provoking meanings of consciously registered triggers tend to be perceived and processed at the deep unconscious level.

When triggers are alluded to manifestly, it is incumbent on a therapist to attend to the patient's themes for relevant unconscious perceptions and their ramifications. But it's also important to search for other active triggers because there is often an additional repressed or denied trigger that may be of greater importance to the patient emotionally. These triggers usually obtain encoded representation and are therefore more difficult to identify than those that are directly mentioned. The search for unmentioned triggers usually begins with a therapist's review of his or her conscious knowledge of existing, active triggers – the therapist's trigger list. It also entails listening to the themes in the patient's material for clues to possible unidentified triggers – themes always reflect the triggers that have evoked them. In this context, it's well to note that a session in which a patient is dealing with but one trigger is extremely rare, although there are many sessions in which a single trigger is by far the most powerful environmental stimulus at the moment – the key is in correctly identifying which one, among several active triggers, it is.

In principle, then, therapists should be ever-mindful of the need to search for triggers that patients do not allude to directly – they may be of great importance. This is often the case when a patient has been subjected to a highly traumatic intervention by the therapist – often in the form of a frame modification. The very fact that the therapist has intervened in a harmful manner makes it especially difficult for the patient to allude to the trigger directly, and even in encoded fashion, much as it makes it difficult for the therapist to recognize communicated encoded clues to its existence. Both patient and therapist tend to repress and/or deny the experience of destructive interventions by therapists.

There are several safeguards against this type of blocking by a therapist. First, there's the examination of the patient's material for signs of non-validation after an intervention has been made – unconfirmed triggers are likely to be both harmful and repressed by both parties to the therapy. Second, there's the therapist's self-examination of his or her interventions for signs of error and harm caused, while a third safeguard involves maintaining an up-to-date trigger list of one's active interventions and extended silences. A fourth protector entails a monitoring of the negative themes in patients' narratives – they usually imply that the therapist has intervened in error and caused harm to the patient. Such themes call for a reexamination of the therapist's trigger list, and if the negative themes cannot be accounted for through known interventions, the search for a missed errant intervention should be undertaken. Lastly, the therapist should monitor the themes in the patient's material for bridging imagery – themes that could represent a missing trigger. For example, themes of being robbed suggest a fee-related overcharge, while those of exposure and nudity suggest a modification of the privacy and confidentiality of the frame. Themes are invaluable clues to missing triggers.

There are several variations on who is and is not aware of a powerful triggering event at any given moment in a session – the patient
and/or therapist. For one, there are many situations in which both
parties to therapy are so informed. This usually means that the patient
has manifestly alluded to the trigger, the therapist has noticed the allusion, and now waits for a cluster of powerful encoded themes in order
to intervene. But there are also sessions in which the patient is aware
of a trigger that the therapist has missed when the patient mentioned
it. These situations are reminders that therapists need to be open to
hearing and consciously registering patients' passing allusions to triggers and to be cognizant of times when they themselves have been
traumatized and are likely to intensify their use of denial and miss
patients' references to powerful triggering interventions.

Actually, matters are even more complicated when the therapist is
aware of a trigger that the patient is consciously unaware of and has
not mentioned. In these situations, the patient's communicative resistances are strong and the trigger is in all likelihood quite powerful and
traumatic. The therapist is obligated to work only with what the
patient communicates and therefore should not unilaterally introduce
the trigger. Instead, he or she is restricted to doing a playback of the
relevant encoded themes as they become available for intervening,
doing so in the hope of eliciting from the patient a direct allusion to
the missing trigger – after which a full interpretation can be offered.
This arises most often when there are signs of illness and other severe
impairments in the therapist.

Finally, in situations in which neither the patient nor the therapist is
consciously aware of an important trigger, the only hope for recovering
it lies with the therapist's monitoring the themes in the patient's
material for images that suggest unnoticed triggering interventions.
This search is very much called for in the presence of unexplained
gross behavioural and/or communicative resistances, as the trigger
that evokes these obstacles to therapeutic progress is usually a highly
traumatic intervention by the therapist – here, too, signs of serious
physical illness in the therapist often serve as the evocative trigger.

All in all, then, the search for missing triggers is an ever-present
challenge for the psychotherapist. They may be identified directly by a
therapist who carefully monitors his or her interventions and keeps
track of those that seem especially powerful. And they can also be discovered by monitoring patients' narrative themes for clues to triggers
of which the therapist him or herself is unaware. Themes cannot be
interpreted and proper rectifications of the frame cannot be carried

out without knowing the accountable triggers. The ability of therapists to forgo their denial of errant and hurtful triggering interventions is vital to the avoidance of misalliances with their patients in which powerful, traumatic interventions are obliterated by both parties to therapy – and, as a result, never identified, processed, interpreted and worked through. This kind of shared blind-spot is an ever-present danger, often the source of many unexplained symptoms and resistances in patients and symptoms and counter-resistances in their therapists.

The conscious recognition of active triggers

As noted, therapists should consciously be in touch with and monitor their most recent interventions, and when power themes appear in patients' material they should be prepared to organize and identify their most likely encoded meanings in light of these triggering stimuli. Strongly evocative triggers must be distinguished from those that are relatively inconsequential, and consciously registered triggers and meanings of triggers need to be differentiated from those that are registered deep-unconsciously. Because of the pervasive use of denial by the conscious mind, the two classes of events and meanings – that is, those that are registered consciously as compared to those that are registered deep-unconsciously – are not at all alike, and the processing activities of the conscious and deep unconscious systems deal with two very different constellations of meanings and handle them very differently. The distinction between manifest and encoded contents is crucial here.

A great challenge for the therapist, then, is to be aware of the significant, active, traumatic triggering interventions, or rare outside catastrophes, that a patient has not alluded to manifestly and that the therapist's own conscious mind may be inclined to ignore as well. To carry out this task effectively, therapists must overcome their own denial-based defences so they can be fully cognizant of their interventions and their most telling implications. It's especially important, as I've been stressing, to develop the capability of detecting erroneous interventions and other possible ways that a therapist has traumatized a patient – for example, through a sudden lapse in anonymity or by appearing to be ill or injured. Keeping track of frame-related interventions is especially helpful in these efforts.

Identifying triggers by monitoring narrative themes

In addition to conscious monitoring, the second way of identifying missing triggers is carried out by listening to the themes in the patient's narrative material and keeping an ear open for themes that might well bridge over and point to an overlooked triggering intervention. This effort is carried out by keeping in mind the four main areas of intervening that might be especially traumatic for a patient:

- first, the mismanagement or violations of the ground rules of the therapy which are inherently harmful;
- second, the validated securing of the therapy frame which evokes secured-frame anxieties;
- third, erroneous verbal interventions which are also intrinsically harmful; and
- fourth, the validated interpretation of disturbing deep unconscious meanings and their connections to past traumas as stirred up by adaptation-evoking triggers – interventions that stir up a dread of deep unconscious meanings.

As we can see, both validated and non-validated therapeutic efforts may evoke anxieties and resistances in patients. It is helpful, then, in searching for overlooked triggers to appreciate the kinds of situations in which these disturbing triggers are likely to be missed. The therapist's unconsciously validated explorations of a patient's activated, anxiety-provoking, repressed or denied, death-related events and their meanings is both vital to the healing process and is one source of considerable anxiety for the patient. This issue is strongest when the ground rules of treatment have been secured or stabilized so that distracting frame violations no longer occupy the patient's deep unconscious mind. The patient's deep unconscious experience of this type of therapeutic work is fraught with emotional dangers. With patients who have acted in a predatory fashion against others, a therapist's pursuit of these efforts tends to be experienced unconsciously as tantamount to trying to murder the patient. This is not a distortion or transference manifestation, but a true reflection of the patient's fear of suicidal fantasies and impulses when his or her deep unconscious guilt is activated in the treatment situation. Interpretation of the patient's trigger-evoked themes must be shaped in a way that takes this factor into account.

Predatory, death-related early traumas may also create similar fears of the therapeutic work and therapist. This arises, for example, in instances when there's an activation of conscious and unconscious memories of violent acts by a parent towards the patient when he or she was an infant or child – for example, attempts at abortion, acts that have severely harmed the child, being born with a congenital defect, and so on. The dread here is of the reexperience of the danger situation along with the related predatory death anxieties and of murderous rage against the parent or other person involved in the damaging incident. It's well to appreciate, then, that the therapeutic pursuit of repressed or denied traumatic, death-related memories is experienced by patients as persecutory despite its ultimate critical healing qualities – it's not a readily welcome curative effort. Work of this kind may be quite difficult for both the therapist and patient, who often tends to become resistant and, at times, psychologically assaultive towards the therapist even though – or because – the patient unconsciously validates the therapist's interpretations and reconstructions. This anxiety-driven opposition occurs despite the therapeutic benefits accrued by the patient.

Technically, therapists should not attempt to force interventions on their patients by introducing ideas that extend beyond the trigger-decoded meanings of the encoded narratives available in a given session. Interventions that are consciously refuted by, or confusing to, a patient should not be repeated by the therapist – instead, he or she should sit back and await further encoded material from the patient to see where the problem lies. There's no need to hurry this kind of work, especially when the therapist is intervening in an appropriate and unconsciously validated manner, and neither frame violations nor interventional errors are involved. Both tact and caution are called for – neither backing away from the available encoded material nor pressing one's interpretations beyond the patient's tolerance. The anxiety-provoking insights so derived are vital to a restructuring of the patient's adaptive resources, but they come at the cost of considerable guilt and anxiety as well.

Along different lines, the search for missing triggers requires that therapists strive to become aware of every nuance of their management and impingements on the ground rules of treatment – be they frame-securing or frame-modifying. Because frame violations are harmful to patients and often register deep-unconsciously rather than consciously in their minds – and in the minds of the therapists so involved as well – there's a need to continually monitor patients' narrative themes for frame-related imagery. Each ground rule is mirrored by a particular set of themes and emergence of these themes in a patient's material – and they fall into a small and manageable number of areas – calls for a careful search for a missed trigger in respect to the ground rule to which the themes point. The following list of ground rules and related themes can serve as a general guideline to the kinds of themes that should alert a therapist to the presence of a missing frame-related trigger:

1   The single, set fee – themes of money, greed (a fee increase), stealing (an overcharge), charitable donations (an undercharge), salary decreases and harmful overindulgences (a reduction in the fee), and earning one's due through benign trickery (increasing a low fee to a reasonable one – that is, breaking the frame to secure it).

2   The locale, which should be a professional setting – themes of exposure and bizarre or dangerous places and structures (for home-office arrangements), or those of new, safe places (for a shift from a home-office to a professional setting).

3   Confinement of contact between the patient and therapist to the time and place of the sessions – themes of seduction, loss of boundaries, being followed or pursued (inadvertent meetings outside of the therapist's office), and themes of rape and exploitation (arranged meetings outside of the therapist's office).

4   A single, set time, length, and frequency of sessions – themes of harmful overindulgence, chemical addiction, seduction (for a change in the time of a session), and themes of safety and trust, keeping appointments, and so on (holding the frame in these areas).

5   Full responsibility for the therapist to be present for all scheduled sessions – themes of loss, death, illness, disappearance, abandonment or irresponsibility (the therapist misses or unexpectedly cancels a scheduled session).

6   Total privacy, with no access to the sessions by third parties in any form – themes of intruders, invaders, spies, third parties to various situations, exposure or exhibitionism (the therapist speaks with a patient's relative or friend, or completes an insurance form), or themes of safety and ensuring the safety of someone's secrets (the therapist does not speak to a third party who tries to contact him or her or does not complete a presented insurance form).

7   Total confidentiality, with no note-taking by the therapist and no release of information in any form – themes of leakage, exposure of secrets, and themes similar to those that emerge when the therapist violates the rule of total privacy (for violations of this ground rule), and themes of keeping matters private and safeguarding secrets (for keeping to this ground rule).

8   The relative anonymity of the therapist, with no deliberate self-revelations, advice, opinions, directives and extraneous comments –

themes of nudity, exposure, exploitation, controlling others, manipulation or infantalization (when a therapist reveals personal information or tells a patient what he or she should or should not do), themes of illness and death (when a healer therapist appears to be ill or injured), and themes of modesty and allowing others their autonomy (when the therapist adheres to these tenets).

9   The absence of physical contact between the two parties – themes of physical harm and sexual contact (inadvertent brushes between patient and therapist) and of rape and violence (deliberate physical contact between patient and therapist).

In addition to these particular bridging themes, which point to a particular frame-violating trigger, all frame-violating acts by therapists evoke predatory themes of harm and seduction. As for frame-securing interventions, they tend to generate a mixture of themes – those of safety and trust, along with themes of entrapment and annihilation related to the existential death anxieties activated by secured frames.

Other helpful clues to triggers

Another helpful tool for identifying triggering events is the various ways that they can be classified. First, there's the important issue of the level of awareness at which a trigger has been perceived and registered by the patient – consciously or unconsciously. There may be full conscious registration of the major meanings of an interventional triggering event, but, more typically, the overall traumatic triggering event registers in awareness, as do some of its lesser meanings, while its most disturbing meanings register at the deep unconscious level. Another scenario entails the unconscious perception and deep unconscious processing of the entire traumatic incident and its meanings – an instance of extreme perceptual denial. This type of response is much more common than generally realized because, as humans, we have no way of knowing that we've completely obliterated a strongly traumatic triggering event – as a rule, these situations can be recognized only if the denied incident is identified by an outside party such as an adaptive-sensitive psychotherapist.

In psychotherapy, then, the therapist may be aware of a traumatic intervention or outside event that the patient is processing deep-unconsciously, of which the patient has absolutely no conscious awareness. In this regard there are two possibilities: first, that the trigger was consciously experienced by the patient and has been repressed, or, second, that the trigger was subjected to perceptual denial and registered deep-unconsciously. In the first instance, the trigger can eventually be recovered, mostly with the help of the therapist's playback of encoded bridging themes. But in the second instance the trigger is unrecoverable – patients cannot become aware of a memory of an event that has registered deep-unconsciously because memory traces that eventually can be brought into awareness require conscious registration at the time of the incident. Since, technically, the therapist should not override the patient's denial and introduce the trigger to the patient, therapeutic work with this kind of triggering event is carried out solely on the encoded level of the patient's communications. Indeed, should a therapist inadvertently mention the trigger to the patient, he or she will have no idea what the therapist is talking about.

Another helpful insight stems from the finding that the conscious mind works over consciously-registered triggering events and meanings, while the deep unconscious mind works over unconsciously-registered events and meanings. As a result, there are many situations in which the conscious system is processing and adapting to one set of trigger events and meanings (those that have been perceived at the conscious level and are weak emotionally), while the deep unconscious system is working over a very different set of triggers (those that have been perceived at the deep unconscious level and are powerful emotionally). Recognition of the triggers that the patient has alluded to consciously should not lull the therapist into turning away from the task of identifying all of the active triggers and meanings that the patient has perceived and processed deep-unconsciously.

Another classification of triggers to keep in mind is their source – that is, either within or outside of the therapy. In keeping with the tendency of the conscious system to scan all manner of triggering events, patients' consciously perceived triggers usually pertain to events outside of therapy, although at times they may concern the interventions of their therapists. In general, however, short of a dramatic intervention by a therapist, for patients in treatment the conscious mind is focused on triggers outside of therapy and, in addition, almost all triggering events outside of the therapy situation are worked over and adapted to by the conscious mind with little or no deep unconscious activity. The exceptions to this rule are, as noted, extremely traumatic triggering events that involve personal and public disasters.

In contrast, it bears repeating that patients' deep unconscious minds are focused almost entirely on their therapists' interventions. These triggering events may register consciously, while their more disturb-ing meanings register deep-unconsciously, or they may register deep-unconsciously in their entirety. The therapist works with them accordingly, making certain to interpret the most powerful themes and the aspects of the patients' emotional problems and genetic history that they touch on. Therapeutic work with unconsciously registered triggers is extremely difficult largely because, first, the patient or client is unaware of the trigger, and, second, the trigger itself is severely anxiety-provoking – which is why it was not allowed to register in awareness in the first place. Examples of this kind of trig-ger include inadvertent indications that the therapist is physically ill or injured, but it may also involve disturbing personal information about the therapist that a patient obtains either directly from the therapist or from third parties who know the therapist personally – especially non-professional information that involves illness in the therapist or a family member, the death of someone close to the ther-apist, and references to other kinds of personal life crises.

Still another way of classifying triggers involves the aspects of emotional life that they touch on. As I have indicated, the deep uncon-scious system is a highly focused system that is sensitive to only a small number of classes of intervention and events. Keeping these areas of experience in mind helps therapists scan patients' material for missing triggers that are being processed by the deep system. As you may recall, the most important group of triggers touch on transactions that involve the rules, frames and boundaries of the therapy situation. The other aspects of interventions made by therapists that are monitored by and responded to by the deep unconscious system are the therapist's level of listening, formulating and intervening – be it manifest contents and conscious material, or encoded and deep unconscious – and the valid-ity of the therapist's interventions. Essentially, the deep unconscious mind validates sound therapeutic work with encoded meanings, but does not affirm work with manifest contents and their implications. Therapists can therefore use the encoded narrative communications from the deep unconscious system as a reliable guide to sound and effective, deeply insightful psychotherapy.

The pool of encoded or derivative themes

The narrative thematic material from a patient in a given session collates into what has been variously called a *pool of encoded themes*, a *narrative pool* or a *derivative complex* – derivatives are disguised themes that are 'derived from' a meaning of a triggering event. There are several useful principles that apply to listening to and formulating the unconscious meanings of this kind of narrative material. For one, themes that are expressed in intellectualized material are either weak or not pertinent to the most compelling, deep-unconsciously active triggers at any given moment in a session. In contrast, themes that are expressed in a dream or story that the patient creates or recounts generally encode unconscious perceptions of important meanings and implications of active, traumatic triggering events.

Another useful concept pertains to the distinction between power-ful and weak thematic material. Power themes are reflections of intensely anxiety-provoking unconscious perceptions that are the substance of deep unconscious experience and processes. Such themes include allusions to death, injury, illness, harm, violence, natural disas-ters and so on, and they should alert the therapist to the existence of a major triggering event. In the absence of power themes, the deep unconscious mind is not being represented. A strong, meaningful and workable derivative (that is, encoded/disguised) network must include at least several power themes; indeed no pool of themes is complete without frame-related and power themes. Nevertheless, there's a strong human tendency to consciously avoid power imagery and dwell on less-empowered emotion-related themes. Sexuality or concerns with self-esteem and relating are substituted for death-related issues. Patients tend to emphasize and self-interpret these relatively weak themes and issues, and therapists need to struggle against their inclinations to follow suit.

In formulating the meanings and implications of active triggers that link to a pool of themes, it's important that the therapist recognize all of the power themes and account for and use them in his or her interpretation or frame-securing efforts. If this appears to be unfeas-ible, it's well for the therapist to consider the likelihood that he or she has overlooked a critical trigger, one that would better account for the unexplained powerful imagery – a fresh trigger search should follow (see above). A useful clue in this regard is the finding that power themes always touch on one of the three forms of death anxiety, so a therapist is well-advised to first search for a trigger capable of arous-ing these concerns.

Therapists should listen to the themes in patients' narrative mater-ial with one basic question in mind: 'What intervention have I made that this theme encodes a valid unconscious perception of me in light of what I've said or done?' A patient's conscious view of a therapist and his or her interventions is unreliable, and generally defensive and deceptive, but deep unconscious views are extremely dependable and well worth listening to. This is because narrative themes encode selected, valid unconscious perceptions of a therapist in light of his or her interventions – frame-related and otherwise. Encoded themes are a rich source of deep unconscious, adaptive wisdom and a very reliable guide on how to do effective insight psychotherapy.

In addition to power themes, the pool of themes should, as a rule, also have *bridging themes* – themes that encode the identity of the triggering event and therefore facilitate moving the disguised themes within the narrative into alignment with the triggering event. For example, the trigger of a fee increase evokes a story about getting a dishonest kick-back from a customer – the theme of getting money in a dishonest, frame-violating manner is the bridging theme (the fee should be set at the outset of a therapy and remain as agreed-upon). Or, a trigger of filling out an insurance form with information about a patient evokes a story of a spy giving the enemy secret information; the inappropriate, frame-violating revelation of what should be kept secret bridges from the story to the trigger. Themes of this kind tend to be frame-related and they provide convincing evidence that the encoded imagery is indeed connected with the evocative trigger. Such themes are called *close derivatives* because their degree of disguise allows for ready decoding. They stand in contrast with *distant derivatives* which are far more difficult to unravel.

The build-up of a strong and usable pool of derivative themes is a vital feature of every meaningful session, and there are several types of interventions that help patients to generate this kind of thematic material. First, there's the *basic rule of guided associations* alluded to earlier – the adaptive precept that advises the patient to begin each session with a dream or a spontaneously made-up story and to then associate fresh stories to the elements of this initial narrative – the so-called *origination narrative* (Langs, 1993, 1999a). This precept is usually introduced in the first session because patients need to be informed that certain types of material facilitate the therapeutic process by helping them to gain access to their deep unconscious experiences and adaptive solutions. Left to their own devices, the conscious minds of patients, with their strong inclination for denial and defence, will avoid generating narrative material, especially stories replete with power themes. The directive to generate as much narrative material as possible is offered to counter this in-built, natural tendency. Thus, while dreams serve well in and of themselves as a conveyor of thematic imagery, they serve even better as the source of fresh associated stories, many of them pertaining to events in the life of the patient. As a rule, these associated narratives tend to have more powerful themes than those found in the dream itself.

Other useful interventions that favour patients' generation of narrative imagery include the therapist's use of silence when a patient is building a strong pool of themes, and when the patient is intellectualizing or generating weak themes. Another helpful intervention involves gently confronting the patient with the absence of narrative material when such is the case. Finally, the offer of validated trigger-decoded interpretations implicitly encourages the patient to communicate further meaningful encoded, powerful narrative imagery.

Factors in overlooking important triggers and themes

As humans, we are naturally-born encoders, but just as naturally we are also poor decoders who are inherently disinclined to learn about and engage in trigger decoding. This avoidance arises because we tend to encode perceptions that are emotionally painful and intolerable to awareness – and by evolved design the emotion-processing mind is configured to keep it that way. This means that trigger decoding, which requires the identification of an unconsciously perceived trigger, is a process whose use goes against human nature – even when it applies to decoding the imagery of someone other than ourselves.

The difficulties in bringing ourselves as therapists to engage in trigger decoding stem from a number of additional, specific sources. The first is the evident fact that, as therapists, we are restricted to using our conscious minds in our work with patients. The cognitive design of the conscious system, the weak triggers and meanings to which it is drawn, its overuse of denial, the relatively simple emotional issues with which it's concerned, and its view of the world is far different from the more effective design and powerful concerns of the deep unconscious mind. But in addition to the natural weakness of conscious cognitive processing in the emotional realm, for the conscious mind the world of deep unconscious experience is unfamiliar, alien, puzzling and dangerous, thereby making it inherently difficult for therapists to tune in to patients' deep unconscious communications and experiences.

Along different but related lines, the contents and meanings of unconscious perceptions are quite disturbing for therapists to decode and bring into awareness for both their patients and themselves.

These images tend to be focused on therapists' errant and harmful interventions, qualities of their work that therapists are often unaware of and are disinclined to search for – or to recognize in patients' encoded material. There's a dread in therapists of experiencing conscious guilt, although deep unconscious guilt and predator death anxiety cannot be avoided through these defensive efforts.

Another deterrent to engaging in trigger decoding stems from the finding that the deep unconscious system copes with and processes perceptions that are always linked to death and death anxieties – areas of concern that therapists strive to avoid for reasons of personal anxiety. There is also the disquieting realization that the consistency with which patients react deep-unconsciously to their therapists' interventions speaks for the enormous influence that they have on the emotional lives and treatment experiences of their patients – this too mitigates against engaging in trigger decoding. And given the extent to which humans experience similar traumas and share common anxieties and conflicts, especially those that are death-related, triggers that evoke undue personal anxieties in patients often have similar effects on their therapists. As a result, therapists unconsciously activate their own conscious-system denial mechanisms to defensively protect themselves from being overwhelmed by these concerns, and avoiding efforts at trigger decoding serves this purpose quite well. Finally, triggers and themes that point to the need for therapists to intervene by securing the therapeutic frame tend to activate their existential death anxieties and prompts them to avoid recognizing the triggers and encoded models of rectification to be found in their patients' disguised narrative material.

This outline of factors mitigating against the adaptive approach to psychotherapy, and to the recognition of active triggers and of encoded, unconscious responses to these triggers, helps us to appreciate why so few therapists engage in this process and why those who do find it so arduous. It asks a lot of therapists to work this way, but, as I have been emphasizing, doing so gives back far more to themselves and their patients than is possible through any other means. In their dread of death and the experience of death anxieties, of unconscious meaning and secured frames, therapists fail to appreciate the enormous amount of healing and personal creativity that comes from dealing with and mastering these most disturbing and ever-present concerns.

10

Three Classes of Intervention

The strong adaptive approach has found that only those interventions that obtain encoded, unconscious validation are truly and deeply healing. In testing out all manner of interventions, it has also found that there are very few types of intervention, correctly applied, that meet this criterion. In turning to therapists' interventions, I shall, then, confine myself to those that meet this stringent but clinically supported criterion. And as for the definition of the term *intervention*, I shall use it to refer to everything that a therapist says and does that is at all connected with a given patient's psychotherapy. This includes everything that touches on the means by which a therapist has arranged to and actually obtains referrals; all of the therapist's direct transactions between him or herself and the patient, in both words and deeds, including extended silences and contacts within and outside of the therapist's office; and any contact or absence of contact after the treatment has been completed.

Types of intervention

The following are the main classes of interventions that have been found to consistently obtain encoded validation:

1 Appropriate silences in the absence of interpretable material.
2 Managing the setting, rules, frames and boundaries of the treatment situation towards their securement.
3 Verbal comments:

(a)   the playback of selected derivatives – that is, encoded themes – organized around an encoded representation of an active triggering event – usually in the form of a prior intervention by the therapist;

(b)   trigger-decoded interpretations and, more rarely, reconstructions;

(c)   interventions like questions and confrontations solely designed to increase the extent to which a patient communicates encoded narrative imagery.

4   Behaving in a manner that respects the patient's human and therapeutic rights, physical and interpersonal boundaries, and needs for a secured set of ground rules of treatment.

In contrast to these unconsciously validated efforts, there are many classes of interventions made by therapists that consistently fail to obtain encoded validation; they include:

1   Managements of the setting and ground rules of therapy that do not comply with the patient's unconsciously sought and validated ideal, secured framework for treatment, and

(a)   additional frame-deviant behaviours such as touching the patient or filling out an insurance form, or answering the telephone during a patient's session.

2   Comments that are not based on or intended to facilitate encoded communication and trigger decoding:

(a)   so-called interpretations that are not based on trigger decoding;

(b)   questions, clarifications confrontations, and reconstructions that are not in the service of increasing or clarifying encoded expressions from the patient;

(c)   all directives, personal opinions, self-revelations and so on;

(d)   interventions that include material from sessions other than the one at hand.

From the vantage-point of a therapist accustomed to working on the manifest level of listening and formulating, the restrictiveness of the list of viable interventions may seem limiting and rigid. Nevertheless, these are clinically tested precepts and they hold true – nature is nature, and what heals is what heals. This handful of interventions are the only efforts by therapists that the extremely wise deep unconscious system of the emotion-processing mind affirms and finds insightful and deeply curative. None of the other types of interventions are afforded such support and many are unconsciously deemed to be overly-defensive and even harmful to the patient. Adherence to the ideal ground rules of therapy and making exclusive use of other interventions that are likely to obtain encoded validation are safeguards that protect the patient from harm – and the therapist as well.

Modes of healing

Sound, unconsciously validated interventions are healing in three interrelated ways. First, through the offer of trigger-decoded interpretations that provide the patient with profound insights into the deep unconscious and historical basis of their emotional issues and their influence on their resistances, behaviours, life decisions, modes of relating and symptoms. Second, through the establishment and maintenance, to the greatest extent feasible, of the ideal unconsciously sought setting and ground rules of the psychotherapy – an offer of inherent support, emotional holding and frame-related healing. And, third, through unconscious, positive, healing identifications with a therapist who is capable of securing the ground rules of treatment and making unconsciously validated interventions. With this in mind, let's take a closer look at three types of interventions that, properly formulated and timed, regularly obtain encoded validation.

Therapists' silences

Therapists' extended silences – silent listening and formulating – are one of a therapist's most basic interventions. They are fraught with meanings and effects on the patient, effects whose nature depends on the status of the patient's material *vis-à-vis* the therapist's failure to intervene actively. On the one hand, a therapist's silence may reflect a failure to understand a patient's material – an erroneous use of silence – or, on the other, may be a response to the patient's not having communicated material that can sponsor an intervention – a valid use of silence. As is the case with a therapist's active interventions, silences are the therapist's adaptive or maladaptive responses to patients' material and they are, in turn, adaptation-evoking triggering events for the patient as well. Consciously, and especially deep-unconsciously, their use and misuse influence what a patient does and does not communicate.

When properly used and unconsciously validated, a therapist's silence implies that an active intervention is not called for because the patient has not fulfilled the recipe for intervening – that is, has not represented the most compelling trigger manifestly or in encoded form, and/or has not generated a pool of encoded themes with power and bridging imagery that is relevant to a trigger at issue at the moment. Indeed, a therapist should remain silent until the patient has fulfilled this recipe – at which point an active intervention is called for.

In principle, whenever a therapist has been silent for an extended period of time, he or she should study the patient's encoded, narrative material for his or her deep unconscious perceptions of the essential qualities of the silence. Is the silence being unconsciously validated through positive imagery, or is it being refuted through themes of blindness, error, missing the point, and so on? This question touches on the need to differentiate two basic forms of silence: *appropriate silence*, which is validated deep-unconsciously, and *inappropriate silence*, which is not. The latter silence actually is an erroneous intervention because the material from the patient evidently is sufficient for an interpretive and/or frame-securing intervention by the therapist – and the patient's deep unconscious system knows that this is the case, while the therapist's conscious system does not. The emergence of negatively toned themes during a therapist's extended silence should therefore alert him or her to the need to reassess the patient's material in order to discover the unrecognized ingredients that make intervening actively possible. Such a search usually begins with a review of currently active triggers and then turns to a reassessment of the decoded meanings of the narrative themes. If the reevaluation indicates that there is, indeed, sufficient material for intervening, the therapist should do so as soon as possible.

In a sense, then, a therapist's valid silence serves as a trigger that indicates to the patient that he or she needs to generate additional meaningful material before an intervention can be made – ingredients are missing from the recipe for intervening on the deep unconscious level. It also indicates that the therapist is not going to intervene on a superficial level with relatively weak or intellectualized material.

On the therapist's side, valid silences are effective efforts to adapt to the incomplete material from a patient, and, in general, to the role of and tasks inherent to being a healer. Given the general need among therapists to be active and to offer something palpable to their patients, sustaining appropriate periods of silence tends to be a difficult task. Nevertheless, the patient should be granted the basic right and prerogative to unconsciously orchestrate the course of each session by unconsciously indicating when he or she does or does not need, or is able or unable to tolerate, a trigger-decoded interpretation or frame-securing intervention. Therapists should follow their patients' implicit directives in this regard. They should also keep in mind that valid silences are deeply effective healing interventions, and that speaking up when silence is called for is harmful to the patient.

Managing the ground rules of therapy

In Chapter 6, I explored in some detail the nature and management of the setting, rules, frames and boundaries of psychotherapy. This relatively unappreciated dimension of treatment brings up some very crucial aspects of intervening. Indeed, managing the ground rules and frame-related interventions take precedence over interpretations of meaning, and they tend to be the grounding for effective interpretive efforts – recall the extreme sensitivity of the deep unconscious system to frame conditions. Thus, regardless of whether or not a ground rule can be secured or otherwise managed, most trigger-decoded interpretations will, of necessity, centre around the patient's deep unconscious responses to the prevailing frame conditions of a therapy and to the prior frame-related interventions of the therapist. For a therapist new to this approach, it is quite surprising to discover the extent to which these issues and their interpretation and management illuminate a patient's symptoms and resistances, and bridge over to the emotional concerns in his or her everyday life.

As I have been emphasizing, the management of the frame should be directed at all times towards maintaining or securing, to the greatest extent possible, the ideal and deep-unconsciously sought ground rules. With the exception of the first session, in which the therapist must unilaterally establish the most ideal conditions for treatment possible for a particular patient, all efforts to manage the ground rules of treatment should be carried out at the behest of the directives that are encoded in the themes to be found in the patient's narrative material – their appearance is assured by the evolved design of the emotion-processing mind. In the presence of an activated ground rule issue, the therapist should engage in two activities: first, securing the frame at the behest of the patient's encoded imagery, and, second, interpreting the meanings of the patient's encoded themes in light of the therapist's prior and/or anticipated ground-rule interventions.

If a patient requests a frame modification, the initial themes are likely to convey the patient's unconscious perceptions of the therapist if he or she were to comply. If the therapist then agrees to modify the ground rule, additional themes related to the deviation will be forthcoming from the patient. If, on the other hand, the therapist intervenes to keep the frame secured, the subsequent themes from the patient will usually reflect the patient's sense of safety as well as his or her secured-frame existential death anxieties. In any case, secured frames or secured-frame moments are a necessary and vital feature of a sound, insightful and relatively complete therapy experience. They activate the patient's secured-frame existential death anxieties, and the patient's genetic history of death and loss, and enable the patient to work through this constellation of issues. In the absence of secured-frame interludes, the patient's secured-frame issues will not materialize because there's no secured-frame trigger to activate them. This is a reminder that patients' material in sessions depends greatly on the interventional triggers created by their therapists.

Therapeutic work in situations in which the basic ground rules are compromised from the outset – so-called *deviant-frame therapies*, as seen in clinic settings or with the use of insurance cover for treatment – tends to be focused on the patient's deep unconscious perceptions of the relevant frame modifications. It follows from this that the therapist's interpretations, which supply insights into the patient's deep unconscious experiences, will usually involve frame-deviant triggering events. The material will be concerned with the patient's trigger-evoked, predatory death anxieties because modified frames are experienced deep-unconsciously as psychologically damaging. Deviant frame forms of entrapment, such as being jailed illegally, will abound. This work should, if at all possible, be supplemented with frame-securing moments and their interpretation and working through.

Secured-frame therapies tend to be focused on the patient's secured-frame, existential death anxieties, and on the death-related traumas that he or she has suffered in the past. With the therapist safely holding the patient and not causing him or her physical or psychological damage, patients who have significantly harmed others will also experience predator death anxieties, deep unconscious guilt and needs for punishment. Because secured frames are safe, calming and growth-promoting, and also evocative of existential and predator death anxieties, they tend to be reacted to ambivalently by both patients and their therapists. In addition, when frames have been secured and stable for an extended period of time, the ground rules tend to recede into the background and the patient's genetic history of traumas and death-related incidents come to the fore. It's important to stress that the critical therapeutic work with these issues must continue to be conducted on the deep unconscious level and with triggers and encoded themes – exploring conscious feelings and issues is insufficient for a truly insightful cure.

In sum, therapists should be ever-mindful of the state of the framework of treatment in each session with each of their patients. They also need to maintain an ear for frame-related issues and themes. Unexpected frame-related themes should alert a therapist to the presence of an unrecognized ground-rule issue and prompt a search for the missing trigger. Managing and interpreting the meanings of ground-rule-related events in a given psychotherapy is a substantial part of the therapeutic process and essential to the healing that takes place on the deep unconscious level of experience and adaptation.

The playback of selected encoded themes

There are many clinical situations in which the patient's indicators – his or her symptoms and resistances – are strong, but there's no manifest allusion to the causative triggering event. Thus, there's a considerable therapeutic need in the patient for an intervention, but there's no manifest representation of the trigger – an essential ingredient in the recipe for intervening. In some of these sessions, the patient fails to generate a workable encoded representation of the activating trigger – a close derivative expression – and intervening is either impossible or extremely difficult. But in a majority of sessions in which the trigger is not alluded to directly, a viable encoded representation of the triggering intervention is communicated and a partial intervention is possible. What's needed from the patient for this effort is a strong and complex pool of encoded themes and a non-specific bridge to therapy – a passing allusion to the therapist or the therapy. This last element serves as a way of tying the disguised themes to the treatment situation and enables the therapist to intervene in that vein.

If all of these elements are available in the patient's material, an intervention called the *playback of selected encoded or derivative themes* is made. Its purpose is to offer a partial, trigger-decoded interpretation in the hope that the patient will then recover and allude to the repressed trigger so that a full and complete trigger-decoded interpretation can be made. Regardless of the outcome, these playbacks of themes allow therapists to do effective quasi-interpretive work on the encoded level. They also are a way of therapists letting their patients' deep unconscious minds know that they have heard and understood their messages and are aware of the triggers with which these encoded communications are concerned.

To cite a brief example, consider the sudden appearance of pallor on a female therapist's face, (unknown to the patient, she's had an episode of vaginal bleeding). In the course of the session, her male patient suddenly announces that he's thinking of terminating the treatment – a very strong gross behavioural resistance indicator. He makes no mention of the pallor, but tells a story about a friend who has cancer whom he can't bear to be with, as watching her die is so painful; she's been bleeding a lot lately and looks terribly pale and ashen.

In this situation, the patient's thought of terminating therapy – a strong resistance indicator – signals a great need for an interpretive intervention. The material strongly suggests that the unconscious perception of the therapist's pallor is evoking existential death anxieties in the patient, and that this is his unconscious motive for wanting to quit treatment. The therapist cannot bypass the patient's defensive denial or modify the frame by pointing out in self-revealing fashion that she herself is pale and/or reveal that she's been ill. Thus, she cannot offer a trigger-decoded interpretation of the unconscious source of the patient's resistance – a direct allusion to the trigger is needed for that type of intervention. Nevertheless, intervening is imperative.

Under these circumstances, a playback of selected, trigger-related encoded themes is the optimal intervention. The intervention should begin with the bridge to therapy, allude next to the best encoded representation of the trigger (the bridging image), then allude to the remaining themes, organizing them around the encoded triggering event. Thus, the therapist might have said the following to the patient:

'You've mentioned thoughts of leaving therapy [the general bridge to therapy], so treatment is on your mind. And in this connection, you're thinking about someone with pallor who looks pale and ashen [the best representation of the trigger] and who is seriously ill with cancer and bleeding [the additional encoded themes]. Something going on here must be prompting the appearance of these themes, something about me, and whatever it is, it must also be what's causing you to think about leaving therapy [using the themes to suggest the unconscious basis for the indicator].'

The ideal validating response would be the patient's sudden realization that the therapist looks pale, which would be a direct representation of the repressed or possibly denied trigger. In the latter case, it would require that the patient suddenly become aware of the trigger which happens to be visible at the moment – once its time has passed, there would be no undoing his use of perceptual denial. A full trigger-decoded interpretation could then be made. Short of that, validation could take the form of further encoded themes pertinent to the triggering event. For example, the patient might next recall that his mother died of a stomach cancer, thereby providing a previously unmentioned genetic link to the trigger – one that helps to explain the patient's need to repress or deny the observed pallor and his wish to flee the therapy in order to not experience a repetition of the traumatic loss of his mother.

Not infrequently, because the triggers that evoke this kind of response in patients are extremely traumatic and anxiety-provoking, the entire working through of the unbearable event – the intervention – will take place on the encoded level. There will be no direct mention of the trigger and not the least indication that the patient is or was aware of the stimulus that he or she is so intensely processing on the deep unconscious level. The failure of the patient to manifestly mention the active trigger is a communicative resistance and, as noted, it tends to occur when the triggering event is especially disturbing for the patient. At such moments, the trigger may be subjected to perceptual denial and not register consciously at all. Or it may register consciously and be immediately subjected to repression.

In the first case, where obliteration has occurred, the trigger is lost to potential awareness and will not be recoverable. Under these circumstances, the therapeutic work remains on the encoded level, even in the face of repetitive encoded representations of the trigger. In the second case, where there's been conscious registration but immediate repression, the trigger may eventually be rescued from repression and emerge in the patient's awareness. The playback of selected derivative themes is designed to facilitate this type of recovery of the repressed experience.

In principle, then, a playback of encoded themes should begin with the bridge to therapy. This alerts the patient to the idea that the intervention pertains to happenings and triggers within the treatment situation. An allusion to the best available encoded representation of the trigger should come next. This is done by reiterating the theme – simply repeating or playing it back to the patient – without decoding its underlying meanings. Finally, the remaining encoded themes are played back to the patient in a way that organizes the themes as conveying unconsciously perceived meanings of the unmentioned but encoded triggering event.

The intervention is offered as an encoded but compelling narrative statement. That is, it takes shape as a stimulus – response tale that is told using the encoded thematic idiom – essentially implying that the therapist did this or that and that the patient responded unconsciously with that or this unconscious perception. The tale is also constructed as a story of valid perceptions, rather than as a product of the patient's imagination or tendency to misperceive or distort. It's critical, too, for the therapist to respect the denial-based defences of the patient that have prompted him or her to deny or repress the existence of the trigger. These defences operate automatically to protect the patient from being overwhelmed by a traumatic triggering experience. The patient alone should be the one to decide, however unconsciously, when and if the anxiety-provoking trigger can enter his or her aware-ness if it is available to do so.

As is the case for all interventions, the themes used by the therapist in offering a playback of selected encoded themes must have been alluded to in the session at hand. There are two reasons for this rule: first, this material is all that the patient can deal with at the moment, and, second, it's been found clinically that when a therapist brings past material into an intervention, it almost always detracts from the inter-ventional effort and reflects a defensive or other kind of inappropriate, countertransference-based need in the healer.

A few additional points. The intervention should, if possible, include all of the communicated power themes and make use of other themes in the form and on the level that they have been generated by the patient. Playbacks should be used only when an active trigger related to the themes has not been manifestly alluded to. If the patient has mentioned the trigger, a full trigger-decoded interpretation is called for. In addition, once the intervention has been made, the responsive encoded thematic material must be assessed for validation – or its lack. The ideal validating response entails the patient's conscious recovery of the missing trigger so that he or she alludes to it manifestly. If this hap-pens, the therapist should then make a trigger-decoded interpretation.

Alternative kinds of encoded validation include allusions to wise and helpful figures (interpersonal validation) and/or fresh themes that move the patient closer to identifying the missing trigger and its more power-ful meanings (cognitive validation). In these cases, the therapeutic work is taking place on the deep unconscious level without conscious insight, but with deep unconscious understanding. This phenomenon is not uncommon in the presence of powerful interventional triggers and such work does have healing qualities. Indeed, in extremely traumatic situations this kind of encoded processing persists for as long as the trigger is being worked over – at times, for an entire therapy experience. This happens largely because the trigger was denied access to the conscious system and never registered in awareness. As noted, triggers that involve signs of illness in the therapist or the revelation by someone else of a death–related trauma in the life of the therapist are often dealt with by patients in this manner.

Finally, in the absence of the conscious recovery of the missing trigger or of encoded validation, the therapist should reassess his or her formulation of the patient's material. This effort should be focused on the search for another trigger that better organizes and gives clearer meaning to the encoded themes – a trigger that the therapist has overlooked, one that's likely to have evoked his or her unresolved death anxieties.

A clinical illustration

The following excerpt illustrates the application of the playback intervention:

Mrs James, a woman in her early forties, is in psychotherapy with Dr Keller, a psychiatrist, for episodes of depression. Three years into her therapy, the patient finds employment for the first time in many years. In her sessions, she begins to encode themes that reflect her deep unconscious view that Dr Keller's fee, which is 50 dollars per session, is extremely low, self-sacrificing and seductive. When the themes also point to the need to rectify the low fee, Dr Keller increases it to 75 dollars per session. Validating themes follow this intervention, as does a mixture of images that portray this intervention – modifying the frame to secure it – as both frame-modifying and frame-securing.

Mrs James begins the session after the fee increase with a dream in which she's walking arm in arm with both her father and her uncle Ted. They're going to buy a drill so her father can repair a broken railing for the stairs that lead to the basement of their home. Associating to the dream, Mrs James recalls that her father hated to spend money; he still has the first nickel he earned. He'd find ways to trick his employer into giving him a raise, things like falsifying his sales reports. He'd kill for a dollar. Her uncle Ted was the opposite. He knew how to handle money and was honest to a fault. He worked for the same company as her father and got raises when he deserved them, like when he did better than his quotas. Looking at her therapist, she then adds that Dr Keller reminds her of her uncle.

When Mrs James begins to ruminate, Dr Keller decides to intervene. He points out that the patient has referred to him, which seems to be her way of connecting the themes in her dream and associations to himself and to the therapy in some way. The images are about spending money, getting a pay raise under false pretences, being ready to kill for a dollar, but also getting more money because it's deserved. Mrs James laughs and says that this must be all about Dr Keller's fee increase. She then thinks about her father again. He did pay for her tuition for college. He was a thief, but he could do good things with money when he wanted to.

Breaking off the vignette at this point, we may note that the use of a playback of encoded themes was called for here because the patient had not alluded manifestly to the activating trigger – the fee increase. The therapist correctly respected the patient's denial and repressive defences and did not introduce the missing trigger on his own. Having obtained a strong encoded representation of the evidently repressed trigger and a workable pool of themes that addressed the fee increase as a frame-modifying way to secure the frame, he also correctly waited for a non-specific bridge to the therapy before intervening. In so doing, he made good use of the bridge to therapy and organized the themes around the best encoded representation of the fee increase trigger – namely, getting a pay increase. The therapist also made sure that he alluded to the only available power theme – the reference to the patient's father's readiness to kill for more money. Notice, too, that even though he told the story of his patient's adaptation to the triggering event using encoded themes, he did so with the idea that the themes reflected deep unconscious perceptions rather than unconscious fantasies.

The intervention brought into play themes that encoded both the positive and negative aspects of the fee increase – as is the case when the frame is modified to better secure it. The frame-deviant aspects of the fee increase are conveyed in the story of the father finding dishonest ways of getting money and in the violence behind his actions. No matter how justified and necessary a fee increase may be, the basic position of the deep unconscious system is that the agreed-upon fee should be sustained for an entire therapy experience – to which it adds necessary perspectives as well. It's for this reason that frame-violating themes of dishonesty appear under these circumstances. Nevertheless, the deep unconscious system also realizes that the low fee also has frame-modifying qualities in that it is not the therapist's usual fee and it therefore has a seductive aspect to it. For this reason, the fee increase is also at the deep unconscious level seen as well-deserved and frame-securing – aspects that are conveyed in the story of the uncle who deserved the raises he got.

In all, the intervention evoked a validating response from the patient in the form of a manifest reference to the unmentioned trigger. After the therapist had intervened, there was also a validating story about the patient's father that again speaks for the mixed picture of the fee change – helpful in one sense, selfish in another. Dr Keller could now wait for fresh encoded material – there's a need for more power themes – and be prepared to offer a subsequent trigger-decoded interpretation when further encoded images would permit.

*   *   *

The selected playback of encoded themes is an invaluable intervention because patients often obliterate or repress one or more important, active triggers. Quite often, the use of this intervention enables patients to modify their use of repression and to consciously refer to the unmentioned trigger. Nevertheless, it bears repeating that if the triggering event is especially disturbing and has been obliterated perceptually, the therapeutic work may be confined to encoded communications from the patient, and playback interventions by the therapist will prevail without the trigger ever finding manifest representation by the patient. While it is trying for a therapist to maintain restraint when he or she is aware of a traumatic trigger to which a patient is responding on the encoded level of communication, it's absolutely essential that the therapist not violate the patient's defences and become self-revealing. To do so is experienced as both frame-modifying – that is, a violation of the rule of relative anonymity – and as an unconscious assault on, and/or seduction of, the patient. Such an intervention would also shift the patient's deep unconscious focus away from the repressed or denied trigger to the therapist's self-revelation, and this would be a most unfortunate and harmful development. In contrast, the judicious use of playback interventions typically has unconscious healing effects, even in the absence of a patient's conscious recognition of the triggering event with which they are trying to cope unconsciously. Such are the ways of the emotion-processing mind.

11

Trigger–Decoded Interpretations

Trigger–decoded interpretations are the most comprehensive means by which a therapist can bring into the conscious awareness of a patient his or her contemporary, trigger–evoked, deep unconscious perceptions and adaptations as they relate to his or her symptoms and resistances. These interventions can also illuminate the unconscious connections between adaptive issues within the therapy with those in the outside life of the patient, including their links to early life experiences and traumas. Trigger–decoded interpretations are, then, the basic means by which the fullness of a patient's world of deep unconscious experience and his or her emotion–related maladaptations are illuminated through genuinely healing, deeply derived insights. And they are offered to patients when they fulfil the *recipe for intervening*: a manifest allusion to an active trigger, and a rich complex and powerful pool of derivative or encoded themes replete with a clear bridging image.

Patients are, at times, capable of consciously recognizing and alluding to an emotionally–charged trigger to which they are responding deep–unconsciously. They may also be able to generate dreams and other types of origination narratives, and guided associations to their elements, and to thereby create strong pools of themes that encode their deep unconscious reactions to a given triggering event. But, with remarkably few exceptions, they are not able to connect the triggers to their themes in a manner that reveals the nature of their deep unconscious experiences of these triggers. It appears, then, that patients are unable to overcome the natural resistances to trigger-decoding built into their emotion-processing minds. This task therefore falls to the psychotherapist.

The job of adaptive psychotherapists is, then, to offer their patients the trigger-decoded insights that they are unable to generate on their own. By evolved design, patients are disinclined to engage in trigger decoding and, when and if they do make the effort, they tend to do so crudely, very simply, badly or erroneously. Furthermore, their unconscious opposition to trigger decoding often quite unknowingly motivates a variety of gross behavioural resistances against, and conscious objections to, the trigger-decoded interpretations of their therapists and the therapies in which they are offered. While their deep unconscious minds and the encoded stories that they create will consistently validate correctly formulated trigger-decoded interpretations and frame rectifications, patients find a variety of ways to justify their many conscious objections to these very same efforts.

The most insidious of these objections take shape as a sudden, uninsightful abandonment of the therapy. Because their unconscious fear of deep unconscious meaning and secured frames is so intense, these patients find ways to avoid a termination session in which they might discover their deep unconscious reasons for wanting to end their treatment. Another difficult group of patients will repeatedly voice outright objections to the very interventions that they have unconsciously validated, a gross behavioural resistance that is, as a rule, motivated by severe forms of death anxiety – most often predator and existential in nature. Another inbuilt, natural type of resistance to the conscious integration of validated trigger-decoded interventions is reflected in the finding that even when a patient consciously affirms and absorbs a trigger-decoded interpretation, their understanding disappears very quickly from conscious thinking. The conscious mind does not sustain most trigger-decoded insights for very long – their half-lives can be measured in minutes and sometimes in seconds. Nevertheless, these validated interpretations do initiate a healing process – much of it operating unconsciously – that has strong constructive effects, including favourable adaptive and behavioural changes.

All in all, then, the same inbuilt resistances in patients that are directed against effective trigger decoding and adaptive forms of psychotherapy are the very reasons why patients need the services of adaptive psychotherapists in the first place. Paradoxes of this kind are commonplace when it comes to the emotion-processing mind and its two often diametrically opposed operating systems.

Some basic precepts

The decision to make a trigger-decoded interpretation is based on two considerations: first, the intensity of the patient's indicators, and, second, the extent to which the patient's material fulfils the recipe for intervening. Recall that indicators – resistances and emotionally-founded symptoms – are the manifest signs of therapeutic need in a patient. Here, too, the more pressing the indicators, the more compelling the need for the therapist to intervene. Thus, for example, a patient who is threatening suicide or who is thinking of abruptly quitting his or her therapy is expressing very strong indicators. Under these circumstances, the therapist should at some point in the session intervene as best he or she can – optimally, with a trigger-decoded interpretation. Serious indicators are driven by unconsciously perceived traumatic triggers, and the interpretation of a patient's unconscious perceptions of these triggers can provide much-needed deep insight into the deep unconscious motives behind a pressing symptom or resistance and resolve the problem insightfully.

To cite a brief example, a patient's suicidal feelings may be triggered by an unnecessary, frame-violating personal self-revelation by the therapist that is at the deep unconscious level perceived by the patient as seductive, abusive and damaging – and as cause for despairing thoughts of wanting to end his or her life. The interpretation of the patient's deep unconscious perceptions of the trigger and a pledge by the therapist to not violate the frame in the future is clearly the most salutary way of dealing with such a threat.

On the other hand, when the level of indicators is low, as seen when there are no notable resistances or acute symptoms, the need for intervention is small and the therapist should intervene only if the recipe for intervening has been fulfilled. This recipe, as spelled out for a trigger-decoded interpretation, begins by requiring a *manifestly represented triggering event*. That is, the patient must allude directly, even if in passing, to an active trigger, which is most likely to be a recent intervention by the therapist. For example, a patient notices that the therapist is wearing a bandage, and then drops the subject, or he mentions that the present session is a make-up session and goes on to talk about other matters. These are manifest allusions to active, frame-related triggers.

The second requisite for the recipe is a *rich pool of encoded themes*. Ideally, this includes a *bridging theme* that connects the storied images to the triggering event. Because frame-related triggers are the rule, bridging themes tend to involve *framework and ground rule images*, so it's important for the therapist to be on the alert for thematic elements of this kind in the narrative material; they serve as markers for the trigger at hand. Also needed is a rich variety of other themes, including *power themes* – allusions to death, illness, injury, harm, violence and so on. As a rule, sexual themes lack power and usually function as a way of denying harm and death, although they may allude unconsciously to a frame violation, as seen in stories of infidelity.

Technically, in offering a trigger-decoded interpretation, it's generally best to mention the trigger first. After all, the trigger is the event that has activated the operations of the deep unconscious system and it therefore organizes and gives meaning to the encoded thematic material – and its decoded interpretation. The reference to the trigger prepares the patient for the remainder of the therapist's intervention. It also enables the patient to readily appreciate the connection between the trigger and the themes – and thereby to understand his or her unconscious perceptions of the triggering event and its meanings.

After identifying the trigger, the themes are *organized into a narrative tale* that recounts the patient's unconscious perceptions of the triggering intervention and how he or she has unconsciously processed its implications. Thus, all trigger-decoded interpretations are delivered as stories of a patient's deep unconscious experience of, and adaptations to, a triggering event. Next, the insights that have been generated are used to explain the deep unconscious sources of the patient's indicators – his or her resistances and/or symptoms. The connection is made on the basis of the understanding that indicators are interactional products – an aspect of the patient's adaptive or maladaptive responses to their therapist's interventions. In addition, if present in the material, connection to events in the patient's outside life, recent and past, are also identified.

The model of an ideal trigger-decoded interpretation, which is always based on material from the immediate session, goes like this:

'I [the therapist] said or did such and such [the trigger aluded to by the patient], which you [the patient] unconsciously perceived in this and that manner [the patient's selected, but valid unconscious perceptions], and as a result, you responded by doing or feeling that and this [the patient's indicator response], all of which is connected to this or that past experience in your life.'

The stress is on the specific unconscious perceptions automatically selected by the patient for representation and response – images that are chosen by the patient from the universal and personal meanings and implications of the triggering event for him or her.

A clinical example

The following material will serve to illustrate the use of trigger-decoded interpretations:

Mr Forrest, a man in his early thirties, is in private psychotherapy for potency problems with Mr Parks, a social worker. About three months into the therapy, the therapist decides to place a framed picture of himself and his wife on his desk where it's visible to his patients. Mr Forrest begins the following session by ruminating and complaining about his continued difficulties sustaining his erections during attempts at intercourse with his wife. He looks at the picture of Mr Parks and his wife and says that his wife is almost as attractive as Mr Parks' wife, so there's no reason he should be having problems sustaining an erection.

His thoughts then turns to his friend, Sammy, who's sexually uninhibited. He's outrageous. He'll be talking to a woman at work and expose his penis to her. The other night, he did a really weird thing: he called the patient on the telephone and told him that he had the cure for his potency problem. He was in bed with his wife and invited the patient to come over and join them. Invitations like that are out of line, crazy. Sammy doesn't know a thing about decency and privacy. He needs to clean up his act. If he doesn't do it, Mr Forrest will stop being his friend.

At this point, Mr Parks intervenes. He points out that Mr Forrest has alluded to the picture of himself and his wife on his desk. He (the patient) then went on to talk about his friend, Sammy, who exposes himself sexually to others and who had invited the patient to join him and his wife in bed. He was a man without a sense of decency or privacy. These themes must reflect Mr Forrest's unconscious view of Mr Parks in light of his placing the picture on his desk. He (the patient) evidently sees this as a way of his (the therapist) exposing himself sexually to Mr Forrest and as a sexual invitation to join him and his wife in bed. Sammy is being used to convey his (the patient's) view of him (the therapist) as someone who doesn't know a thing about privacy and proper boundaries. And his remark that Sammy needs to clean up his act is also addressed to him (the therapist), as is the threat to stop seeing him if he doesn't do it. His (the patient's) point is well-taken. Mr Parks then takes the picture and places it in his desk drawer.

Mr Forrest pauses and then says that for some reason he's thinking about another friend of his who is also named Sam. Only this Sam has a good head on his shoulders and knows where to draw the line – he's a stickler about privacy and won't even watch porno movies when the guys get hold of some. People like that are rare these days.

At this juncture in the session, Mr Forrest suddenly recalls an incident he hadn't thought of in years. Once, when he was a late teenager, he'd gotten involved in some sex play with his early adolescent sister. At the very moment that they were exposing their bodies to each other in his bedroom, their father came into the room. His father lost control and started beating Mr Forrest and didn't stop until the patient passed out. After the incident, he discovered that for the first time in his life he couldn't get an erection no matter how he tried to arouse himself.

To comment: Mr Parks' picture of himself and his wife on his desk is personally self-revealing and violates the ground rule relating to his relative anonymity; it also brings a third party into the therapy situation, thereby violating the ground rule related to total privacy. A therapist with a weak adaptive orientation might well hear this material as a reflection of the patient's inner fantasies about his therapist, his memories of his sister (which are manifest and conscious), and his intrapsychic sexual conflicts. If such a therapist accepted sexual frame violations as non-pathological and as part of life (a view that would not be shared by his or her own or his patient's deep unconscious system of morality and ethics), he or she might even see Mr Forrest's reluctance to join his friend Sammy in a menage-à-trois as a sign that the patient was sexually inhibited – a view that also could be used to explain his impotency. These possibilities reflect the arbitrary qualities of weak adaptive approaches to psychotherapy.

Focusing on the mental state of the patient detracts from looking at the therapist and his need to violate the framework of this treatment situation. This is the prime mover of the patient's deep unconscious experience of the therapist at the moment – and his narrative material. Formulations of this material should begin, then, with this frame violation and with the realization that it undoubtedly is countertransference-based. The self-revelation speaks for active intrapsychic and interpersonal sexual conflicts in the therapist that in all likelihood have been activated by one or more triggers in his therapeutic work, his daily life and his own personal therapy. Indeed, his therapist had placed a picture of his wife and children on his desk a week earlier – a not uncommon source of frame breaks among psychotherapists.

The therapist's need to expose himself and his wife, and to bring her into his office, is a traumatic triggering event of great power. The inappropriate exhibitionistic and perverse qualities of this event will have strong effects on the emotional lives of both the patient and the therapist, and gravely affect the therapeutic situation – as seen in the patient's encoded threats to quit treatment. The patient's deep unconscious view that the picture represents the therapist's sexualized exposure of himself, and a sexual invitation as well, are not distortions or unconscious fantasies, they are valid unconscious perceptions of actual, personally selected unconscious meanings of the trigger – themes of this type are universal responses to this kind of trigger, and they will appear again and again in the imagery of patients following this kind of triggering event. Deep unconscious experience is raw, sensitive to the implicit, unconsciously mediated instinctual-drive meanings of frame-deviant behaviours, and focused on powerful issues – that is, on the kinds of meanings and experiences that empower emotional life.

Technically, there was a passing but direct allusion to the frame-deviant trigger and it served as its manifest representation – a key ingredient for the recipe for intervening. The interpretation offered by Mr Parks correctly took the themes and organized them as a narrative story of the patient's valid unconscious perceptions of the actual implications of this triggering event. It began, as it should, with a reference to the trigger, alluded next to the main power themes, and then transposed these themes into the therapy situation as unconscious perceptions of the meanings of the triggering event. In substance, the essence of the interpretation followed the model:

> 'I [the therapist] broke the frame – you [the patient] unconsciously perceived that I did so – and you [the patient] experienced the frame break as a sexual exposure and invitation to join me [the therapist] and my wife in bed. You see this as my [the therapist] not knowing how to maintain privacy and it prompts you to think of stopping therapy [the indicator and its unconscious basis].'

Mr Parks also rectified the frame break at the behest of the patient's encoded directive to clean up his act, doing so by putting the picture into his drawer. He correctly adhered to the principle that interpretations must be supported by available frame rectifications and that the guidelines to rectification are to be taken from the patient's encoded narratives.

The patient unconsciously validated Mr Park's trigger-decoded interpretation and frame-securing effort both interpersonally and cognitively. Interpersonal validation came forth in the allusion to the wise Sam who knows how to draw proper boundaries. The cognitive validation was conveyed in the recovery of a previously repressed memory that touches on the theme of inappropriate exposure and illuminates the onset of the patient's main symptom. The symptom-promoting unconscious equation between Mr Forrest's sister and his wife had not come up previously in the therapy and was a revelation of great importance in helping the patient to insightfully understand and resolve his potency problem.

This interlude also serves as a reminder that effective therapeutic work can unfold in response to therapists' errors in technique and frame violations. But this can happen only if the errant trigger is identified and properly interpreted – and the frame is rectified if that too is at issue.

Summing up, a trigger-decoded interpretation can and should be made whenever there's a manifest representation of an active trigger and a rich and strong pool of encoded themes. If a frame modification is involved, the interpretation should be supported by frame-securing efforts when feasible. Such interventions uniformly obtain deep unconscious, encoded validation, and they shed light on the deep unconscious sources of a patient's maladaptations. They are a vital part of the insight-oriented healing process and bring a measure of emotional health to the patient – and, secondarily, to the effective therapist as well.

12

The Validating Process

The strong adaptive approach endorses as salutary and healing only those interventions that obtain encoded unconscious validation. While conscious minds vary greatly in respect to the interventions that they accept or confirm directly and manifestly, the deep unconscious mind shows an enormous degree of consistency in this regard. This, too, is evidence for the diversity of conscious-system operations and the universal attributes of deep unconscious processing. Thus, narrative responses to the great variety of consciously fashioned interventions of therapists tend to uniformly encode validating imagery for trigger-decoded efforts, be they interpretive or frame-securing, and non-validating imagery for almost everything else that a therapist says or does that is not in the service of securing the frame or promoting narrative expression.

As described in the previous chapters, the lexicon of unconsciously validated interventions includes appropriate silences in the absence of interpretable material, properly formulated trigger-decoded interpretations, playbacks of encoded derivative themes, management of the ground rules towards their securement, questions and confrontations solely designed to enhance the patient's communication of a rich pool of narrative themes, and on very rare occasions reconstructions from the encoded imagery that pertain to the early life traumas of relevance to the patient's symptoms and resistances. In addition, as noted, all validated interventions draw their material from the session at hand.

All other types of intervention fail to obtain encoded confirmation because they do not properly deal with the patient's empowered deep unconscious experiences. This includes departures from the ideal frame of treatment and a wide variety of weak adaptive interventions, most of which are in common use today. These manifest content-oriented interventions are compromised efforts that serve in part to avoid working with deep-unconsciously experienced triggers and their meanings. They tend to be laced with denial and other defensive qualities, and are often harmful to the patient. The relief that they may bring is not based on genuine deep insight, but mainly on the punitive aspects of these efforts and the means by which these interventions help patients to avoid secured frames and their evoked existential death anxieties.

The validating process

The basic principle of the validating process is that the material from a patient that comes after an intervention of any kind made by a therapist should be explored for confirmation of the intervention – or its lack. This effort begins on the manifest-content level by listening for conscious responses, albeit keeping mind that these reactions are not, as a rule, a reliable guide to an intervention's accuracy or helpfulness. The far more certain means of validation pertain to affirmations from the deep unconscious system and are determined by attending to the patient's narrative responses which encode and convey the patient's *valid deep unconscious commentaries on, and adaptive responses to, the therapist's efforts*. This imagery is studied in two ways: first, for themes that are positive and affirming, or negative and disconfirming; and, second, for fresh encoded meanings that further illuminate and extend the unconscious insights conveyed in the intervention just offered.

There is perhaps no more important time in a therapy session than the minutes following an intervention. Whatever else is being communicated, the therapist must evaluate the material from the patient in order to determine the validity and other effects of his or her immediately preceding therapeutic effort. And, in doing so, it's critical to maintain a humble and open ear for non-validating responses – refutation is every bit as important as confirmation.

Technically, after intervening the therapist should allow the patient ample time to respond. It's generally inadvisable to elaborate on an intervention that seems to consciously puzzle or confuse the patient. Instead, judicious silence and waiting is called for, but if the patient becomes hesitant or falls silent, the best intervention appears to be advising the patient to continue to say whatever is coming to mind.

In most instances, even when patients ruminate for a while – a likely sign of pending non-validation – some type of anecdote or dream will eventually emerge. Most of these narratives will materialize spontaneously in the patient's mind, as if they came from 'nowhere'. This and all subsequent stories must be taken as encoded deep unconscious assessments of the therapist's most recent effort.

Conscious validation

In using the strong adaptive approach, patients' *manifest and direct reactions to interventions* are attended to, taken with a grain of salt, understood for what they say about an intervention, but are not considered to be the ultimate basis for determining the accuracy and validity of an intervention. In adaptive forms of therapy, patients generally do not make direct comments about an intervention after it is made. If they do so, the therapist listens and learns, but nevertheless waits for narrative responses before deciding how the patient has truly and deeply received the therapeutic effort.

Conscious acceptance of an intervention is reassuring, but is of little if any value unless followed by encoded confirmation as well. Conscious affirmation speaks for a cooperative attitude in the patient, but says nothing about the deep unconscious basis and motives for this cooperation. Caution is necessary in evaluating this kind of affirmation because it is often based on conscious-system denial and needs for punishment – in essence, an unconscious need to support erroneous and harmful therapeutic work. The nature of the themes in subsequent narrative communications, when and if they appear, facilitate the differentiation between a genuine conscious affirmation of an intervention – as seen with positively toned narratives – and conscious affirmation that serves the defensive and punishment needs of the patient – in which case the narrative themes will be negatively toned and disconfirming. Because weak adaptive forms of psychotherapy do not address these distinctions and tend to accept conscious responses at face value, they are inherently arbitrary; conscious responses to interventions may be valid or quite invalid and deceptive, and there's no way of telling which are which in that type of therapy.

The manifest rejection of an intervention tends to be supported by the subsequent absence of encoded validation; negatively-toned surface reactions tend to speak for therapist error. In addition, intellectualized ruminations following an intervention and the absence of narrative expressions are considered to be non-validating responses.

They often arise when the therapist has made an intellectualized comment of his or her own. All in all, in attending to conscious reactions to interventions, it's well to keep in mind the fundamental commitment of the conscious system to defence and denial, and the strong influence on conscious-system responses exerted by deep unconscious guilt and needs for punishment. These needs often unconsciously prompt a patient to accept or support a deeply harmful intervention – as measured by deep unconscious standards and subsequent encoded themes. Overall, then, the conscious system is by no means the kind of system on which to rely as a guide as to how to intervene in the future, or as a judge of the qualities and effects of an intervention already made.

Encoded validation

Once a therapist has intervened verbally or behaviourally, including periods of silence, he or she is obliged to listen to the subsequent narrative material and themes from the patient as an incisive deep unconscious commentary on the qualities of the intervention. Deep unconscious responses to intervention are, as a rule, non-defensive, highly perceptive and quite dependable – they reflect a wisdom that stands far beyond anything the conscious mind can muster. This means that it's incumbent on the therapist to determine if there's a narrative response, and, if so, to then carefully assess its nature and meanings.

Given therapists' natural tendencies to seek affirmation of their efforts, it is as well to carry out the search for encoded validation or its lack with not only an open mind, but with a sensitivity for non-validating responses. Non-confirmation is a narcissistic blow. But in a field in which it's all too easy to fossilize one's thinking, aside from sound personal therapy, non-validation is perhaps the single best means through which a therapist can make fresh discoveries and engage in a learning process that enhances his or her emotional growth and mental health. Recognizing encoded, non-validating responses is also a vital means of identifying and correcting harmful interventions so as to prevent their repetition. They're also an invaluable way of keeping a therapy experience on an even keel and moving it ever forward on the basis of unconsciously confirmed, deeply insightful, healing interventions.

In evaluating the implications of encoded themes, we must reject the thesis that the emergence of fresh or previously repressed material is, *per se*, a form of validation. The themes in the material must be examined for their encoded commentary, which may be affirming or disconfirming. Beginning with Freud, therapists who work within weak adaptive frameworks have suggested that the very emergence of previously unreported incidents and memories speak for the accuracy and helpfulness of an intervention. But adaptive clinical studies have shown that this is not at all the case. Many newly-recovered memories with powerful themes come to the minds of patients following seriously harmful and erroneous interventions – these narratives are replete with non-validating, negative imagery. The true nature and functions of these images can be appreciated only in an adaptive context and by recognizing that, in these instances, the themes convey valid perceptions of the hurtful qualities of the therapist's efforts. It is equally true, of course, that if the recovered memory is positively cast, it can then be taken as an encoded, deep unconscious validating response to the intervention at issue.

Validating themes

There are two forms of deep unconscious, encoded validation. The first is called *interpersonal validation* because it reflects a positive view of the therapist in light of the offer of a sound intervention. It's conveyed through stories with themes about people who are insightful or wise, rewarding or offering gifts, supportive or caring, or helpful in any number of other ways. It may also emerge as an allusion to rewarding events, accomplishments, moments of satisfaction and gratification, and other positively-toned images. This is seen, for example, when following a trigger-decoded interpretation a patient recalls the smartest person in their high-school class – or his or her best teacher, a wise religious leader, a competent physician, or even something that they did well themselves.

The second type of encoded affirmation is called *cognitive validation* because it reflects the operations of the deep unconscious wisdom system as it endeavours to add new insights to those just provided by the therapist. It's conveyed through encoded stories that reveal fresh aspects of the patient's resistances and symptoms – historical, contemporary, psychodynamic and so on. The encoded material is truly fresh and provides unforeseen insights for both the patient and therapist.

We saw an example of this kind of validation in the vignette offered in Chapter 8. It arose after Dr Wren had kept the frame of Mr Arp's therapy secured by using the patient's material as a basis for not changing the day and time of the following session. The patient suddenly realized that he was asking to change a session that fell on the anniversary of his brother's death. This new cognitive material was crucial to understanding the patient's current deep unconscious issues and the deep unconscious motives for his wish for a frame change. Cognitive validation through the recovery of an important genetic experience also emerged in the vignette presented in Chapter 11, when Mr Forrest responded to his therapist's frame rectification – Mr Parks putting the picture of himself and his wife in his drawer – by recalling an impotency-causing incident of discovered sexual play with his sister during his teenage years.

Non-validating themes

Themes that reject the validity of an intervention tend to be negatively toned. *Interpersonal non-validation* is conveyed in three ways: first, through the absence of narrative material; second, by default through the absence of positively-toned, validating imagery; and, third, through negatively-toned themes such as people who are blind, deaf, insensitive, unwise, defensive, wrong about something, off the mark, unhelpful, and so on. *Cognitive non-validation* is conveyed through the absence of freshly illuminating encoded material. Patients' non-validating responses call for the reformulation of known triggers and existing imagery and guidance from the patient's subsequent narrative material. The best way to begin this corrective effort is by engaging in a search for an interventional trigger that has been overlooked. Efforts at both direct recall and the use of the patient's narrative themes for clues to the missing trigger are called for, and a reassessment of the encoded meaning of the thematic material should follow.

Follow-up efforts

Technically, when a patient responds to an active intervention with encoded validating themes, the therapist should simply continue to listen. He or she may then make one or both of two further interventions. The first is an attempt to underscore the patient's validating response so he or she is fully aware that they have indeed confirmed and supported the previous intervention. To do this, the therapist will usually review the patient's responsive themes, showing how they affirm the prior intervention. This should be done tactfully and entirely for the patient's benefit. An important use of this intervention is seen with a validated frame-securing intervention where it's essential to help the patient appreciate his or her own deep unconscious needs and wishes for this type of framework for their therapy – and their lives.

The second supplementary intervention involves interpreting any fresh encoded material that the patient communicates after the initial intervention. Encoded cognitive validation always offers new insights that need to be identified and imparted to the patient through further trigger-decoded interpretations. After they are offered, it is especially important for the therapist to listen to the patient's subsequent material for indications of the validation of the new interpretation – or its lack.

Matters are quite different when a patient has responded to an active intervention with non-validating imagery. In these situations, the therapist's main responsibility is to reformulate the material and his or her thinking. There are two types of issues here. The first arises with non-validated extended silences, as seen with negative themes such as people who are in a fog, asleep, not listening, missing the point, and so forth. These images indicate that an active intervention – interpretive or frame-securing – has been missed. The therapist's search is therefore directed towards finding the evocative trigger that he or she has overlooked, and finding the bridging and power themes that connect to it. Once these elements have been identified, a trigger-decoded interpretation and/or frame-securing intervention can be made.

It is quite uncanny to see how often the deep unconscious mind of a patient is incisively aware of a missed intervention. As I've been saying, deep unconscious intelligence is a resource to be envied and respected by the less-intelligent conscious mind. The deep unconscious system is a superb guide to when and how to intervene – an inner supervisor, if you will. Remember, too, that each session is its own creation as orchestrated by the patient's deep unconscious system, and that interventions must be based on the material available in the session at hand.

The second type of situation arises with non-validated verbal interventions and frame-management efforts. If the invalidated intervention was a verbal comment or frame-related decision by the therapist, it's again incumbent on the therapist to reformulate the material. If the refuted intervention was frame-violating, there's a need to both rectify the frame break if at all possible, and to interpret the patient's deep unconscious perceptions of the therapist in light of the frame modification. If these efforts prove to be feasible, they become fresh triggers that need to be subjected to the patient's subsequent deep unconscious assessments. On the other hand, if the intervention was frame-securing, non-validating themes suggest either the presence of a frame violation regarding a ground rule other than the one that has been secured, or that the therapist has actually not secured the frame as he or she thought – the patient's deep unconscious mind is a lot wiser than the therapist's conscious mind in this regard.

With invalidated verbal interventions that have not been based on trigger decoding, there should be an attempt to reformulate the material using the adaptive approach so that a sound trigger-decoded formulation and intervention can then be made. Along different lines, with rejected interventions that were based on trigger decoding, the effort to reformulate the patient's material should begin, as I said, with a reconsideration of the trigger that was used to organize the thematic material and to render its decoded meanings. The most common error in this regard lies with the therapist's selection of the wrong trigger with which to organize the decoded meanings of the available themes. In most instances, a less-important trigger has been used for the interpretation, while a more powerful and often more harmful triggering intervention has been overlooked. If such a trigger is discovered and seems to give cogent, integrated meaning to the encoded themes, the therapist should offer a fresh interpretation or frame rectification. He or she should do so using the newly recognized trigger to decode and organize the meanings of the thematic material, or to direct his or her frame-securing activities. Once this intervention has been made, it's necessary, of course, to listen to the patient's further material for validation or its lack – and to proceed accordingly.

Validating planned interventions

The validating process is the basic means by which therapists can, to the greatest extent humanly possible, ensure the accuracy and helpfulness of their efforts. It's a continuous process that should be invoked not only after an offered intervention, but also during an ongoing session as a therapist develops *silent hypotheses* about, and formulations of, the unfolding material before imparting them to the patient. As a rule, these silent formulations are made in the form of a narrative, trigger-decoded interpretation, frame-securing effort, or playback of themes – they are privately considered practice runs.

The key to this effort involves the *silent validation* of a tentative intervention – an initial test of the correctness of planned comment. Thus, once a formulation has been settled on, the therapist attends to the subsequent material from the patient to observe if the intervention that he or she is thinking of offering is being validated by the patient's fresh imagery and themes. When the new encoded material supports and extends the proposed intervention, the therapist is well-advised to intervene. In contrast, when the fresh material seems to be discordant with the potential intervention, it's wise to reformulate. Here, too, the effort begins with the search for a new trigger with which to organize and understand the material to that point in the session. The outcome is likely to be the development of a fresh proposed intervention, which can then be put to its own test of silent validation.

An illustrative vignette

Ms Wohl, an advertising executive, is in once weekly psychotherapy with Dr Bart, a psychologist, because she's been having problems relating to her clients and men friends – she blushes easily and feels terribly self-conscious and embarrassed when she does. About eight months into the therapy, she begins her session with a dream in which she's walking along a dark street, exposing her breasts to several men who are walking past her. The dark street brings to mind a movie she saw the previous weekend in which prostitutes were walking up and down a dark street trying to solicit customers. One of the women was married and when her husband found out what she was doing, he felt betrayed, flew into a rage and murdered her.

When she was a child, Ms Wohl's father would parade around their house naked and she'd feel embarrassed for him. She has a memory of her mother yelling at her father that he shouldn't be exposing his body to his daughter like that. The patient speculates that her father's exposing himself like that must have something to do with her shyness with men and her blushing.

Dr Bart responds by pointing out that her dream supports this idea. She seems to have unconsciously thought of her exposed father as a male prostitute. She also seems to have identified with him and to feel like a prostitute herself when she's with men and her clients – which is why she blushes and feels embarrassed around them.

Ms Wohl pauses and then says that all of that makes sense, even though it's kind of dumb of her to identify with her father because he really is a very stupid man. He'd do something wrong and then deny he'd done it, and when that didn't work, he'd blame someone else for what he'd done. Like once, when Ms Wohl was about 10 years old, he was driving his car and was pulled over in town for speeding. He got into an argument with the police officer, denied that he'd been speeding even though he'd been clocked by radar, and made such a fuss that he was briefly jailed. The incident was reported in the local newspaper and was a great embarrassment to her entire family. Her father blamed the officer for the ruckus, not himself. Ms Wohl couldn't look any of her friends in the eye for months afterwards and she found it especially difficult to look at or talk to her father after what he'd done. With that she falls silent.

Dr Bart interprets that Ms Wohl, who's in face-to-face therapy, has now stopped talking to, and is looking away from, him. In the transference, then, she seems to reacting to him as if he were her father and in her confusion imagining that he (Dr Bart) is prostituting himself. This must be similar to what happens with the eligible men she meets – in her mind, they must also be identified with her prostitute-father.

Ms Wohl blurts out a question: 'How can an idiot have so much effect on a person?' With that the session comes to an end.

To comment, Dr Bart conducted psychotherapy and intervened based on a psychoanalytically-oriented, weak adaptive model of the mind. He had, however, as we shall see, recently begun supervision with an adaptive therapist. Nevertheless, at the time of this session his deeply ingrained weak adaptive approach was the basis for his interpretations. In this regard there was a predominance of themes of exposure and prostitution, and a clear genetic link to the patient's father. The interpretation of the patient's identification with her father is reasonable, but it's based on a model of the mind that accounts for emotional maladaptations – here, the patient's blushing – in terms of intrapsychic conflicts and inner identifications. These formulations are also based on readings of the manifest material, their implications and their links to the patient's early life. The interpretation does not in any way attempt to formulate the material in terms of efforts to adapt to an emotionally-charged triggering event. Indeed, an adaptive therapist would be asking him or herself what intervention he or she has made to trigger these themes.

The therapist's transference interpretation speaks for the same weak adaptive model of the mind in which the patient's unconscious misidentifications play a role in the development of untoward behaviours and in misperceptions of the therapist. Here the idea is that, unconsciously, the patient identifies both the therapist and men with her father. As a result, they inappropriately fall victim to perceptions and reactions that belong to the father rather than to themselves.

It can be seen, then, that repression, unconscious memories and fantasies, and memory-driven distortions are the central dynamics inherent to these interventions. The patient consciously accepts and agrees with the therapist's initial interpretation. In weak adaptive approaches, this would be taken as confirmation, all the more so because fresh material of some import follows. But the negative nature of that material and it's likely non-validating encoded meanings are not considered. Thus, the patient's conscious agreement with her therapist's comments is contradicted by the non-validating encoded themes that follow.

As noted, in principle the encoded stories that follow an intervention should first and foremost be explored for indications of encoded deep unconscious validation or refutation – that is, assessed for positive and negative themes. In this case, the initial interpretation is followed by stories about the patient's father and his many faults – his stupidity, use of denial, tendency to blame others for what he himself did, and his doing something that embarrassed his entire family. These are negative themes and strongly suggest that the patient's deep unconscious perception of the therapist in light of his interpretation was that he's all of the above – stupid, uses a lot of denial, blames others for his errant ways (here, the therapist is evidently blaming the patient and her father for problems that he himself has caused – whatever they may be), and he's a source of embarrassment for the patient. Essentially, then, this is a clear example of a non-validating encoded response to an interpretation that was affirmed consciously.

In the absence of deep unconscious validation, a therapist is well-advised to reformulate. Many therapists working with weak adaptive approaches would see no need to reassess; even if they somehow felt that something was amiss, they may be at a loss to detect why. In contrast, a therapist working with a strong adaptive approach would immediately recognize that Dr Bart had made no allusion to a trigger or to unconscious perceptions, and that trigger decoding was not involved in making this evidently invalidated intervention. The search for a trigger – an intervention of the therapist's – that has evoked this imagery would begin in earnest.

Dr Bart, however, believed that his initial interpretation had found support from the patient because new material had emerged, and paying no attention to the thematic content of this new material, he pressed forward and added a transference interpretation. The patient's terse allusion to an idiot is well-taken as an encoded, non-validating response. Nevertheless, without knowing the trigger for this material, an adaptive therapist would be at a loss to say what exactly is needed here. Weak adaptive therapists tend to bury active triggers under a mountain of non-validated interventions.

It is worthy of note, too, that the therapist did not interpret the most powerful theme in this material – the murder of the prostitute by her husband. This avoidance of death and other power themes is common in weak adaptive approaches, largely because they have not established a hierarchy of emotional traumas or thematic contents. Such therapists also do not appreciate that powerful encoded themes should alert them to the existence of strong and emotionally import-ant triggers constituted as their own damaging interventions.

Also overlooked are the allusions to frame violations – the father's exhibiting himself to his daughter, his speeding, the prostitution and the murder – themes that speak for some kind of deviant ground-rule issue and trigger. This oversight arises because therapists who use weak adaptive paradigms are relatively insensitive to frame references and to the critical role played by the ground rules and boundaries of psychotherapy in the unfolding therapeutic experience. To continue the vignette:

Dr Bart presented this material to his supervisor in his supervisory hour. The supervisor, Dr Lester, was, as mentioned, a strong adaptive psychotherapist. He identified the themes in the patient's dream and associations, and pointed out that the images in the patient's associ-ations were more powerful than those in the dream – a typical clini-cal finding and a reminder of the importance of getting patients to generate guided associations to their dream elements. Then, using a Socratic-like, questioning method, he elicited from Dr Bart the main themes in the patient's material: the power themes of exposure, pros-titution, incestuous-like nakedness, betrayal and murder, and the frame-related themes alluded to above.

Dr Lester asked Dr Bart how these themes might connect to the therapy and what the evocative trigger might be – what intervention he had made that could account for these encoded thematic threads. Dr Bart thought for a while and said that he could see that the themes spoke to and evidently encoded some kind of frame violation in the therapy, and that the violation seemed to have to do with his having exposed himself inappropriately to the patient – but he had no idea what he had done to deserve this picture of himself. His patient's unconscious mind (and his own deep unconscious mind as well) knew the answer, but their conscious minds did not. Dr Lester pointed out that this was all the more reason to not intervene until the trigger was unearthed and represented in the patient's material. Dr Bart's erroneous interventions were moving the patient away from unconsciously working over and getting to the missing trigger and it must be the key to the patient's material and her achieving deep insight.

Taking notice of what Dr Bart had left out, Dr Lester also pointed out that the trigger – Dr Bart's frame-violating intervention – was not only self-revealing, but also seems to have involved prostituting himself and doing violence to the patient. Furthermore, the patient evidently feels betrayed by what he's done and is ready to murder him because of it. Dr Lester also indicated that these are the kind of powerful themes that the conscious minds of therapists tend to overlook and deny – after all, they speak for a powerful indictment of the therapist as an exhibitionist, prostitute, criminal and murderer. Much to the detriment of themselves and their patients, therapists readily defend themselves against recognizing interventional triggers that fully justify this kind of picture of themselves.

After making several other observations, largely about the patient's non-validating responses to Dr Bart's interpretations, Dr Lester again asked the key question: What, then, is the trigger for this imagery? The themes, he reiterated, are encoding a valid deep unconscious perception of one or more of Dr Bart's interventions, and in raw uncompromised language they are characterizing its seductive and murderous qualities. What had Dr Bart done to deserve these encoded perceptions of himself? What intervention has the patient perceived and processed deep-unconsciously in this manner?

Dr Bart still could not find an answer to these critical questions. He accepted the idea that he was dealing with a missing trigger and realized that he must have known and repressed its nature. He also understood that his repressing the trigger had made it impossible for him to decode the themes in his patients material or to think in adaptive terms as he was being taught to do. Indeed, even a playback of these themes would require that he consciously know the nature of the trigger so he could properly organize the thematic elements. It was a very frustrating situation.

Dr Lester extended these realizations by suggesting that harm was being done to the patient by some intervention that Dr Bart, unwittingly and at present unknowingly, had made. If Dr Bart remained unable on his own to consciously identify the missing trigger, he needed to turn to his patient's deep unconscious system for help – the best and most reliable resource he has. He should listen carefully to the patient's encoded narrative imagery in the next session and take the themes as clues to the missing trigger – and to continue to do so until he discovers what it is. In the meantime, he'd be wise to avoid intervening, especially if he was inclined to do so without having the missing trigger in hand.

Ms Wohl begins the following session with another dream. She's watching a television advertisement for a salve that stimulates hair growth and she has the thought that the promoter, a middle-aged man, is lying – that he's a fraud. The night of the dream, she'd been surfing her television set, going from channel to channel, when she noticed an ad for a massage parlour. They must be lying about giving massages, was her thought, this must be a way that prostitutes solicit customers. You can't trust ads these days. She also watched a made-for-television movie about a salesman who kept promoting himself by lying and cheating; he ended up being murdered by an investor from whom he stole a lot of money. It was like a small morality tale: crime doesn't pay, be honest, earn less, but live to see another day. She gets a lot of phoney ads and promotions in her email – there's also a lot of deceptive advertising on the internet. Everyone's out to make a dollar no matter what they have to do to get it. Dr Bart may be the only person on earth whom she can trust.

At this point, Dr Bart, who was monitoring these themes for clues to the missing trigger, was jarred into realizing what it must be. He was stunned by the fact that he hadn't thought of it earlier, but about two months prior to these sessions, he'd arranged to have a web site created for himself. On the site, he offered articles on mental health, gave advice on common emotional problems, and indicated that he was available for on-line, telephone, and direct consultations and psychotherapy. Several of his colleagues had done something similar and had gotten referrals – it seemed to be the way to build a practice these days. Was it possible that Ms Wohl had seen the web site? Her encoded themes sure as hell fitted that trigger like a hand into a glove.

To comment, assuming that he is correct in his silent hypothesis, we may note here that Dr Bart is dealing with a self-revealing, frame-violating trigger that has not been mentioned manifestly by the patient. Instead, she has in this session given it a strong or close (thinly disguised) encoded representation through the mention of the solicitous television advertisements and of the deceptive ads to be found on the internet. The proposed trigger also organizes the material in the present and previous session in a very meaningful fashion. But the absence of a manifest representation of the trigger means that according to the rules of intervening, in speaking up, Dr Bart should not introduce or allude to it directly – he should respect the denial-based defences of the patient. Alluding to the trigger would also modify the ground rules of the therapy because it would be personally self-revealing and therefore a violation of the ground rule pertaining to his relative anonymity. The fact that the therapist could be wrong about the trigger is also relevant to this point, but it's not the primary issue.

In sum, then, in the absence of a manifestly represented trigger, Dr Bart needs to offer a quasi–interpretive playback of these encoded themes organized around the best encoded representation of the hypothesized trigger. Validation, ideally, would take shape as the patient's direct mention of the trigger – the lifting of her veils of denial and repression – and were this to occur, further interpreting would be feasible. Let us return the session:

Dr Bart prepares to intervene. He realizes that the reference to himself is a non-specific bridge to therapy that connects the themes to the treatment situation and that this bridge opens the door to a playback of the themes in a way that links them to himself and something he's done. He therefore points out that Ms Wohl has just mentioned him and in that way has connected her earlier images to the therapy situation and himself. And while she consciously alludes to trusting him, the themes are about mistrust, especially when it comes to ads on television and on the internet. There are also themes of solicitation, prostitution, dishonesty and deception. There must, then, be a trigger – something he's done – that has elicited this imagery, something that he's done that is self-promoting, dishonest, deceptive, and in some way exploitative of the patient as seen in the story of the salesman – something she'd like to murder him for.

Ms Wohl laughs nervously and says that she'd completely forgotten to mention something that happened a couple of weeks ago. Her friend Tom, who's an avid internet surfer, had told her that he thought he'd come upon a web site set up by her therapist. She really didn't want to check it out, but soon found herself doing just that. It was a little upsetting, seeing Dr Bart hustling for and soliciting new patients. But she figured that these days therapists need to find new ways to get patients and she'd let it go at that. Was all that stuff last week about prostitution and her father exposing himself also about seeing the web site?

Dr Bart says that it certainly was. The web site is being unconsciously experienced by her as his way of exhibiting himself inappropriately, much as her father had done in her childhood – he was in fact repeating in this way her father's seductive behaviour. The site had also prompted Ms Wohl to see him as deceptive and lying about what he had to offer her. While claiming to be honest, the web site was a way of making him into a liar and a cheat because it was a way of soliciting patients for what Ms Wohl saw unconsciously as a seductive, sexual encounter – he was prostituting himself. In addition, she felt victimized by his behaviour and wanted to murder him for it. She had also mentioned that criminals like him are better off having less and surviving longer, which indicates her view that he would be well-advised to remove the web site and clean up his act. It was advice well worth his taking.

Ms Wohl suddenly remembered that she had also had a dream fragment last night about a male prostitute. She had once met a man who had been a male prostitute. What was really strange about him was that he also was a genius designer of women's clothes. She hadn't thought about it in a long time, but once when she was a teenager and her mother was away visiting her own mother in another city, her father had tried to lure her into bed with him. Maybe she has, after all, been blushing in embarrassment for her father all these years. And no wonder she doesn't trust men.

To comment further, let's first note that Ms Wohl's conscious comment in this session, after she had encoded a powerful deep unconscious indictment of her therapist, was to the effect he's about the only person she can trust. This is, of course, a clear instance of conscious system denial in the face of deep unconscious perceptions of the therapist as a murderer and prostitute. Similarly, when the evocative frame-violating trigger finally comes to her mind, she consciously excuses Dr Bart for the very same act for which she unconsciously feels justified in murdering him. Let the consciously flattered and consciously excused therapist beware!

Dr Bart needed to resolve his own conscious-system defences before he was able to offer a sound intervention to Ms Wohl. Therapists need to stay in touch with all of their deliberate and inadvertent frame-modifying and frame-securing interventions, including those that are not directly conveyed to their patients in sessions, but are open to patients' discoveries. Whatever a therapist's personal secrets may be, as long as they might be found out by or known to others, whenever themes begin to emerge that touch on one of these secrets, the therapist's suspicion and silent hypothesis must be to the effect that somehow the patient has found out about it in some manner – on their own or through a third party.

The predator death anxiety and deep unconscious guilt evoked in therapists by frame-violating and other types of secrets are particularly troublesome. They prompt strong degrees of conscious-system defensiveness that will, of course, interfere with their doing sound therapeutic work. The secret motivates the use of self-protective, errant interventions that cause therapists additional deep unconscious guilt and intensifies their efforts to punish themselves. It also prompts the therapist to unwittingly turn a deaf ear when patients begin to encode their knowledge of this kind of trigger – typically, patients are as fearful of the conscious acknowledgment of these triggers as are their therapists so they resort to encoding rather than direct confrontations. All of this transpires without either party consciously knowing what's going on. These situations are a frequent cause of major resistances and symptoms in patients, and counter-resistances and symptoms in therapists. The best available resource in these situations is the patient's thematic material which may, if the derivatives become strong and close enough to the nature of the trigger, wake up the therapist to what is going on beneath the surface of the therapeutic situation.

This brings up another important therapeutic principle, namely, that deeply understanding the encoded meanings in patients' material depends on therapists' abilities to meet patients' themes half-way. It is as if therapists have to have their antennae set in the proper direction to pick up and decode the encoded signals coming from their patients. Sound listening and formulating requires both generating well-defined silent hypotheses about the meanings of a patient's material – without which the therapist often misses or is severely delayed in making necessary interventions – and an openness to unexpected themes that call for reformulating the hypothesis at hand – without which a therapist will often fail to recognize a critical trigger. Therapists must know and yet not know and be open to learning at one and the same time.

Dr Bart's playback of derivatives or encoded themes was properly organized around the best representation of the unmentioned trigger – the allusion to internet solicitations. Ms Wohl responded with the ideal validating response for such a playback – a manifest allusion to the missing trigger. The frame violations involved in this trigger include modifications of the ground rule that restricts contact between patient and therapist to the therapist's office and the appointed time of the sessions; the implicit ground rule that asks therapists to accept only professional or neutral referrals and to not solicit patients; and the relative anonymity of the therapist, through professional self-revelations that range from the articles offered on the web site to the information as to how to reach him.

Once the trigger had been manifestly alluded to by his patient, Dr Bart correctly offered a definitive trigger-decoded interpretation of the patient's material, using the themes that were available in the session. He included some material from the previous hour because the patient had mentioned it in the current session. It's critical to note that this intervention included indications that Dr Bart would be rectifying his frame violation. If rectification is at all possible, it must be agreed to and added to the interpretive effort. If the frame is not rectified, the interpretation is belied by the failure to rectify, and much of the therapeutic effect is lost. As a result, there will either be a failure to validate the fresh trigger-decoded interpretation no matter how correct it may be, or a mixture of validating and non-validating responses that reflect the patient's experience of the therapist's confusion. The curative effects of the interpretation will also be either diminished or entirely lost.

Dr Bart's interpretation obtained both interpersonal and cognitive-encoded validation. The former was conveyed in the allusion to the genius qualities of the male prostitute. The latter was conveyed in the recall of the previously repressed dream of the male prostitute, in the later allusion to Ms Wohl's father's attempt to seduce her, and to some extent in the patient's conscious insight about a likely unconscious source of her emotional difficulties. All in all, then, once he engaged in interpreting and rectifying the frame, the patient offered an apt deep unconscious description of Dr Bart as a genius male prostitute. In light of the web site and his interpretation and decision to rectify the frame, this combination of features speak to a valid view of the therapist. In doing psychotherapy, unconsciously, therapists get what they deserve.

13

The First Session

The initial contacts between patients and their therapists are among the most compelling and influential moments in a treatment experience. The ways in which a therapist arranges for referrals, and handles the first telephone call and first session, are overflowing with both conscious and unconscious meanings and consequences. These interventions tend to set the tone for all of the therapeutic work that's to follow – if any. Indeed, the manner in which these opening moments are handled will not only determine whether a patient agrees to enter treatment, but will also speak for how the therapist will go about helping the patient to find relief from his or her emotional difficulties.

There are many therapists who handle the initial consultation in a manner that is different from their way of conducting ongoing sessions. Some therapists will not charge a fee for this session, others will offer elaborate formulations of the patient's emotional problems, and still others adopt a personal, self-revealing (and seductive) approach to the initial hour. There are many variations on this theme, and none of them find support through deep unconscious validation and, therefore, they are not to be recommended. Indeed, the emotion-processing mind and its deep unconscious system operate with the same perceptive capabilities, needs and preferences regardless of which session is at hand. Thus, the principles of technique that apply to ongoing sessions also apply to the initial hour – be it in a clinic or private office. Even so, as we shall see, there are several ways in which the first session calls for exceptions to the usual rules of intervening, although the listening and formulating processes remain unaltered.

Some basic precepts

The basic principles that guide the handling of the initial contacts between patients and therapists can be stated quite succinctly, even though their elaboration and application takes some effort. The first precept is that, with only a handful of well-defined exceptions (see below), it's essential to adhere to the same principles of technique that a therapist applies to all other sessions. To the greatest extent feasible, the ideal, secured frame for therapy should be created and sustained in the initial contact, which usually is by telephone, and it should also be offered to the patient in the consultation session. Therapists are also well-advised to be mindful of their interventions, frame-related and verbal, from the very first moment of contact with a patient. And in attending to potential patients' communications and observing their behaviours, it's advisable to adopt a listening process that takes into account the manifest as well as possible encoded meanings of the communicated material – even during the first telephone call. As always, this should be done in light of prevailing triggers, which find expression beginning with the nature of the referral source and unfold from there.

While the called-for principles of technique are identical for all settings, the issues that tend to arise in clinics as compared to private settings for therapy tend to be both similar and different. For this reason, I'll proceed by first establishing the precepts that apply to all therapy situations, and then discuss the issues that seem to be distinctive for public versus private treatment settings.

The initial contact

With rare exceptions, the initial contact and arrangements for the first consultation session should take place solely between the potential patient and the therapist. Third parties should not be involved. On the patient's side, short of a dire emergency or a severe infirmity, or in dealing with children under the age of 12 or so, the therapist should avoid making these arrangements with a family member or a referring physician or his secretary or nurse. On the therapist's side, answering machines are to be preferred to answering services or secretaries – which are, in general, frame-violating third-party pres- ences. Thus, opportunities should be afforded to clinic therapists to make their own appointments rather than leaving it in the hands of other clinic personnel. If a potential patient appears unannounced at a therapist's office, it is best to *not* make an appointment and to instruct the individual to call the office telephone number. To do otherwise is to support the patient's frame-violating behaviours – intrusion into a therapist's office risks contact with another patient and is inappropriate. In addition, it violates the implicit ground rule that contacts between patients and therapists take place by appointment only.

The first telephone call should be handled as professionally as possible and be brief as is reasonable. Both self-revelations and discussions of the potential patient's emotional problems are to be avoided. It's necessary, however, to ask several key questions such as who made the referral, to implicitly or explicitly assess the risk of suicide, and to make certain that a mutually agreeable time is available for ongoing treatment if the patient so chooses.

Referrals from professionals of all kinds – for example other therapists, physicians, religious leaders and so on – are usually uncontaminated and acceptable. Referrals from a therapist's relatives and from other patients are contaminated – that is, they violate the patient's need for privacy and the relative anonymity of the therapist; ideally, they should not be accepted. The same rule of exclusion applies to any potential patient with whom the therapist has had or may have outside personal contact, such as co-workers and individuals with close ties to someone with whom the therapist is involved. In declining to see a potential patient, it's best that the therapist simply state that he or she is not able to see the individual in therapy without explaining the underlying reason.

It's quite important for a therapist to be clear about the presence of any possible suicide threat. This can usually be ascertained indirectly from the tone and manner of the caller's request for treatment. If there's any uncertainty in this regard, direct questioning is called for. If there's the least sign of a threat to the life of the potential patient, the therapist should ask for firm assurances that he or she will not act on these impulses and will definitely come to the arranged consultation session – which should be scheduled at the earliest possible time and certainly within 24 hours of the call.

As for the requisite that the therapist have a suitable time available in which to see the potential patient on a regular basis, consultations without a time slot for a patient's subsequent therapy are frame-violating and very destructive. They imply either a long delay in beginning therapy with the consulting therapist, or a referral to another therapist which means that the consulting therapist is abandoning the patient after what is certain to be experienced unconsciously, if not consciously, as an exploitative contact. In addition, short of an emergency it's best to schedule the first session at a time that both parties will be able to commit to should the therapy go forward – that is, ideally the day and time of the consultation should be used for all future sessions.

The therapist should get a telephone number from the caller in case a personal emergency arises and there's a need to cancel the appointed session. The caller must also, of course, be given the therapist's office address, told how to enter the building and office waiting room, and instructed to wait there until the therapist comes to escort him or her into the consultation room. It is generally advisable to inform the caller that the time for the consultation session is being set aside for him or her and that they must assume financial responsibility for that time. Further, it's best for a therapist to not present or discuss his or her fee during this call. If asked about the fee, the therapist's usual fee should be indicated without further elaboration. Questions about a therapist's personal life, like his or her religion, should go unanswered. Those about the therapist's professional training are best handled with a general assurance that he or she has the proper credentials rather than with a detailed description of their training and experience.

All in all, it is well to be aware that every comment and intervention made by a therapist in the course of this initial telephone call is an interventional trigger that the patient may or may not process consciously, but will most certainly process at the deep unconscious level. This principle applies to the nature of the referral source and to any outside information that the potential patient has obtained about the therapist. The more important of these triggers are likely to be represented and encoded by the patient in the consultation session and, if so, will require interpretation – as well as rectification if they are frame-violating.

The therapist's goals

The therapist usually has several goals in mind as he or she approaches the first session. They include determining the patient's need for therapy; making a multi-levelled diagnosis; getting a sense of the nature of the patient's emotional problems; and deciding if there's any call for hospitalization or psychotropic medication – steps to be avoided if at all possible, but to be taken when absolutely necessary.

There is also the intention to get a sense of the patient's conscious attitudes towards treatment and the type and extent of his or her gross behavioural resistances, if any, and to mark them for possible interpretation in this first hour, doing so in light of an already existing trigger. For example, patients who call to reschedule their first appointment, who delay making the appointment because they will be away for a period of time soon after calling to arrange a consultation, and those who are late to the first session are exhibiting gross behavioural resistances. The basis for their actions needs to be interpreted to them in light of their encoded themes and the triggers, frame-securing or frame-deviant, that are being responded to in this way. The dread in these patients of secured frames and deep unconscious meaning are prominent motives for this kind of early acting out. However, these motives can be superseded by therapists engaging in frame-violating approaches to the consultation session, in which case the deviant trigger – that is, the therapist's frame violation – is to be held accountable for the patient's actions.

Therapists should also plan to indicate to the patient his or her belief that they can be of help to the patient – when this is the case – and to recommend and offer an ongoing psychotherapy experience. Along different lines, the therapist should endeavour to determine the patient's communicative style, mainly the extent to which he or she tends to produce narrative material and to represent active triggers. In addition, it's well for the therapist to monitor the patient's conscious and deep unconscious attitudes towards the unfolding frame conditions of the treatment. For example, the setting of the office says a lot about the basic conditions of therapy, which are frame-secured in a fully private office, and inherently frame-deviant in situations where the therapist shares the office space and waiting room with other therapists, has a home-office arrangement, or works in a clinic type of situation. Attending to the patient's history of death-related traumas will indicate the extent to which a given patient is likely to be fearful of a secured or modified frame. Patients who have suffered major death-related traumas are vulnerable to fleeing secured frames, much as patients who have been severely traumatized by others will fear the deviant frame. With both groups of patients, the therapist should be prepared to anticipate their gross behavioural and communicative resistances and interpret their deep unconscious sources as early as possible – material from the patient permitting.

Throughout the first session, the therapist is actually listening to two stories being told by the patient. The first is the conscious and manifest narrative, which usually recounts the history of the patient's emotional difficulties and reveals their present status, and touches on his or her prior experiences with and attitudes towards the present psychotherapy. In this regard, it's well for therapists to be cautioned that manifest criticisms of prior therapists are often unconsciously recruited by patients to encode negative unconscious perceptions of the consulting therapist, as evoked by his or her interventional errors and frame-deviant conditions. It is also advised that therapists be wary of such communications and search for evocative triggers when stories of that kind emerge from the patient.

In keeping with this last point, the second story that the patient tells is an encoded narrative of his or her deep unconscious responses to the active, interventional triggers that the therapist has created during the referral, first telephone call, any subsequent contact between the patient and therapist, and during the unfolding initial session itself. Most of these triggers pertain to the therapist's frame-management efforts and they may have been enacted prior to the first session or revealed during its unfolding, or even promised for the future by the therapist. These triggers also call for intervening in the course of the session based on the material from the patient.

In this session alone, the therapist does not wait for encoded direct-ives from the patient in respect to establishing the frame conditions for the therapy; it is absolutely necessary to define all of the ground rules of treatment in the first hour. The failure to do so is unconsciously perceived by the patient as creating a highly deviant, structureless and boundariless treatment situation, and some patients will make the sound adaptive decision to not enter therapy with a therapist who fails to offer the best possible conditions for treatment. It is, however, equally true that for maladaptive defensive and self-destructive reasons, many patients will enter treatment only if it is frame-deviant from the outset.

As for listening and intervening – interpreting and managing the frame – if a patient represents a triggering intervention either manifestly or in clear encoded form and also provides a strong pool of themes, the therapist should respond with a trigger-decoded inter-pretation and/or frame-management effort. As a rule, the encoded material will deal with existing frame-related triggers and interven-tions that were or were not made during the consultation session itself. The encoded material will also touch on the ground rules that are and are not offered by the therapist, all of it in keeping with the patient's deep-unconsciously sought ideal framework for treatment.

As a final goal of the therapist in the initial hour, we may note his or her need to establish a cooperative, professional relationship with the patient that is essentially geared towards the resolution of the patient's emotional maladaptations. Much of this is accomplished with the way in which the therapist conducts him or herself in the course of the session. It is also reflected in his or her manner of intervening and in the therapeutic skills that he or she manifests. There's a strong need to gain the patient's trust and confidence in the therapist as a healer.

The initial contact in private settings

There is, then, much to be accomplished in a first session. Achieving these goals is facilitated by adhering to the unconsciously validated principles of technique that have been developed throughout this book, but there are also a number of precepts that apply specifically to the first session. I shall take private psychotherapy as my initial model, and propose a number of deep-unconsciously validated principles.

To begin at the beginning, in entering the waiting room to first greet the patient, the therapist should address the patient by name and introduce him or herself by name as well. In a shared waiting room, it's best for the therapist to announce his or her name, and not the name of the patient. If there's a third party with the patient, he or she should not be addressed or acknowledged. That is, the therapist strives to avoid participating in or sanctioning this frame-deviant, gross behavioural resistance and, instead, marks it as an indicator – an expression from the patient of a strong need for a trigger-decoded interpretation. The most likely triggers for this deviation is the expectation of a deviant frame, as with a third-party payer, or an already existing frame deviation by the therapist.

To continue with the waiting-room scene, an initial handshake – arguably the only moment of physical contact between the therapist and patient – with the patient is optional. The therapist then allows the patient to be the first person to enter the consultation room – it's more appropriate for the therapist to watch what the patient does than the other way around. This arrangement also enables the therapist to close and secure the door or doors to the consultation room, which is his or her responsibility.

Once inside the consultation room, the patient may find his or her assigned chair if it is obvious, as is the case with a chair across from a therapist's desk. If the patient moves towards the wrong chair, the therapist should indicate which chair the patient should use. Once settled in, the therapist should speak first. The ideal query is: 'With what can I be of help?' This question establishes the nature of the relationship as therapeutic, the respective roles of the two participants, and the initial framework of their work together. With that said, the therapist should sit back and listen. As always, this is done on the two levels of communication, manifest and encoded.

The therapist should listen silently until one of three contingencies arises. The first involves the patient's falling silent. If this happens, the best intervention usually is the invocation of the fundamental rule – explaining to the patient that he or she should say whatever is coming to mind. The second contingency that calls for comment occurs when the patient fulfils the recipe for intervening. The material in the first session may well include a manifest or encoded allusion to an inter-ventional trigger and several strong encoded themes. The therapist should then offer a trigger-decoded interpretation or playback of encoded themes depending on how the trigger has been represented. This type of situation is most likely to arise when there's an active frame issue that needs to be dealt with.

For example, a male patient who wants to use insurance coverage is, in making the proposal, manifestly representing the anticipated trigger of his therapist's compliance. He then tells a story about the harm that was done to him after he told his boss in all confidence about a per-sonal crisis he was facing, one that involved a known criminal. He later found out that the boss had leaked the story to another man in their office, who then told it to several other co-workers. The patient felt betrayed and that his reputation had been badly damaged by the leak-age – the boss shouldn't have said a word about what the patient had told him, he'll never trust him with a secret again, and he's thinking of looking for another job with a boss he can trust to keep his secrets.

The trigger-decoded interpretation from the therapist would go like this:

> 'You've asked me to complete insurance forms to help you pay for your therapy. But your story about your secrets and your boss's betrayal indi-cates that if I complied, you'd see me betraying you and as revealing your secrets to third parties who will do you harm. You're story indicates that if I did that, you'd never trust me again and that you'd want to go to another therapist whom you could trust to keep your secrets. Your comment that your boss shouldn't have said a word to anyone about what you told him is a clear directive to me to do much the same – to not complete the insurance form so you can place your trust in me.'

This is an apt trigger-decoded interpretation and frame-securing intervention and we'd expect it to obtain encoded validation. Whether the patient would then heed the advice of his own deep unconscious wisdom system is another matter. As we saw earlier in the vignette about Ms Benson's therapy with Dr Wall (Chapter 6), this kind of frame issue may take a fair amount of time to process and secure.

The third call for therapists to speak up occurs around the midpoint of the session. At this juncture, it's advisable for the therapist to indicate his or her belief that he or she can be of help to the patient, to recommend ongoing psychotherapy, and to obtain the patient's commitment to accept the recommendation. If this is the case, the therapist should proceed to define the ground rules of the treatment. This structuring would include a recommended frequency, time and length of sessions, and a statement of the therapist's fee. This should be the therapist's usual fee and, ideally, there should be no negotiating of the fee or discussion of this requisite which is, of course, a mandated amount in the case of insurance coverage. In this regard, therapists are well-advised to adhere to the rules set by these third-party payers and not collude with the patient in any way to bypass or alter them. It is also best for the therapist to inform the patient that he or she will not be receiving a bill, that they should keep track of the number of sessions held each month, and that they should pay for the previous month's session at the beginning of the first session of the new month. There's no need for a bill because the patient can easily keep track of the number of sessions held each month and the bill is sometimes kept by patients as a transitional object. The stated fee for the consultation should be identical to the fee for ongoing sessions and payment by cheque or money order is preferable to cash payments, for which a patient should be given a receipt. The patient's full financial responsibility for all scheduled sessions also needs to be stated. In keeping with the principle of crafting the first session as closely as possible to the design of all future sessions, the length of the initial session should be identical to that of future sessions.

In regard to responsibility for sessions, the therapist needs to indicate his or her vacation policy. A rough guide calls for some three to four weeks out of the office each year and requires that these vacations be announced well in advance. It is also necessary to advise the patient that sessions will not be held on major legal holidays. Implied ground rules, such as the therapist's relative anonymity and the absence of physical contact between the two parties to treatment do not need to be stated, because the responsibility to enforce them generally lies with the therapist – they usually are demonstrated rather than articulated.

With patients who decide not to go forward with therapy, the therapist is well-advised to ask to be paid for the consultation session when it's nearing its end. It is, however, inadvisable to keep time open for these patients until they make up their minds about continuing with treatment. They should be told that they should call if they decide to go forward, and that the therapist will make every effort to accommodate their time needs. If they do call and decide to proceed with treatment, the time of future sessions should be established during that telephone call.

Another pair of ground rules that need to be spelled out are the requisites for total privacy and total confidentiality by both parties to the therapy. In stating these rules, it needs to be said that nothing connected with the sessions will be recorded by the therapist and that the patient make a similar commitment. If need be, the only information that the therapist should record is the name, address and telephone number of the patient.

The therapist should also introduce the *fundamental rule of free association*, namely, that the patient should in each session say whatever comes to mind. But there's also reason to supplement that rule with the *basic rule of guided associations* – advising the patient to begin each session with a dream or story, and with narrative associations to their elements, in order to build a strong narrative pool of themes that facilitates psychotherapy that addresses patients' deep unconscious experiences and their ramifications.

It bears repeating that the principles that guide a therapist through the initial telephone call and first session are, in substance, the same as those that apply to ongoing sessions. There's considerable temptation in therapists conducting initial sessions to try to lure the patient into accepting therapy though frame-violating, seductive comments and promises. Therapists are also inclined, early-on, to be lax about adhering to the ideal frame in other ways, and are often unusually active, seeking facts and details rather than allowing the patient to free-associate. Some therapists will inappropriately conduct a formal mental assessment instead of doing it by observing the patient as he or she speaks – the exception being any suspicion of an organic brain disturbance in the patient. All types of interventions that would be precluded in the course of an ongoing therapy should meet the same fate in the first session. This is especially the case with blatant departures from the unconsciously sought ideal frame, which should be avoided at all costs – their deep unconscious effects can be devastating for all concerned.

In structuring the treatment situation, therapists should be wary of offering unnecessary frame modifications lest the patient accept therapy for unconscious, maladaptive reasons. These departures from the ideal frame create the deep unconscious expectation that additional frame modifications will be forthcoming and frame violations will become the preferred mode of attaining maladaptive relief from existential and other forms of death anxiety. Under these circumstances, patients' requests for further frame modifications abound. And even though the patient's deep unconscious system will emit encoded messages that speak for holding the frame secured, he or she will usually be consciously adamant about having his or her pathological, frame-violating needs satisfied. While these frame modifications will be accessible to repeated working through – patients will encode their deep unconscious experience of these errant interventions from time to time throughout their therapies – these early frame modifications are very difficult to rectify and they cause no end of trouble for both patient and therapist. Predatory and predator death anxieties in both parties to the therapy will play a notable role in their responses to these disruptive frame deviations because each participant is being predatory towards the other.

In contrast, the offer of an ideal, frame-secured treatment experience will always evoke, and will be a test of the extent of, a patient's secured-frame death anxieties. There will be the typical ambivalent unconscious response to ideal conditions for therapy – a strong sense of holding, healing and security on the one hand, and the activation of existential and predator death anxieties on the other. The patient is therefore likely in the first hour to generate a series of encoded themes in light of this interventional trigger. Lest the patient's entrapment and existential anxieties become too intense and he or she flee treatment, the themes need to be subjected to trigger-decoded interpretation. Encoded validation is likely to follow, but even so the intervention cannot be expected to resolve in a single stroke the patient's intense deep unconscious death anxieties and the emotional events and issues to which they pertain. Indeed, such work will occupy much of the future therapy. The main goal in the first session is to offer the patient sufficient insight into these anxieties to enable him or her to continue the therapy under secured-frame conditions.

The initial contact in clinic settings

I shall use clinic settings as the model for all non-private settings in which psychotherapy is conducted – outpatient clinics, half-way houses, in-patient settings, government-run facilities, and so on. There are a number of problems that tend to arise in these compromised but socially necessary settings, but there are also principles of technique that can serve as guidelines to making these therapeutic experiences as non-damaging and insightful as possible. The simplest and most basic precept for clinic therapies is this: every effort should be made to create conditions and offer ground rules that come as close as possible to the ideal therapeutic frame, and to approximate as closely as possible the ideal conditions available in a private therapy situation.

While some frame modifications are inevitable – for example a third-party presence, low fee, the therapist's recording a minimal note for each session – there are many frame violations, as measured by deep unconscious standards, common to clinic settings that are frivolous and unnecessary; they should be avoided and corrected as much as possible. Of note in this regard is the practice of having secretaries and other third parties make appointments with patients instead of their therapists; giving third parties responsibility for collecting the fee; requiring detailed notes of sessions, far more than the necessary minimum; keeping patients' records in locations where non-professionals have access to or can see them; using large public waiting rooms instead of small waiting areas outside of each therapist's office; the lack of adequate soundproofing for the therapy offices; unnecessary if not outrageous casual discussions of patients with colleagues and other clinic personnel – all too often in earshot of patients and/or others; the leakage to patients of personal information about the therapist and other clinic workers; the improper, unauthorized release of information about patients to third parties – a practice that should be kept to a minimum and require a written, informed release from the patient; and arranging for a therapist to see in treatment two members of the same family or two people who know each other socially.

The list of frivolous but deeply affecting frame violations in clinics is seemingly endless and bears grim testimony to therapists' conscious neglect of the ground rules of psychotherapy, the power of their secured-frame anxieties and dread of secured frames, and their need for excessively deviant conditions for treatment. Every therapist who works in this type of setting is well-advised to review clinic policies and the behaviour of clinic personnel for frame violations and to do as much as possible to correct these harmful departures from the ideal, healing frame. Nevertheless, I must offer a word of caution about such efforts because, for most people, secured-frame existential and predator death anxieties are far stronger and more threatening than predatory death anxieties. This means that most of the individuals who work in a clinic – professionals and non-professionals – suffer unconsciously from significant amounts of secured-frame anxieties and have a strong conscious preference for deviant frames. As a result, the reformer is almost certain to meet conscious opposition and to evoke angry responses from clinic personnel, reactions that are unconsciously driven, unrecognized for their deep unconscious sources, and irrational. One must proceed with great caution in trying to bring about vitally necessary frame-securing changes in clinic policy.

As for doing psychotherapy in clinics, the basic principle is that, given the natural focus of patients' deep unconscious systems on ground rules issues, much of the therapeutic work will, of necessity, revolve around the frame deviations built into the treatment situation and experience. This work should, of course, be guided by patients' representations of triggers and their pools of encoded themes. Clinic therapies are deviant-frame therapies, and the trigger-decoded interpretations and deep insights that therapists are able to offer their patients will be based on each patient's selective deep unconscious experience of the particular deviant conditions of treatment. Nevertheless, it has proved possible to link these experiences and their trigger-decoded interpretations to the patient's symptoms and resistances, as well as to their core, death-related traumas and conflicts. Such therapeutic work should, if at all possible, be supplemented by *secured-frame moments*, during which the patient's secured-frame anxieties and their history are mobilized and can be interpreted, worked over and resolved to the greatest extent feasible under these conditions. The opportunity for this type of therapeutic experience generally arises when a patient requests a fresh frame modification – for example a change in the time of a particular session, a reduction in the fee, a meeting between the therapist and a third party – and the therapist, using the patient's encoded themes as directives, turns down the request. Properly managed and interpreted, these interludes are quite healing for the patient – and quite rewarding for the therapist or counsellor as well.

The dynamic and interactional nature of clinic therapies serve to remind us that the psychotherapy experience is by no means constituted as a simple unfolding of the inner life of a patient. The therapeutic experience is a mutual creation of both patient and therapist.

And given the conditions for treatment that the therapist must offer in a clinic setting and the untoward effects of frame modifications on all concerned, it's well to appreciate that doing psychotherapy in these settings is one of the most arduous tasks a therapist can take on. Nevertheless, done wisely, a therapist can transform these same difficulties into insightful healing experiences that make this work all the more rewarding.

14

An Unnatural Profession

I have now presented the basic theoretical edifice of the strong adaptive approach and the principles of technique that have been forged through its listening, formulating and validating processes. In this final chapter, I shall cover a number of additional, relatively neglected topics that have a bearing on the efforts by all types of therapists to help their patients resolve their emotional maladaptations to the greatest extent possible today.

Defying the design of the mind

Doing psychotherapy under secured-frame conditions and with the goal of interpreting the deep-unconsciously perceived meanings of triggering events is an undertaking with a quite unusual requisite: the therapist must behave – listen and intervene – in a manner that is quite unnatural and different from his or her usual way of framing, thinking and adapting. Thus, the adaptation-oriented psychotherapist who strives to offer patients deep unconscious insights must go against the grain of nature and the evolved design of the emotion-processing mind, especially the defensive operations and deviant-frame preferences of the conscious system. Rather than accepting the natural protection, however emotionally costly, offered by the MAC as a way of sparing the conscious mind from system overload and dysfunction, the strong adaptive therapist must find ways to bring forbidden knowledge about death-related traumas and other emotional issues – that is, grim power themes – dynamically into awareness under secured-frame conditions that the conscious mind also inherently dreads and tends to oppose. Indeed, recent clinical evidence indicates that the prospect of entering the deep unconscious realm under secured-frame conditions is experienced unconsciously by many patients as a threat to their mental stability and integrity. Themes of madness and psychosis, and of mental disintegration, are not uncommon when the offer of this kind of therapy is even hinted at.

Many of the same anxieties connected with the dread of deep unconscious meaning also arise in connection with the secured frame. As a denial-prone adaptive entity, the conscious system prefers to embrace therapy situations that support its defensive and obliterating needs, which are largely related to the experience of death anxieties and madness, especially as they pertain to the awareness of personal mortality. It is therefore quite natural to avoid seemingly entrapping secured frames, lest they activate unmanageable existential – and predator – death anxieties. And, again, regardless of the cost in emotional suffering, it's also natural for therapists to create modified frames and to modify ground rules in order to create the denial-based illusion or delusion that they are exceptions to the unconsciously defined ideal rules of therapy – and thus to the existential rule that death follows life. Working under secured frame conditions and securing such frames for patients therefore requires that therapists stand bold and strong against their natural obliterating defences and tolerate the existential angst that this inevitably arouses – doing so, not in the name of masochism or unnecessary suffering, but in the name of offering their patients optimal, deeply insightful, secured-frame healing experiences.

In sum, human nature stands opposed to sound adaptive forms of psychotherapy. By evolved design, we humans fight against the very conditions and deep understanding that are most healing for our emotional ills. Put another way: optimal forms of psychotherapy must be structured and carried out in ways that overcome the dysfunctional and self-defeating aspects of the evolved design of the emotion-processing mind which is one of the basic causes of human emotional pain.

Despite the cost, it is quite difficult for therapists to resist working within the framework of weak adaptive approaches to psychoanalysis and emotional life. These approaches are consonant with the ultimately defensive design of the conscious system. In substance, then, these manifestly-oriented efforts are ways of avoiding the most anxiety-provoking meanings of traumatic events and their deep unconscious impact on the human psyche. And while defences of this kind may bring temporary relief to all concerned – both patient and therapist – they do so at enormous cost. Denial of sources of anxiety and conflict do not make the issues disappear; they remain in the psyche and cause a great deal of harm, even as that very harm is being denied and overlooked. Denial creates unnoticed maladaptations, opens an individual to repeated acts of personal damage from denied sources of harm, and precludes insight, growth and preparedness for future traumas. There are, then, great rewards for therapists who are able to forgo their overuse of denial mechanisms and work within secured frames and engage in the pursuit of sound trigger-decoding insights. Still, it's very difficult for the conscious mind to grasp the truth of this statement.

Adopting a strong adaptive approach is not, however, simply a matter of conscious choice for a therapist. While every therapist should make use of the vast array of insights that have been derived from this approach, its clinical use may not suit everyone. In addition to the universal, basic design features of the emotion-processing mind and its conscious system, a therapist's personal history of death-related traumas plays a significant role in his or her choice of therapeutic model and, more basically, his or her tolerance for deep unconscious meaning and secured frames. Experiences of loss through death, especially early in life, of being predated and harmed by others, and of causing significant harm to others, all tend to affect the operations of the emotion-processing mind. In most cases, the experience of death-related traumatic events intensifies the use of conscious-system denial and obliteration. It follows from this that making use of an adaptive approach is especially threatening for the traumatized therapist.

Paradoxically, these same traumas sometimes create deep unconscious needs that render certain individuals strongly inclined to seek and offer secured frames and trigger-decoded, deep unconscious insights. The adaptive techniques are often recruited for self-processing (see below) as well as for their therapeutic endeavours with patients – the goal of healing emotional wounds is present in both quests.

The direction that a given therapist chooses – that is, towards or away from the strong adaptive approach – is based on many factors, some of them yet to be determined. It is evident that death-related traumas may evoke either an intensification of the use of denial-based obliteration, or a compelling unconscious need to understand the death-related concerns buried in the deep unconscious mind. What is not clear is the nature of the other factors that influence this choice. Discovering what they are is quite critical because, with few exceptions, psychotherapists have to-date chosen denial, deviant frames and weak adaptive approaches, instead of insight, secured frames and adaptive efforts. In my view there is a great loss in both healing power and insight into the design of the emotion-processing mind and the nature of emotional life in this decision. Knowing more about what motivates it unconsciously may well help improve the quality of psychotherapy – and of life itself.

In this context, it is well to appreciate that given the evolved design of the emotion-processing mind, a strong adaptive therapist – and all mental-health professionals regardless of their orientation – must be forever vigilant against naturally-driven lapses in managing the ground rules and intervening. This is especially necessary when a therapist suffers a personal death-related trauma to him or herself or to some-one close to them – and when death begins to cast its shadow over the world at large. The activation of personal death anxieties always unconsciously presses an individual towards frame modifications and the denial of deep unconscious meaning – both are ways of denying the reality of personal death and death-related harm to others, along with their many disturbing ramifications.

In principle, then, the vicissitudes of a therapist's personal life, especially in respect to death-related traumas – and secondarily, in respect to available outside satisfactions – have a powerful influence on how he or she manages the ground rules of therapy and intervenes. The psychotherapy experience does not unfold in an isolated office far from the maddening effects of everyday life. Instead, for all concerned, it is a special segment of that life, set apart from yet inherently embed-ded within the unfolding drama of the participants' very existence. For all concerned, effects pass both to and from their outside lives and their life within the treatment situation. Past traumas play a real but secondary role in this regard – the power of life lies in the immediate moment.

The fate of therapists who defy human nature

A few words need to be said about the effects of the universal dread of secured frames and deep unconscious meaning on the professional rela-tionships and everyday lives of adaptive psychotherapists. In the 35 years during which the strong adaptive approach has been blossoming as a new paradigm of psychoanalysis, it has redefined the unconscious domain; linked psychoanalysis to biology by placing conscious and deep unconscious adaptation at the heart of emotional life; brought a lawful formal science to both psychotherapy and biology; identified and mapped the adaptive module with which humans cope emotionally and traced its evolutionary history; developed new forms of psychotherapy; generated a host of unprecedented insights into both daily emotional life and the therapeutic process; provided the field with unprecedented realizations about the role of rules, frames and boundaries in all forms of psychotherapy and in everyday life; identified three basic forms of death anxiety, each with its own threat to emotional equilibrium and each evoking a different basic response in humans; and forged new links between psychotherapy and religion in ways that have enriched both disciplines.

Despite these accomplishments and in the absence of a single definitive negative critique of its methods, findings or theory, the strong adaptive approach has been marginalized and largely rejected and ignored by the vast majority of mental-health professionals. This is especially true of psychotherapeutic and psychoanalytic writers who almost never reference the large number of books and papers that have been written from the adaptive vantage-point. In addition, on the personal level, therapists who work in this manner often find themselves alienated from their colleagues and peers. Why so?

The answer seems to lie in the aforementioned defiance of the natural design and defences of the emotion-processing mind that underwrites the theory and the work of practitioners of the adaptive approach. This most necessary feat evidently evokes strong and unwitting anxieties in, and hostilities from, a vast majority of mental-health professionals. The dread of both secured frames and deep unconscious meaning, and of the various forms of death anxiety, plays an unrecognized role in their turning away from the adaptive approach and its advocates.

To some extent, then, accepting the precepts of the strong adaptive approach requires that a therapist be able to both tolerate the often overwhelming meanings and anxieties that the approach arouses in them, and endure the hostilities and rejections of other therapists. Enlightenment of psychotherapists may, with time, help to alleviate this situation, but pockets of resistance are likely to persist for many years to come. The inherent support and affirmation of the adaptive approach that comes from patients' encoded, deep unconscious validation of trigger-decoded interventions and the strong adaptive therapist's personal knowledge that he or she is being truly and deeply helpful goes a long way towards supporting such work and making the anxiety-founded opposition to the approach tolerable although always disquieting. As is true of so much in emotional life, satisfaction comes at a price.

The constructive aspects of therapists' lapses and errors

Given the evolved design of the emotion-processing mind, errors in managing the ground rules of therapy and in intervening are inevitable. These very human lapses can, however, be turned to therapeutic advantage as long as they are recognized either directly or with the help of patients' non-validating, encoded responses. On this basis, they can then be interpreted and/or rectified in keeping with the nature of the error and the patient's responsive encoded advisories. To facilitate this kind of therapeutic work, we may review some of the most common, often overlooked, momentary errors made by therapists who work according to adaptive principles. They include inadvertent and uncalled for frame lapses, such as accidentally beginning a session late or ending it early or late, leaving the telephone in the ring-on mode, instead of ring-off so it doesn't ring during a session. (A therapist should not answer the telephone during sessions – doing so allows third parties into the patient's session and takes the therapist away from the patient even though the patient is paying for the time and for the therapist's undivided attention.) There may also be lapses in relative anonymity such as an inadvertent personal comment, agreeing to a patient's request to modify the frame for one session, for example by changing the time of a session, and many other similarly unguarded if temporary frame modifications.

Another list pertains to errors in intervening, which includes missing a critical triggering event, one that usually involves an intervention that is anxiety-provoking for the therapist; failing to consciously notice powerful encoded themes that are also usually especially disturbing for the healer (current traumas tend to give therapists tin ears for patients' themes related to the trauma); missing an opportunity for a trigger-decoded interpretation and/or frame-securing activity; lapses in which an adaptive therapist makes an intervention that is not based on trigger decoding – and so on.

The effects of, and issues raised by, these inadvertent lapses are somewhat comparable to those that arise in instances of unanticipated but necessary frame breaks by the therapist, as happens for example with an unexpected illness in the therapist or a family or some other kind of emergency. These lapses are also not unlike situations in which it is seemingly necessary for a therapist to begin a patient's treatment under compromised frame conditions – as happens in clinic settings and with patients who, out of utmost necessity, must have help from insurance companies in order to enter and remain in treatment. In all of these situations, the patient at the deep unconscious level experiences and encodes a measure of predation, harm and predatory death anxiety – whatever additional perspectives they may have. These departures from the ideal frame need to be interpreted and rectified if at all possible, using the patient's encoded narratives as the basis for intervening. The intensity of the effects on the patient – on his or her symptoms and resistances – will depend on the nature of the frame lapse, the extent to which the therapist could or could not have avoided the deviation, the particular sensitivities of the patient, and the extent to which the frame violation can be rectified.

In all of these situations, the modification in the frame has a negative impact on both parties to therapy, much of it derived unconsciously by the death anxieties it arouses. But at the same time there are two potentially healing aspects to many of these frame-deviant situations. The first is based on the finding that modified frame conditions makes therapy available for many patients who would not otherwise be able to enter therapy. Some of these individuals are unable to afford treatment on their own. Other potential patients have suffered severe, early death-related traumas – as victims and/or perpetrators – and are unable to tolerate, accept or remain in a secured-frame therapy situation. They are, however, able to engage in a frame-modified therapy which affords them an opportunity to develop insights based on trigger-decoded interpretations related to their modified treatment conditions. Eventually, some of these patients are able to better cope with their secured-frame, existential death anxieties, and they either accept a fully-secured treatment situation or allow themselves to experience and process critical secured-frame moments.

The second advantage to be gained from frame deviations applies to all frame-modified conditions for therapy and to all of the frame-deviant lapses and technical errors made by therapists. These triggering events tend to activate deep unconscious experiences of patients that are linked to traumatic memories and issues that would not find expression during an entirely secured-frame treatment experience. This is the case because the conflicts and unconscious issues that are factors in patients' maladaptations remain in a latent state – unarticulated and unencoded – until they are activated by a triggering event. As a result, the frame lapses and errors of therapists, while certainly harmful, also offer crucial opportunities for trigger-decoded interpretations and frame-securing interventions that touch on areas of healing that might not emerge under non-deviant frame conditions.

The healing aspects of frame-modified conditions depend, of course, on the therapist's ability to process and interpret the patient's deep unconscious, encoded responses to the activating, deviant triggering event. In addition, this kind of therapeutic works requires that the therapist be consciously aware of his or her own predator death anxieties and guilt over having caused a measure of harm to his or her patient. The conscious experience of guilt is far more adaptive than the experience of this guilt at the deep unconscious level. Conscious guilt is based on recognizing that harm has been done and it facilitates ameliorative actions. In contrast, deep unconscious guilt occurs without conscious articulation or knowledge of its existence; it exerts its self-punishing effects unconsciously and therefore does not promote conscious understanding or efforts to correct the damaging situation. While the minds of therapists seem to naturally favour experiencing guilt deep-unconsciously rather than consciously, effective coping and unencumbered therapeutic work are best done on the basis of the painful but positively motivating experience of conscious guilt when called for. Here, too, therapists do well to defeat the evolved preferences of the emotion-processing mind.

Personal self-processing

How then can therapists personally safeguard the offer of adaptive forms of psychotherapy – and any other treatment modality of their choice? How can they protect themselves against excessive therapeutic errors and discover the deep unconscious basis for their lapses in intervening and holding the frame secured? Every erroneous intervention should be understood to be unconsciously motivated by unresolved conflicts and anxieties within the therapist as triggered by the patient's material. In addition, each of these errors evokes within the therapist, however unconsciously, a measure of predator death anxiety and deep unconscious guilt. Because he or she cannot learn from experiences that are processed unconsciously, it is essential to have an effective means of both consciously recognizing these often overlooked harmful errors and discovering their personal, deep unconscious sources. Such a process fosters the rectification of the error, the ability to curtail its repetition, the resolution of unmastered unconscious conflicts and death anxieties in the therapist, and his or her insightful healing and emotional growth.

The strong adaptive approach has discovered two especially salutary ways of achieving these goals. The first lies with engaging in a process of self-exploration based on adaptive principles; that is called *self-processing*. Elsewhere I have spelled out in some detail the means by which a mental-health professional – or anyone else, for that matter – can conduct a self-healing form of personal psychotherapy based on the adaptive approach (Langs, 1993). The process requires setting aside a set amount of time – some 30 to 50 minutes – and a particular number of days – somewhere between two and five – for this activity. The minutes before going to bed or to sleep often serve this need quite well.

The self-processing session should begin with the recall of a dream from the previous night or with spontaneously making up a story that will be used as a dream equivalent – a so-called *origination narrative*. Once this is done, the next step is to generate a series of *narrative guided associations* to the elements of the origination narrative. Many of these associated stories are taken from the personal life of the self-processor, but other sources of narrative are also of value. The alternative of extracting meanings from the surface of a dream or initial story is a resistance and a way of preventing access to one's own deep unconscious perceptions and processes – it is to be avoided as much as possible.

After engaging for a while in this effort to develop a *meaningful pool of encoded themes*, it's necessary to step back to determine if the pool has both frame imagery and power themes. If not, more guided associations are called for. If so, the next step involves identifying the most compelling, currently active triggers, keeping in mind the need to search for those that are frame-related and/or likely to evoke some type of death anxiety. This done, the next step is to decode the themes in light of each of the active triggers in order to become consciously aware of the deep unconscious perceptions and processing of the triggering events. There then follows an effort to search for encoded genetic connections to this constellation of triggering event and decoded meanings – adding them to the self-interpretation. If a frame modification is at issue, the themes should also be decoded as directives to secure the deviant frame, be it in a therapy that the therapist is conducting or in his or her everyday life. After this is done, there's a need to associate further to the origination narrative and to examine these fresh themes for validation of the self-interpretation and/or frame-rectifying effort – or its lack. Non-validating imagery calls for a search for a possible missed trigger or for the reformulation of the meanings of the encoded themes. If encoded validation has emerged, it's advisable to continue the process with fresh guided associations and the search for additional trigger-decoded insights.

Psychotherapists are in an advantageous position to carry out self-processing efforts because the triggers that arise in their therapeutic work tend to be especially powerful and to be processed by their deep unconscious minds. In addition, traumatic events in their daily lives, especially those with frame-deviant qualities and that arouse death anxieties, also lend themselves to these efforts. When successful, self-processing serves to acquaint therapists with their deep unconscious issues and the effects of their life traumas on their lives and work. It should also help them to reduce the level of death anxiety that they experience and to better manage these anxieties to the point where they only rarely motivate technical errors and frame modifications harmful to their patients. The process can also reduce or alleviate therapists' emotionally-founded symptoms and other forms of mal-adaptation, lessen the extent of their counterresistances and counter-transferences, and greatly improve the quality of their therapeutic work and personal lives.

Strong adaptive forms of therapy

The second approach to personal insight and emotional healing involves engaging in one of the three forms of strong adaptive psychotherapy that exist at present. The first uses a *standard model of adaptive therapy* based on a 45 or 50-minute session and adopts both the fundamental rule of free association and the basic rule of guided associations. The second is called *self-processing psychotherapy* and, ideally, it's carried out using a 90-minute session, but works well in frame-works of 60 or 75 minutes. The third and last is called *self-processing psychotherapy-supervision*, which is a treatment form that combines therapy with supervisory work.

Self-processing psychotherapy is structured in a manner that turns over the first 40 minutes to the patient, who is taught how to engage in the self-processing effort (see above). The therapist is entirely silent during this time. He or she then intervenes as needed during the balance of the session. The reason for such a lengthy session is that, empirically, it's been found that patients' resistances to accessing deep unconscious meaning and frame-securing directives are so severe that it takes an extended session for the patient to fulfil the recipe for intervening and for the therapist to bring the patient to solid moments of deep-unconsciously validated insights. For therapists who conduct therapy based on adaptive theory and principles of technique, self-processing psychotherapy is very helpful – as it is for mental-health professionals who wish to have a strong adaptive form of treatment without a supervisory component.

Self-processing psychotherapy-supervision is an optimal treatment modality for therapists who need both of these aides. The structure of this situation calls for allowing the patient-supervisee 30 minutes of self-processing on their own, 40 additional minutes of therapeutic work with the therapist-supervisor, and 20 minutes of supervision (see Langs, 1994, for details). The great advantage of this modality is that it facilitates the revelation of the deep unconscious sources of the supervisee's erroneous, countertransference-based interventions in a way that is immediate and alive, truly experiential and reflective of deep unconscious experiences and processes.

The reason that this is the case lies with the interactional-adaptive aspects of deep unconscious experience. If a therapist – I'll call him Dr Jones – is in therapy with one therapist and in supervision with another, defining the triggers that detrimentally affect his therapeutic work with his patients is all but impossible. Adaptively, the evocative triggers related to Dr Jones' therapy – most of them frame-related – are active only in the treatment setting; they are not active in the supervisory situation. This puts Dr Jones' supervisor at a great disadvantage. On the other hand, the evocative triggers that are created by the supervisor's efforts – and they too are mostly frame-related (Langs, 1994) – are not actively available in Dr Jones' psychotherapy, which puts his therapist at a great disadvantage.

The only sound solution, then, is to combine the two offerings into one situation and to have but a single therapist-supervisor who works with Dr Jones within a single frame. The result is but one set of triggering events activating Dr Jones' deep unconscious system, which is, or can be, known to his therapist-supervisor who can interpret Dr Jones' thematic imagery accordingly. From there, it's a small step to showing Dr Jones how his therapist-supervisor's interventions – validated or erroneous, verbal or frame-related – have affected Dr Jones' therapeutic work with the patient he chooses to present in the supervisory part of the session.

The nature of the therapeutic space

Another issue of great importance is the nature of the therapeutic space created by strong and weak adaptive psychotherapists and called for by their respective theories. Before turning to the therapeutic situation, it is well to note that we have just been witness to the nature of these differences. Weak adaptive therapists would see combining therapy with supervision as a contaminating interference of both efforts. In contrast, strong adaptive therapists who understand that all inner mental processes are evoked by interventional triggers, see no effective means of gaining deep insight into the personal problems and difficulties in doing psychotherapy of a given student-therapist than having the same therapist engage with the patient in both efforts.

As for psychotherapy, comparative clinical studies have shown that private secured-frame strong adaptive modes of treatment create therapeutic spaces in which patients consistently express an abundance of narrative imagery that encodes their deep unconscious experiences of their therapists' interventional triggers. This allows for a full processing of these incidents and for extensive work on the deep unconscious level of experience, including deep unconscious issues of guilt and death anxiety. Essentially, this type of therapeutic space implicitly encourages the unencumbered encoded communication of deep unconscious perceptions and meanings, and supports the healing that can take place on that basis. But in addition to its seemingly more effective healing powers, the adaptive therapeutic space is also a place where the operations of the two systems of the emotion-processing mind – and its deep unconscious system in particular – is patently visible and readily observed. It's a world that's quite unfamiliar to the conscious mind and to weak adaptive therapists and its particulars permit a detailed investigation of the mental realm. The many new and consciously unfamiliar observations, concepts, structures and ideas offered in this book bear testimony to this claim.

Weak adaptive treatment situations, which are generally replete with frame modifications and which direct listening, healing and possible discovery to the manifest level of communication, create a very different kind of therapeutic space – a superficial world in which the unconscious dimension is very close to the surface instead of deeply buried as in the strong adaptive space. This is a world that restricts patients' expressions of deep unconscious perceptions and adaptive responses to interventional triggers, virtually shutting off any opportunity to observe these processes. As a result, the available view of the emotion-processing mind is shallow and virtually restricted to the conscious system; the complexities of the emotion-related mind and emotional life simply cannot be seen in this space, nor is deep unconscious healing feasible.

These differences in the therapeutic worlds in which strong and weak adaptive therapists work are one way of accounting for the strangeness that strong adaptive ideas and therapeutic techniques have had for weak adaptive therapists, and for the tendency of strong adaptive therapists to look past weak adaptive clinical findings in their search for the more powerful issues that arise in the world that they occupy. The differences also have something to say about the comparative richness of the strong adaptive compared to the weak adaptive approach, and about why every weak adaptive psychotherapist can learn a great deal from strong adaptive writings.

The limitations of strong adaptive psychotherapy

Every system in the universe, in whatever form it takes, has its limitations. The emotion-processing mind, for example, can process only a finite amount of information and meaning, beyond which the system becomes overloaded and malfunctions – for example through a deterioration of conscious-system functioning or the excessive use of denial and obliteration. Despite the protection offered by the MAC, traumas tend to overload the processing efforts of the conscious mind, and thus failures in conscious-system processing appear to be one basis for symptom formation.

Much the same applies to scientific theories. As data and information accumulate, they test their explanatory powers and the effectiveness of their practical applications. These principles very much apply to the many diverse theories of emotional life and to the clinical practices that they have spawned – including the adaptive approach. It is, however, extremely difficult for impressionistic sciences, like those that sponsor the various forms of psychotherapy, including psychoanalysis, to discover their own flaws and limitations. These quasi-sciences lack the quantitative, mathematical measures and mathematically-grounded methods that could enable them to make definitive predictions and to be in a position where they are confronted with failed results that speak for erroneous assumptions and theoretical and clinical errors. Impressionistic theories are notoriously rife with unrecognized errors that prove to be all but impossible to identify from within their own confines. These discoveries rely on rare, rebellious, individuals who are able to find cause for a paradigm shift (Kuhn, 1962), a new view of the same territory that readily exposes the flaws in previous and alternative ways of thinking. Such basic changes in theory and practice, however, tend to evoke enormous amounts of resistance in those committed to the usual way of thinking, so fundamental changes in impressionistic sciences are difficult to effect and develop very slowly.

The adaptive approach has made special efforts to discover its own limitations and flaws. It has developed a formal, quantitative science of human communication and created likely measures of both counter-transference and effective modes of treatment. While these studies did not test specific aspects of the adaptive and other theories of psychotherapy, the results were nevertheless interpreted by neutral observers to significantly support the adaptive paradigm and its therapeutic techniques (Langs *et al.*, 1996). Indeed, the very fact that the adaptive approach has been the basis for finding communicative measures that facilitated the discovery of laws of the mind speaks for its viability.

Clinically, the adaptive approach has established encoded, deep unconscious validation as a basis for assessing the soundness of all types of interventions and has used this method to test both its own clinical precepts and theoretical propositions and those of other approaches to therapy. Granted that these methods are not quantitative in nature and are open to bias and error, they nevertheless are an effort in the right direction. The search for unconscious validation has enabled adaptive therapists to recognize the kinds of therapeutic interventions that consistently do and do not obtain encoded valid-ation – and to question the correctness and usefulness of non-validated efforts as well as the theoretical constructs on which they are based. And when it comes to the adaptive approach's search for its own inexplicable findings and limitations, its focus on interventional trig-gers for all manner of resistances and paradoxical reactions in patients has placed it in a favourable position to examine its own theoretical and clinical difficulties. Where other theories tend to hold a patient's pathology or inner conflicts primarily accountable for adverse responses to treatment, the adaptive approach focuses first on the contributions of the therapist and only secondarily on how his or her interventions impact negatively on patients.

In the clinical arena, then, investigations of this kind carried out by the adaptive approach have indeed revealed certain limitations in the applicability of its techniques in respect to who can benefit from its secured frameworks and interpretative ministrations. As I have indi-cated, patients who have suffered intense death-related traumas – as victims or perpetrators – resist this type of treatment and often refuse to remain in its therapy situations. Strong adaptive therapists have not found the interpretive means of enabling these patients to do so, a situ-ation that suggests limitations in both technique and theory. These problems arise with individuals with extremes of both existential and predator death anxiety. Indeed, with such patients, securing the frame and offering unconsciously validated interpretations tends to increase their feelings of entrapment and/or sense of danger of self-harm. On the other hand, modifying the ground rules or forgoing a called-for trigger-decoded interpretation convinces these patients unconsciously that their therapists have a greater dread of secured frames and encoded meaning than they do – and with that comes the feeling that it may be senseless to remain in treatment.

Along different but related lines, there are the above-noted observations that many patients dread that the experience of deep unconscious meaning and/or secured frames will drive them into madness and cause their psychic disintegration. The basis for this apprehension, which may be connected to the various forms of death anxiety, is not entirely clear, nor is its presence easily modified. All of these observations suggest that there is a major piece of understanding missing from strong adaptive thinking.

Another sign of difficulty is that adaptive theory is to some extent able to account for factors that damage the MAC and emotion-processing mind, but has been unable to come up with a consistent means of effectively repairing that damage – the approach understands an illness, but not its cure. Thus, it seem well-established that death-related traumas of all kinds cause changes in the MAC, which raise its threshold for the events and meanings that it passes on to the conscious system for hopefully effective adaptive processing and response. In substance, these traumas result in a lasting intensification of an individual's use of conscious-system denial and obliteration. But, that said, no means of consistently reversing this self-damaging change has emerged. The best that adaptive therapists have been able to do is to offer these patients a secured frame and to engage in repeated therapeutic efforts to demonstrate to them their excessive use of denial mechanisms and tendencies towards self-punishment, and to uncover and process the deep unconscious sources of these trends. Some diminution of the use of denial and self-harm has been observed and, in some patients who have harmed others, themes of absolution, repentance and forgiveness have emerged after many years of treatment. The lack of clear insight into how to heal this very common and basic emotional problem challenges adaptive therapists to search for flaws in their theory and thinking and to find new means of creating fundamental, healing changes in the emotion-processing mind.

The continual confrontation with therapeutic failures that are taken as indications of significant missing pieces in adaptive theory and practices is compensated for by its many therapeutic successes and by its many new insights into the emotional domain. This brings us to one last sign of insufficient adaptive understanding – the failure of its theory and practices to gain broad acceptance among psychotherapists and in the world at large. As noted earlier, without being able to articulate their motives, many therapists turn away from and marginalize the adaptive approach. And here, too, adaptive therapists have managed to understand a great deal about the unconscious sources of this rejection of its precepts and techniques, but it has not found a cure – that is, a way of reversing this trend. Adaptive techniques consistently obtain deep unconscious validation, but almost as consistently are met with conscious resistance. The inability of the approach to resolve this impasse is another limitation that is quite painful for adaptive therapists to face. Paradoxically, it is at the same time the source of powerful motives to question the approach and to search for deeper understanding. Unsolved puzzles are painful to behold, yet they are a welcome reason to probe deeper – they are the disturbing sponsors of new insights, growth and development.

A final comment

As a means by which we can deeply understand the emotion-processing mind and both emotional life and the therapeutic process, there's every reason to believe that, at present, the strong adaptive approach has no peer. As a form of therapy it also claims to being the most effective and least harmful form of treatment available today. But carrying out such work asks a great deal of both patient and therapist – even as it gives a great deal more back in return.

In light of its burdensome attributes and the emotional issues it activates in its practitioners, we can appreciate that conducting an adaptive form of psychodynamic, insight-oriented psychotherapy may not be the unconsciously driven choice of every mental-health professional. But, at the same time, we all need to appreciate that truly fresh and rich insights into emotional life and the therapeutic process are quite difficult to come by these days. Because of this, and because the strong adaptive approach has so much to offer, it seems fair to say that it is incumbent on every mental-health professional today to study and master its theories, ideas and principles of technique. It is my deepest hope that this book has made such a quest possible and rewarding for those who have come to its pages.

Glossary of Terms

The Strong Adaptive Approach

synonyms:

> *The Communicative Approach*
> *The Adaptive Approach*
> *The Adaptational-Interactional Approach*

Adaptation – The attempt to effectively cope with and survive environmental challenges. Adaptation is the prime function of all living beings, including humans.

Adaptive context – Synonymous with 'trigger', the term alludes to an event to which the deep unconscious system is responding – the context that defines the disguised meanings of responsive encoded, narrative messages.

Approach, strong adaptive – The theory and therapy of human emotional life that adopts the basic premise that the emotion-processing mind has evolved primarily to cope with environmental events, and only secondarily with inner mental fantasies, memories and conflicts.

Approach, weak adaptive – The theories and therapies of human emotional life that minimize or ignore adaptations to environmental events and tend to stress the role of inner mental life in this regard.

Associations, free – Unencumbered communications from patients who are saying whatever comes to mind without censorship.

Associations, guided – A technique used in psychotherapy and self-processing which requires patients to associate to the elements of a dream or story with fresh narratives. These associations are guided by and are a response to dream images and themes of stories that patients make up in sessions – so-called origination narratives. Guided associations promote the expression of encoded stories that tend to be more powerful than the dreams and origination narratives to which they are connected. They are an invaluable and essential part of working with dreams in the effort to interpret the most powerful meanings of the deep unconscious experiences connected with emotional disturbances.

Bipersonal field – A term used to describe the therapeutic setting and context, one that emphasizes the systemic aspects of the relationship and interaction between patient and therapist in which both parties are seen to contribute to all of the happenings in a treatment experience.

Countertransference – See therapist madness.

Cure, modes of – The optimal means by which patients find lasting relief from their emotional disturbances include therapists' offers of unconsciously validated, trigger-decoded interpretations, the healing qualities of the secured frame and the therapist's sustaining or establishing as many of the ideal ground rules of therapy as possible with a given patient, and via patients' unconscious introjective identifications with their well-functioning therapists.

Cure through nefarious comparison – A patient's achievement of symptom relief through an unconscious comparison with the therapist at a juncture in the therapy when the therapist's madness or countertransferences are active.

Death anxiety, existential – The universal, entrapping, claustrum-related anxiety evoked by the realization of ultimate personal demise. This type of anxiety mobilizes a variety of forms of denial and obliteration through the use of both mental defences such as perceptual blindness and denial-based actions such as manic flights.

Death anxiety, predatory – The anxiety caused by threats of harm and death from others and from natural disasters. This type of anxiety evokes a mobilization of mental and physical resources in preparation for fight or flight.

Death anxiety, predator – The anxiety activated when we harm others psychologically or physically. This type of anxiety evokes conscious and deep unconscious guilt and an unconscious need for punishment that tends to lead to guilt-motivated acts of self-harm. Unconscious guilt is a major problem for humankind to this very day.

Denial – A psychological mechanism through which many unbearable incoming reality-based events and meanings are barred from conscious registration. Because adaptation to external events is the primary function of the emotion-processing mind, denial is seen as the basic human psychological defence. It is also our prime defence against existential death anxiety and its use is often supported by obliterating actions such as ground-rule violations, manic activities, and a shutdown of encoded narrative communication.

Derivative – An encoded theme in a dream or narrative that is derived from and thereby serves to disguise an unconscious perception, or one meaning of an unconscious perception.

Domain, encoded deep unconscious – The world of deep unconscious experience that is accessed through trigger decoding. It stands in contrast to the implied superficial unconscious domain which is accessed through extracting implications from surface messages and observed behaviours.

Domain, implied superficial unconscious – The realm of unconscious experience that is accessed by extracting purported implications of manifest messages. It stands in contrast to the encoded deep unconscious domain that is accessed by decoding narrative themes in light of their evocative triggering events.

Evolutionary biology – The most fundamental of the biological sub-sciences, one that deals with both the nature of organismic adaptations and their long-term histories, including the forces or selection factors that have led to changes in adaptive structures, functions and strategies. There is a consensus that a full and indepth appreciation of biological structures and operations – including those that are mental, psychological and emotional – must include an understanding of the selection factors and evolutionary history of these structures and their operations.

Existential death anxiety – See death anxiety, existential.

Emotional mind – Those components of the human mind that are involved in the production of affects or feelings. This mental module, which has strong physical links and involves the expression or discharge of affects, is to be distinguished from the emotion-processing mind which has evolved to adapt to emotionally-charged events or triggers. This distinction revolves around the differences between the expression of feelings and efforts to cope with traumas through mental and physical activities designed to master the traumatic event.

Emotion-processing mind – The organ of adaptation, the mental module, that has evolved in humans to cope with environmental conditions, events (triggers) and their meanings.

Emotion-related mind – A term used to allude to those components of the human mind that deal with emotionally-charged events or triggers. The two main modules that have evolved for this adaptive purpose are the emotional mind and the emotion-processing mind.

Empowered psychotherapy – A synonym for self-processing psychotherapy.

Encoded messages – Narrative communications with both manifest or surface/conscious meanings and latent or encoded/unconscious meanings. The encoded meanings are decoded in light of the triggers that have activated the deep unconscious system which has, in turn, generated the encoded imagery.

Fantasies, conscious and unconscious – Products of the human imagination, often in the form of daydreams, these mental contents are motivated externally by triggering events to which they are manifest and encoded adaptive responses, and internally by instinctual drive needs. Fantasies come in two forms: conscious and unconscious. Unconscious fantasies are encoded in dreams and stories, and are far more powerful than conscious fantasies.

Fear – guilt subsystem – A term used to allude to the deep unconscious subsystem of morality and ethics.

Frame, ideal – The set of universally and unconsciously validated ground rules. This includes a set fee, frequency, time and length of sessions; total privacy and confidentiality; the relative anonymity of the therapist; the absence of physical contact between patient and therapist; and the use of neutral interventions based on trigger decoding patients' material. See also: frame, secured.

Frame, modified – A set of ground rules for psychotherapy or counselling in which one or more of the ideal, unconsciously validated ground rules is either not invoked or is altered. The use of a modified ground rule obtains non-validating, encoded, unconscious responses. This type of frame evokes

predatory death anxieties in patients and predator death anxieties in the therapist who has altered the frame and who is thereby seducing and harming
the patient – however inadvertently and unconsciously.

Frame, secured – The ideal, soundly holding set of ground rules that
are universally supported and validated by patients' responsive encoded or
unconscious narrative imagery. There is, then, a universally and unconsciously confirmed and unconsciously sought set of rules and boundaries
that promote trust and emotional healing. These frames also, however, activate notable existential death anxieties that often cause an unconscious dread
of the optimal conditions for a psychotherapy or counselling experience.

Frame, therapeutic – The ground rules and setting of a therapy as they create the context for the ongoing therapeutic exchanges and experience.

Ground rules, of therapy – The ground rules of psychotherapy frame
and afford background meaning to the therapeutic experience. They have
multiple functions. When properly secured, they establish sound physical and
psychological boundaries between patient and therapist; create the holding –
healing qualities of the therapist's relationship with the patient; establish
a basic trust in the patient towards the therapist; and facilitate the patient's
openness to communicate to and with the therapist.

Indicators – The signs of disturbance in patients. They include frame
modifications and other forms of resistance, emotional-related symptoms and
interpersonal disorders. Indicators are the target of trigger-decoded interpretations which are designed to illuminate the deep unconscious basis of
these maladaptations and to enable patients to insightfully resolve them.

Intellectualizations – The generic term for all non-narrative communications – the opposite of narratives. Intellectualizations include general
descriptions, speculations of all kinds, analyses and evaluations, formulations,
interpretations, and so on. These communications have little or no deep
meaning in that they tend to convey single-meaning messages that generally
lack encoded implications.

Intelligence – The means by which we analyse and grasp the meanings of
our environments and inter-current events, and find the means of responding
to them adaptively. There is both a conscious intelligence or wisdom and
a deep unconscious intelligence and wisdom. In the emotional domain, the
latter is far more effective than the former.

Interpretation, communicative – The means by which deep unconscious
perceptions and processing activities are decoded in light of their triggers.
Interpretations usually illuminate a patient's indicators – his or her resistances
and emotional symptoms.

Intervention – An all-inclusive terms that refers to everything a therapist
says and does, as well as the conditions he or she sets for a given therapy.
There are two basic classes of interventions: verbal comments, and managements of the ground rules. Comments range from questions to interpretations, but only trigger-decoded interpretations obtain encoded/unconscious
validation and they are therefore seen as the healing class of comments made

by therapists. Frame-management activities that secure the ideal grounds rules obtain encoded/unconscious validation and are also healing, while departures from the ideal frame lead to non-validating responses and are harmful to patients.

Intervening, recipe for – A valid communicative interpretation requires that a patient express deeply meaningful, power-laden derivative/encoded themes and either allude manifestly to their evocative trigger, or encode the trigger in the imagery in a form that is easily decoded. A therapist keeps this recipe in mind in deciding whether or not to intervene.

Memories, conscious and unconscious – Recollection of past events which come in two forms: conscious and unconscious. Unconscious memories tend to be highly traumatic, emotionally powerful, and are encoded in dreams and stories.

Mind-centred approaches to psychotherapy and counselling – Theories of psychotherapy and counselling that propose that emotional maladaptations arise primarily from intrapsychic conflict and anxiety-provoking, unconscious fantasies and memories. These theories are all weakly adaptive in nature.

Misalliance cure – Symptom relief experienced by a patient on the basis of the unconscious experience of the countertransferences or madness of the therapist. See for example, Cure through nefarious comparison.

Misalliance, therapeutic – An unconscious collusion between patient and therapist designed to undermine therapeutic progress.

Module, mental – A collection of mental faculties – for example, perception, thinking, reasoning, and so forth – organized around a central adaptive task. The mental module that has evolved to adapt to emotionally-charged events and their meanings is called 'the emotion-processing mind'.

Morality and ethics, deep unconscious subsystem of – An unconscious system of the mind that sets moral and ethical standards and enforces them by unconsciously orchestrating self-punishments and self-harmful actions and choices for non-compliance, and self-directed rewards and sound decisions for compliance. Unconscious guilt is its hallmark. In psychotherapy, this system's values are represented by the ideal frame and the system operates accordingly – unconsciously rewarding frame-securing efforts and punishing deviations.

Natural selection – The natural process first described by Darwin and Wallace through which organisms with mutations and variations that enable them to survive best under prevailing environmental conditions are favourably reproduced.

Narrative – The generic terms for all storied communications – the opposite of intellectualizations. Narratives are adaptive responses to triggering events and are two-tiered messages, in that they convey a manifest set of directly-stated meanings (along with their implications) and a more powerful, latent, indirectly-stated or encoded set of meanings that are camouflaged in the manifest themes.

Narrative, origination – Any story or fantasy that a patient composes in the course of a therapy or self-processing session that is then used as a source of guided associations. These stories are used in narrative-driven, self-processing psychotherapy when a patient does not recall a dream.

Non-validation, of therapists' interventions – Encoded storied responses to therapists' interventions in which negatively-toned themes such as harmful, inappropriately seductive, blind or ignorant people appear. These themes indicate that the therapist has intervened erroneously and they call for refomulation.

Origination narrative – A story composed by a patient or client that serves as a dream equivalent and, thereby, as a source of guided associations. Typically, they are generated at the beginning of an empowered or self-processing psychotherapy session when a recent dream is unavailable.

Perception, conscious – An all-inclusive term used to convey the reception of incoming stimuli – visual, auditory and otherwise – that register in awareness, along with their directly experienced meanings and implications.

Perception, subliminal – See perception, unconscious.

Perception, unconscious – An all-inclusive term, identical to subliminal perception, that alludes to the reception of all incoming stimuli – visual, auditory and otherwise – that register outside of awareness, along with their unconsciously experienced meanings and implications.

Predator death anxiety – See death anxiety, predator.

Predatory death anxiety – See death anxiety, predatory.

Psychoanalysis – Defined by Freud as the study of the unconscious, transferences, resistances and infantile sexuality, it is redefined by the strong adaptive approach as the investigation of emotional cognition. That is, psychoanalysis is the study of conscious and unconscious human adaptations to emotionally-charged triggering events – their universal features, evolutionary history, and personal history and variations.

Psychodynamic – A term used to describe approaches to the emotion-related mind in which conscious and unconscious conflict are seen as the driving forces of emotional life.

Psychotherapy – An effort by a therapist to help a patient to favourably resolve and modify emotional maladaptations.

Reality-centred approaches to psychotherapy and counselling – Theories of emotional maladaptation that are centred around failures to cope with traumatic environmental events. These theories adopt a strongly adaptive approach and stress the role played by unconscious perception in emotional life and treatment.

Rectification, models of – A term that refers to the finding that when a ground rule is modified and departs from the unconsciously sought ideal frame for therapy, patients consistently encode correctives – images that point to securing the deviant ground rule and frame.

Repression – The obliteration of inner mental contents such as traumatic fantasies and memories. Repression is a second-order defence, denial being

Glossary of Terms 211

the more fundamental of the two. Repressed contents, which are activated by ongoing events, do however find encoded expression in patients' dreams and narratives.

Resistance, communicative – An obstacle to the progress of a psychotherapy in which the patient does not express viable encoded themes and/or a clear indication of the activating trigger for those themes. That is, he or she does not fulfil the recipe for intervening.

Resistance, interactional – Obstacles to progress of a therapy that are products of the bipersonal field, and thus those to which both patient and therapist have contributed.

Selection factor – An environmental challenge, broadly defined, that must be successfully mastered by a group of living organisms. Those organisms that have mutated and passed on to their progeny the most effective responses to such challenges are favourably reproduced largely because they survive best in face of the environmental threat.

Self-processing psychotherapy – A new form of therapy created through the new psychoanalysis. It involves a 90-minute session and concentrates on the build-up of narrative themes and their decoding in light of their evocative triggers. It may also be carried out personally, although this is done in the face of strong conscious-system resistances.

System, conscious – The adaptive system of the emotion-processing mind that operates within awareness with contents that are directly or potentially known or knowable. This system has a superficial unconscious subsystem as well.

System overload – A general term to refer to situations in which the processing capabilities of the emotion-processing mind are taxed well-beyond its adaptive resources. The protective use of denial and obliteration of incoming events and their meanings is a common response to this type of situation.

Strong adaptive approach, the – A synonym for a new paradigm of psychoanalysis whose basic thesis is that conscious and unconscious efforts to adapt to environmental conditions and events (triggers) is the fundamental task of the emotion-processing mind.

Themes, bridging – A term used to refer to themes found in patients' dreams and stories that connect or link up to meanings of the their evocative triggers. For example a dream of being robbed bridges to a trigger in which a therapist has overcharged the patient.

Therapist madness – A non-intellectualized term that refers to therapists' countertransferences as expressed through unneeded frame modifications, erroneous verbal interventions (essentially those that do not utilize trigger decoding), and errant forms of behaviour like physical contact with the patient and ending a session early.

Trauma – An emotionally-charged event that is sufficiently harmful as to activate not only conscious adaptive reactions, but also unconscious perceptions and adaptive responses. By and large, the emotion-processing mind has evolved to deal with traumas, psychological and/or physical.

Trigger or triggering event – An emotionally-charged incident, verbal or physical, that activates the emotion-processing mind. These events are, with few exceptions, traumatic in nature.

Trigger decoding – Deciphering the disguised meanings of a dream or story by using its activating trigger as the decoding key.

Unconscious mind – A mainstream psychoanalytic term that refers to all manner of contents and processes that exist or operate outside of awareness, but are lacking in intelligence and adaptive capabilities.

Unconscious, deep system – The unconscious mind as conceived of by the new psychoanalysis. This system takes in information and meaning subliminally, processing these inputs with a highly intelligent wisdom system, checking out the inputs for moral and ethical implications, and then encoding these processes and their outcome in dreams and narratives. The conceptualization of this system is to be distinguished from that of mainstream psychoanalytic views of the unconscious mind in that this system has adaptive capabilities absent in the old view.

Unconscious, superficial subsystem of the conscious system – An unconscious reservoir of contents and images that easily access awareness either directly (having been preconscious) or in obvious encoded form (for example a teacher who represents or encodes a therapist).

Validation, of therapists' interventions – The unconscious confirmation of the correctness and healing qualities of an intervention, which takes the form of encoded stories that feature helpful and wise people, rewarding events and other positive themes. This response indicates that an interpretation or ground-rule securing effort has been correctly carried out and is serving the healing process.

Weak adaptive approach to psychotherapy and counselling – A term that applies to the wide spectrum of treatment modalities in use today with the sole exception of the communicative or strong adaptive approach. In these forms of therapy, mental efforts at adaptation are implied, but they are not central to the theory that is advocated, nor to the clinical thinking derived from that theory. In essence, these are not adaptation-centred approaches to therapy.

Wisdom, deep unconscious subsystem of – A term used to allude to the remarkable knowledge-base and adaptive resources of the deep unconscious mind and its processing activities. In the emotional realm, deep unconscious wisdom far exceeds conscious wisdom, and its operations are reflected in trigger-evoked narratives which encode its processing of, and adaptive solutions for, traumatic triggering events.

Bibliography

Arlow, J. and Brenner, C. (1964) *Psychoanalytic Concepts and the Structural Theory* (New York: International Universities Press).

Atwood, G. and Stolorow, R. (1984) *Structures of Subjectivity: Explorations in Psychoanalytic Phenomenology* (Hillsdale, NJ: The Analytic Press).

Bacal, H. and Newman, K. (1990) *Theories of Object Relations: Bridges to Self Psychology* (New York: Columbia University Press).

Badcock, C. (1994) *PsychoDarwinism* (London: HarperCollins).

Baranger, M. and Baranger, W. (1966) 'Insight in the Analytic Situation', in R. Litman (ed.), *Psychoanalysis in the Americas* (New York: International Universities Press), pp. 56–72.

Beck, G. and Habicht, G. (1996) 'Immunity and the Invertebrates', *Scientific American*, 274, pp. 60–4.

Becker, E. (1973) *Denial of Death* (New York: Free Press).

Bickerton, D. (1990) *Language and Species* (Chicago: University of Chicago Press).

Bickerton, D. (1995) *Language and Human Behavior* (Seattle, WA: University of Washington Press).

Corballis, C. (1991) *The Lopsided Ape* (New York: Oxford University Press).

Dawkins, R. (1976) *The Selfish Gene* (New York: Oxford University Press).

Dennett, D. (1995) *Darwin's Dangerous Idea* (New York: Simon & Schuster).

Dixon, N. (1971) *Subliminal Perception: The Nature of a Controversy* (London: McGraw-Hill).

Dixon, N. (1981) *Preconscious Processing* (London: Wiley).

Donald, M. (1991) *Origins of the Modern Mind* (Cambridge, MA: Harvard University Press).

Freud, A. (1936) *The Ego and the Mechanisms of Defense* (New York: International Universities Press).

Freud, S. (1900) *The Interpretation of Dreams, Standard Edition,* Vols IV and V, (London: Hogarth Press).

Freud, S. (1913) 'On Beginning the Treatment (Further Recommendations on the Technique of Psychoanalysis I)', *Standard Edition*, Vol. XII, pp. 121–44 (London: Hogarth Press).

Freud, S. (1923) *The Ego and the Id, Standard Edition* (London: Hogarth Press).

Gabbard, G. and Lester, E. (1995) *Boundaries and Boundary Violations in Psychoanalysis* (New York: Basic Books).

Gedo, J. and Goldberg, A. (1973) *Models of the Mind* (New York: Basic Books).

Glantz, K. and Pearce, J. (1989) *Exiles from Eden* (New York: Norton).

Goleman, D. (1985) *Vital Lies, Simple Truths* (New York: Simon & Schuster).

Greenson, R. (1967) *The Technique and Practice of Psychoanalysis* (New York: International Universities Press).

Haskell, R. (1999) *Between the Lines: Unconscious Meaning in Everyday Conversation* (New York: Plenum/Insight).

Holt, R. (1967) 'The Development of the Primary Process: A Structural View', in *Motives and Thought*, Psychological Issues, Monograph 5, (New York: International Universities Press).

Kernberg, O. (1975) *Borderline Conditions and Pathological Narcissism* (New York: Jason Aronson).

Kohut, H. (1971) *The Analysis of the Self* (New York: International Universities Press).

Kuhn, T. (1962) *The Structure of Scientific Revolution* (Chicago: University of Chicago Press).

Langs, R. (1976) *The Bipersonal Field* (New York: Jason Aronson).

Langs, R. (1986) 'Clinical Issues Arising from a New Model of the Mind', *Contemporary Psychoanalysis*, 22, pp. 418–44.

Langs, R. (1987) 'Clarifying a New Model of the Mind', *Contemporary Psychoanalysis*, 23, pp. 162–80.

Langs, R. (1982) *Psychotherapy: A Basic Text* (New York: Aronson).

Langs, R. (1985) *Madness and Cure* (Lake Worth, FL: Gardner Press).

Langs, R. (1992a) *Science, Systems, and Psychoanalysis* (London: Karnac Books).

Langs, R. (1992b) '1923: The Advance that Retreated from the Architecture of the Mind', *International Journal of Communicative Psychoanalysis and Psychotherapy*, 7, pp. 3–15.

Langs, R. (1993) *Empowered Psychotherapy* (London: Karnac Books).

Langs, R. (1994) *Doing Supervision and Being Supervised* (London: Karnac Books).

Langs, R. (1995) *Clinical Practice and the Architecture of the Mind* (London: Karnac Books).

Langs, R. (1996) *The Evolution of the Emotion-processing Mind: With an Introduction to Mental Darwinism* (London: Karnac Books).

Langs, R. (1997) *Death Anxiety and Clinical Practice* (London: Karnac Books).

Langs, R. (ed.) (1998a) *Current Theories of Psychoanalysis* (Madison, CT: International Universities Press).

Langs, R. (1998b) *Ground Rules in Psychotherapy and Counseling* (London: Karnac Books).

Langs, R. (1999a) *Dreams and Emotional Adaptation* (Phoenix, AZ: Zeig & Tucker).

Langs, R. (1999b) *Psychotherapy and Science* (London: Sage).

Langs, R. (2002) 'Three Forms of Death Anxiety', in D. Leichty (ed.), *Death and Denial: Interdisciplinary Perspectives on the Legacy of Ernest Becker* (Westport, CT: Greenwood), pp. 73–84.

Langs, R. (in press a) 'Death Anxiety and the Emotion-processig Mind', *Psychoanalytic Psychology*.

Langs, R. (in press b) 'Relational Perspectives and the Strong Adaptive Paradigm of Communicative Psychoanalysis', in J. Mills (ed.), *Relational and Intersubjective Perspectives in Psychotherapy* (Hillsdale, NJ: Aronson).

Langs, R., Badalamenti, A. and Thomson, L. (1996) *The Cosmic Circle: The Unification of Mind, Matter and Energy* (Brooklyn, NY: Alliance Publishing).

LeDoux, J. (1996) *The Emotional Brain* (New York: Simon & Schuster).

Lieberman, P. (1991) *Uniquely Human* (Cambridge, MA: Harvard University Press).

Liechty, D. (ed.) (2002) *Death and Denial: Interdisciplinary Perspectives on the Legacy of Ernest Becker* (Westport, CT: Greenwood).

Little, M. (1951) 'Counter-transference and the Patient's Response to it', *International Journal of Psycho-Analysis*, 32, pp. 32–40.

Lloyd, A. (1990) 'Implications of an Evolutionary Metapsychology for Clinical Psychoanalysis', *Journal of the American Academy of Psychoanalysis*, 18, pp. 286–306.

Mitchell, S. (1988) *Relational Concepts in Psychoanalysis* (Cambridge, MA: Harvard University Press).

Mithen, S. (1996) *The Prehistory of the Mind* (London: Thames & Hudson).

Nesse, R. (1990a) 'Evolutionary Explanations of Emotions', *Human Nature*, 1, pp. 261–89.

Nesse, R. (1990b) 'The Evolutionary Functions of Repression and the Ego Defenses', *Journal of the American Academy of Psychoanalysis*, 18, pp. 260–85.

Nesse, R. and Lloyd, A. (1992) 'The Evolution of Psychodynamic Mechanisms', in J. Barkow, L. Cosmides and J. Tooby (eds), *The Adapted Mind* (New York: Oxford University Press), pp. 601–24.

Noy, P. (1969) 'A Revision of Psychoanalytic Theory of the Primary Process', *International Journal of Psycho-Analysis*, 50, pp. 155–78.

Orange, D., Atwood, G. and Stolorow, R. (1997) *Working Intersubjectively: Contextualism in Psychoanalytic Practice* (Hillsdale, NJ: The Analytic Press).

Pinker, S. (1994) *The Language Instinct* (New York: Morrow).

Plotkin, H. (1994) *Darwin Machines and the Nature of Knowledge* (Cambridge, MA: Harvard University Press).

Potzl, O. (1917) 'Experimentell Erregte Traumbilder in Ihren Beziehungen Zum Indirekten Sehen', *Zeitschrift Für die gesamte Neurologie and Psychiatrie*, 37, p. 278

Raney, J. (1984) 'Narcissistic Defensiveness and the Communicative Approach', in J. Raney (ed.), *Listening and Interpreting* (New York: Aronson), pp. 465–90.

Rose, S. (1997) *Lifelines: Biology Beyond Determinism* (New York: Oxford University Press).

Slavin, M. and Kriegman, D. (1992) *The Adaptive Design of the Human Psyche* (New York: Guilford Press).

Smith, D. (1991) *Hidden Conversations: An Introduction to Communicative Psychoanalysis* (London: Routledge).

Stolorow, R., Brandchaft, B. and Atwood, G. (1987) *Psychoanalytic Treatment: An Intersubjective Approach* (Hillsdale, NJ: The Analytic Press).

Szasz, T. (1963) 'The Concept of Transference', *International Journal of Psycho-Analysis*, 44, pp. 432–43.

Name Index

Arlow, J.   33, 213
Atwood, G.   7, 213, 215, 216

Bacal, H.   5, 8, 213
Badalamenti, A.   215
Badcock, C.   3, 83, 213
Baranger, M.   103, 213
Baranger, W.   103, 213
Beck, G.   84, 213
Becker, E.   91, 213
Bickerton, D.   85, 213
Brandschaft, B.   216
Brenner, C.   33, 213

Corballis, C.   85, 213

Dawkins, R.   5, 84, 213
Dennett, D.   5, 84, 213
Dixon, N.   51, 213
Donald, M.   85, 213

Freud, A.   7, 213
Freud, S.   4, 6, 7, 17, 30, 31, 32, 33, 34,
  35, 36, 37, 38, 39, 40, 114, 161, 213

Gabbard, G.   60, 213
Gedo, J.   4, 33, 213
Glantz, K.   83, 213
Goldberg, A.   4, 33, 213
Goleman, D.   33, 42, 213
Greenson, R.   7, 214

Habicht, G.   84, 213
Haskell, R.   52, 214
Holt, R.   33, 34, 214

Kernberg, O.   5, 7, 214
Kohut, H.   5, 7, 99, 214

Kriegman, D.   3, 4, 83, 84, 216
Kuhn, T.   81, 201, 214

Langs, R.   3, 4, 5, 6, 8, 9, 17, 23, 33,
  34, 41, 42, 46, 49, 51–2, 60, 83,
  84, 87, 91, 100, 101, 103, 104, 133,
  197, 199, 202, 214–15
LeDoux, J.   87, 215
Lester, E.   60, 213
Lieberman, P.   85, 215
Liechty, D.   91, 215
Little, M.   4, 215
Lloyd, A.   83, 215

Mitchell, S.   5, 8, 99, 215
Mithen, S.   85, 215

Nesse, R.   83, 215
Newman, K.   5, 8, 213
Noy, P.   33, 34, 215

Orange, D.   5, 8, 215

Pearce, J.   83, 213
Pinker, S.   85, 215
Plotkin, H.   5, 84, 215
Potzl, O.   3, 215

Raney, J.   9, 215
Rose, S.   5, 84, 215

Slavin, M.   3, 4, 83, 84, 216
Smith, D.   4, 9, 51, 60, 216
Stolorow, R.   8, 213, 215, 216
Szasz, T.   4, 216

Thomson, L.   215

217

Subject Index

adaptation   84–94, 192, 205
  and death issues   86–94
  conscious   4, 20, 122, 130
  deep unconscious   4, 20, 122, 130
  emotional   4, 5, 6, 31, 57, 82, 83–94,
    120, 192
anxiety, death   *see* death anxiety
approach, communicative   *see*
  approach, strong adaptive
approach, strong adaptive   4, 7, 9–11,
  12–15, 22, 24–5, 60, 81, 83, 99,
  191, 192–3, 196–9, 201–4, 205,
  210, 211
  limitations of   201–4
approach, weak adaptive   7–9, 11–12,
  14, 15, 22–3, 24, 28, 30, 32, 33, 40,
  50, 60, 72–3, 99–101, 158, 159,
  161, 165–8, 190, 191, 192–3, 205,
  209, 210, 212
approach, weak and strong adaptive,
  compared   11–15, 66, 104,
  118–19, 154, 166, 167, 191–2,
  199–201, 202

biology, and the mental realm   3, 28,
  29, 30, 41, 53, 57, 76, 82–93, 192,
  202, 206
bipersonal field, in therapy   103, 205
bridging, themes   *see* themes, bridging

clinics, as locales for therapy   25–9, 63,
  64, 69, 194, 175, 176, 179, 185–8
  see also session, first
communicative approach   *see*
  approach, strong adaptive
conscious system   *see* system, conscious
contents
  extracted meanings (implications) of
    8, 22, 23
  latent/encoded   7, 10, 21, 40, 200–1;
    see also listening/formulating
    process
  manifest   7, 8, 21–4, 45–6, 101–12,
    114, 158, 166, 200

countertransference   40, 83, 112, 124,
  125, 145, 154, 169–70, 172, 173,
  199, 202, 205, 211
cure   *see* healing, therapeutic (cure)

death   64, 65, 70, 74, 75, 76, 78, 79, 80,
  86–94, 117–19, 165, 168
  and evolution of the mind   87–94
  as physical danger   87–9
  as psychological danger   86, 88–9
  denial of   65, 70; *see also* denial
    (mental obliteration)
  personal (one's own)   70; *see also*
    death anxiety
death anxiety   43, 86–94, 103, 108,
  109, 111, 132, 150, 190–2, 195,
  203
  and creativity   87, 94, 135
  and frames (ground rules)   *see*
    frames, of psychotherapy
  and language acquisition   86
  and resistances   *see* resistances, and
    death anxiety
  and symptoms (maladaptations)   *see*
    symptoms, and death
    anxiety
  as a selection pressure (in evolution)
    87
  existential   49, 61, 65, 67, 70, 71, 72,
    73, 88, 91–3, 94, 95, 100, 103,
    108, 109, 111, 112, 113, 141,
    143, 158, 202, 206
  in therapists   *see* therapists, and death
    anxiety
  predator   49, 55, 59, 71, 73, 89–91,
    93, 94, 95, 107, 108, 111, 112,
    135, 141, 173, 203, 206;
    see also guilt, deep unconscious
  predatory   49, 55, 71, 73, 87–9, 92,
    93, 94, 95, 107, 111, 112, 126,
    127, 141, 206
  types of   87–94
  unconscious mediation of effects
    87, 93–4; *see also* death

harm (predation)
  as predatory acts   49, 55, 59,
    70–1, 72
  caused by modified frames   50, 62,
    64, 67, 72, 73, 78–9, 91
  caused by patients to others in daily
    life   55, 59, 70, 71, 103, 108,
    126, 141
  caused by therapists to patients   29,
    55, 64, 67, 70–1, 72, 73, 78, 91,
    100, 105, 106, 122, 123, 126,
    130, 135, 138, 140, 148, 158,
    160, 164, 168, 169–74, 191
  denial of actual   64
  in psychotherapy   78–9, 100
healing, therapeutic (cure)   9, 48, 49,
    51, 53, 55, 56, 57, 58, 63, 64, 65,
    66, 67, 68, 70, 99, 100, 101, 107,
    108, 109, 110, 111, 114, 115,
    126, 127, 135, 136, 138, 140,
    142, 146, 148, 149, 150, 157,
    160, 174, 191, 192
  maladaptive forms of (relief)   100,
    108–9, 114, 158, 190, 206,
    209
  modes of, in psychotherapy   138,
    199–201, 205–6
  of secured frames   62, 64, 70, 95,
    138
  weak adaptive forms of   100–1

immune system   46, 87
indicators   99–119, 208
  as targets for interpretation   140,
    142, 149, 151, 157, 175
  intensity of   151
  unconscious basis of   161–2, 175
  see also symptoms; resistances
insight   102, 107, 110, 119, 138, 149,
    151, 156, 163
  as cause of anxiety   127, 189–92
  deep unconscious (trigger decoded)
    77, 156
interaction, therapeutic   17, 141, 152,
    195, 200
  bipersonal field   103, 205
interpretations
  by patients, unconscious   18–19
  trigger decoded (strong adaptive)   9,

    13, 63, 71, 74–5, 76, 78–80, 117,
    120, 137, 140, 149–56, 171–4,
    208; *see also* approach, strong
    adaptive
  weak adaptive (classical)   37–8; *see
    also* approach, weak adaptive
intervening, recipe for (from patient)
    105–6, 110, 115–16, 139, 142, 149,
    151, 209
interventions, by therapists   63–4,
    136–48, 208–9
  erroneous   137, 169, 194–6; *see also*
    validation, absence of
    (non-validation)
  types of   126, 136–8
  validated (deep unconsciously)
    136–7; *see also* validation, deep
    unconscious (encoded)
  see also interpretations; playback, of
    encoded themes; silence,
    therapist's
intrapsychic focus, classical   6, 7, 8,
    30–3, 34–5
  see also approach, weak adaptive

knowledge reduction   *see* system
    conscious, knowledge of the
    environment, reduction in

language, acquisition of   85–6
  see also evolution
listening/formulating process   17–29,
    122–5, 127–9, 131–3, 138–40,
    164–5, 170, 172, 173
  hypothesizing (silently, by therapist)
    164–5, 170, 173
  manifest level of   101–12, 137
  strong adaptive   8, 61
  weak adaptive   11–12, 165–8

manifest contents   *see* contents, manifest
meaning, deep unconscious, dread of
    189–93, 203
memories, unconscious   *see*
    fantasies, memories, wishes,
    unconscious
message analyzing centre   *see* mind,
    emotion-processing, message
    analyzing centre (MAC)

message units
 double (encoded) 18–21, 24–5, 52,
  56, 83, 96, 206, 207; *see also*
  narratives
 single (manifest) 18–19, 21–4,
  45–6, 56, 83, 114, 208
mind, emotion processing 3, 9, 41–50,
  77, 207, 209
 death anxiety and 86–94, 95–6,
  190, 192–3
 design of 41–50, 82, 88, 95–6, 107,
  110, 112, 120, 134, 140, 150,
  189–93, 203, 204
 evolution of 84–6, 87–94, 109, 189;
  see also evolution
 message analyzing centre (MAC)
  42–5, 51, 52, 89, 91, 96, 189,
  201, 203
 output centre (OC) 58–9
 synthesizing centre (SC) of 42
 universal features of 41, 45, 53,
  61–2, 64, 83, 91, 100, 107, 109,
  114, 134, 150, 155, 157,
  189–93
mind, formal (quantitative) science of
  82–3, 192
mind, models of 3, 4, 30–40
 structural, classical 4, 30, 32–3, 37,
 topographic, adaptive 7, 9,
  33–5
 topographic, classical 6, 30–2, 33–5
mind-centred approach *see* approach,
  weak adaptive
misalliance, patient–therapist 38, 73,
  95, 100, 116, 123, 125, 135, 173,
  209
morality, conscious *see* system,
  conscious, morality of
morality, deep unconscious *see* system,
  deep unconscious, morality and
  ethics subsystem

narratives 209
 as communicative vehicles 10, 13,
  24–5, 63, 120–2
 as encoded directives (guides) 63,
  66, 69, 75, 113, 131, 133, 135,
  140, 162, 163, 169
 origination 63, 133, 197, 210

pool (collection) of *see* themes,
  pool (network) of encoded
 see also dreams; message units, double
  (encoded); themes

perception, conscious 31, 42, 52, 210
perception, deep unconscious
  (subliminal) 6, 34, 35, 38–40,
  42, 51, 89, 120, 121, 129, 132,
  139, 145, 147, 152, 154–5, 163,
  169, 210
playback, of encoded themes 77, 106,
  124, 130, 137, 142–8, 171–4
predator death anxiety *see* death
  anxiety, predator
predatory death anxiety *see* death
  anxiety, predatory
psychological defences *see* defences,
  psychological
psychotherapy 210
 mode of, as offered by therapists
  99–101, 189–93
 self-processing 191, 196–9, 211
 structured 99–101
 unstructured 99–101
puzzles, adaptive
 solutions to 94–6
 unsolved 81–2, 83, 84, 201–4

reality, external (environment) 5, 90,
  96, 103, 120
recipe for intervening *see* intervening,
  recipe for (from patient)
repression 210
 by conscious system 38, 40, 45, 47,
  148
 classical 31, 32
resistances 58, 71, 102, 103–10, 120,
  122, 124, 125, 126, 127, 143, 202,
  204
 against trigger-decoding, in patients
  149–50
 against trigger-decoding, in therapists
  see therapists
 and death anxiety 79, 90, 202
 and frame modifications 104–5,
  106–7, 112–19, 143
 as conscious refutation of validated
  interventions 107–8